A TRANSFORMING FAITH

D1557467

DAVID HARRINGTON WATT

A
Transforming
Faith

EXPLORATIONS OF
TWENTIETH-CENTURY AMERICAN
EVANGELICALISM

Rutgers University Press
New Brunswick, New Jersey

BR
1642
.U5
W38
1991

Copyright © 1991 by David Harrington Watt
All rights reserved
Manufactured in the United States of America

Library of Congress Cataloging-in-Publication Data

Watt, David Harrington.
    A transforming faith : explorations of twentieth-century American
evangelicalism / David Harrington Watt.
        p.   cm.
    Includes bibliographical references and index.
    ISBN 0-8135-1716-8 (clh)   ISBN 0-8135-1717-6 (ppr)
    1. Evangelicalism—United States—History—20th century.
    2. Sociology, Christian—United States—History—20th century.
    3. United States—Church history—20th century.   I. Title.
    BR1642.U5W38   1990
    277.3′082—dc20
                                                                90-29098
                                                                    CIP

British Cataloging-in-Publication information available

To Cydney

CONTENTS

ACKNOWLEDGMENTS

THE RESEARCH ON WHICH this book is based was supported by grants from Temple University, the Lilly Endowment, Harvard University, and the Institute for the Study of American Evangelicals. Portions of it were read, at various times, by Alan Brinkley, Joel Carpenter, Jeff Charles, Howard Eilberg-Schwartz, D. G. Hart, David Herbert Donald, William R. Hutchison, Neil Jumonville, Henry May, Michael Simon, Russell Sizemore, Timothy B. Spears, Evelyn B. Tribble, and Robert Wuthnow. Their criticisms were enormously helpful. Nadia Kravchenko prepared the typescript with care and zeal.

A TRANSFORMING FAITH

INTRODUCTION

THIS BOOK USES RESEARCH in the popular literature produced by men and women associated with that variety of American Protestantism called the "evangelical mainstream" to explore some of the changes that took place within conservative American Protestantism between 1925 and 1975.

To judge by how often they discussed them, conservative Protestants thought each of the four areas where I looked for change and continuity—politics, the private and public spheres, women's proper role, and modern psychology—to be of great importance. Indeed, a substantial proportion of all of the articles and books that constitute the popular literature of the evangelical mainstream deal—either directly or indirectly—with these issues. But conservative Protestants' perceptions did not by themselves determine my field of inquiry. I chose my four subtopics largely because I thought that looking at them would shed some light on the way that dominant and subordinate cultures relate to one another in twentieth-century America. In this introduction I am going to advance some preliminary observations about that relationship and about the changes that illustrate it. I am also going to note some of the book's limitations and outline its structure.

CHANGE

In 1960 the Billy Graham Evangelistic Association began publishing a magazine called *Decision*. Although one seldom runs across quotations from it in monographs—much less in textbooks—on the United States in the twentieth century, many Americans know the magazine quite well: in the middle 1970s, its circulation stood at approximately five million. On the masthead of the first issue of *Decision* (just beneath Billy Graham's explanation of why he thought America needed such a magazine) was a slogan: "The Unchanging Gospel for a Changing World."

The part about the changing world jibes with the way almost everyone thinks about the United States in the twentieth century: American society and American culture have both been changing, it is generally agreed, with ever-increasing celerity. Most people who are not conservative Protestants used to assume, too, that contemporary conservative Protestantism differs in no important respect from the conservative Protestantism of the 1920s. They tended to picture that form of Christianity as having been put in a deep freeze in 1925 (the year of the famous Scopes trial) and thawed out, unchanged, in 1976 (the year which the American middlebrow press dubbed the year of the evangelical and in which Americans witnessed the first of a series of presidential campaigns in which conservative Protestant candidates and concerns played a major role).[1] Although this view is now certainly fading, it has held on longer than it should have. Indeed it is embedded in the very language used to describe people like Graham; they are adherents of the "old-time religion"; they are—to use once again that misleading but indispensable term—"conservative" Protestants.

This inability to discard the deep-freeze metaphor stems, in part, from the way that the scholarly literature on conservative Protestantism developed. Useful popular accounts of contemporary conservative Protestantism were published as early as 1974, and a number of similar works have been published in recent years. Moreover, in the last decade hundreds of scholarly studies of contemporary conservative Protestantism, written by sociologists, anthropologists, and political scientists, have appeared. Some of these works—I am thinking particularly of those by Nancy Tatom Ammerman, Steve Bruce, Susan Harding, James Davison Hunter, Alan Peshkin, Susan Rose, Ellen Rosenberg, and R. Stephen Warner—are terribly impressive. Sophisticated accounts of the history of conservative Protestantism in the years between 1870 and 1925 began to appear as early as 1970 and scores of works on that topic—most notably, of course, George Marsden's extremely influential *Fundamentalism and American Culture*—have appeared since. By comparison first-rate studies of what happened in the years between 1925 and 1975 such as Marsden's *Reforming Fundamentalism*, Robert Wuthnow's *The Restructuring of American Religion* (1988), and Joel Carpenter's *Revive Us Again* (1991) did not begin to appear until later, and there are still relatively few of them. As a result, few non-specialists are familiar with the history of conservative Protestantism in the years between William Jennings Bryan's declamation in Dayton and Jimmy Carter's campaign for the White House.[2]

The books Marsden, Carpenter, and Wuthnow wrote have made it clear that conservative Protestantism simply was not frozen in those years. Rather it was, to use a phrase that Ellen Rosenberg uses in another context, a subculture in transition. Their works furthermore suggest that tracing out what changed—with as much specificity as possible and in a way that does not neglect the real elements of continuity in the subculture—is one of the more important items on the agenda for students of conservative Protestantism.[3] So it is only natural then that one of the two questions I use to organize my discussion of the fifty years with which this book is concerned is: in what respects do the ideas and attitudes of the evangelicals of the 1960s and 1970s differ from those of their predecessors?

There were, as the chapters that follow make clear, some important continuities between the ideas and attitudes of the men and women associated with the evangelical mainstream in the 1970s and those of their predecessors. Both groups placed great emphasis on the possibility of finding private hopes in the midst of public despair. There were also some obvious similarities between the social and political views of the two groups. But on the whole my account stresses change. By 1975, the group I study had begun to suspect (in a way that their predecessors only sporadically had) that Christians should devote a very large proportion of their energy to political matters. Their strategies for finding private hopes had come to focus increasingly on the family and decreasingly on the second coming of Christ. To a much greater degree than is generally recognized they had come to accept the changing role of women in American society. And they had abandoned their predecessors' antipathy to those attitudes and practices associated with modern psychology; indeed, they had come to regard such attitudes and practices as allies rather than adversaries of the Christian faith.

POWER

The factors that produced the changes I study were extraordinarily complex. But they stem in large measure from the evangelical mainstream's half-conscious willingness to allow itself to be shaped by the various dominant cultures of twentieth-century America. Indeed, my particular approach to understanding the changes with which I am concerned rests on a belief that it is helpful to think of American cultural history as a field of conflict upon which a number of competing ideologies struggle. Each ideology seeks to control as much of the field as possible. Each tries to establish itself as the best—perhaps even the only plausible—interpretation of the world in which we live. Each tries to discredit competing, incompatible ideologies. Those ideologies that excel in this competition can be called "dominant;" those that do not, "subordinate." Sheer weight of numbers counts for something in the contest to control the field of battle: all other things being equal, the more adherents a particular ideology possesses, the more plausible it seems. Cultural dominance is not, however, primarily a matter of numbers. Ideologies which manage to win the allegiance of the majority of a society's inhabitants do not by virtue of that fact become culturally dominant. Cultural dominance depends largely upon establishing close and friendly relationships with powerful men and women. Dominant cultures, by definition, are closely tied to those groups that have the most authority and prestige in a given society. They shape and are in turn shaped by the society's political, intellectual, and economic elite.[4]

My use of this angle of attack in analyzing evangelicalism—my concern in other words with hegemony—connects my work to that of a number of other historians. The concept of hegemony is used with great frequency in much recent historical writing (indeed Gramsci, the theorist with whom the concept is most closely identified, has been enshrined on the cover of the *American Historical Review*). Sometimes its use is merely faddish. At other times, though, hegemony is used in ways that are genuinely helpful. Historians' fascination with the term in the 1980s was largely rooted in their impatience with a common and sterile dichotomy, that which would divide history into separate realms of power and culture, and in their hope that thinking about hegemony could help overcome that dichotomy. The first realm is supposed to refer to military, economic and political matters; the second to the world of ideas, meanings, aesthetics and religious beliefs. Before the word hegemony came into common use, it sometimes seemed as if a deal had been struck exempting historians of the realm of culture from ever having to think about power. Power was "something with which the other group was concerned." Or, more pointedly, power was, as the famous phrase from countless unimaginative prefaces puts it, something "beyond the scope of the present inquiry."[5]

But throughout the 1980s, historians became increasingly aware that questions of power were not limited to matters treated in standard works on politics and economics. They became convinced that most, perhaps all, of the cultural artifacts that historians study have been shaped—and in most cases decisively shaped—by the fact that they were produced in societies where power was distributed asymmetrically. Throughout the decade a number of scholars were persuaded that writing cultural history could not proceed without coming to terms with the linkage between culture and power. At first glance, that should have been a terribly difficult project. There are, after all, established traditions within certain segments of academia which support the idea that all cultural configurations are—not to put too fine a point on it—ruling-class swindles, or ruling-race swindles or ruling-gender swindles. But few cultural historians would be content with painting their portraits of the past with such a wide and monochromatic brushstroke. They need a less reductionist way of writing about culture and power, hence hegemony's great allure.

Questions of cultural authority are, as sociologists such as James Beckford and Phillip Hammond, and historians such as George Marsden and R. Laurence Moore have suggested, particularly important to ask when studying conservative Protestantism.[6] The link between culture and power in that context is not something scholars have to go to any great lengths to uncover, for traces of these links are plainly visible in the primary sources with which they work. For instance, Joel Carpenter has pointed out that it is hard to avoid noticing how often "power" comes up in one particular set of conservative Protestants' descriptions of the work of the Holy Spirit. It was as Carpenter notes a traditional usage to which the debased status of the fundamentalists gave a new significance. The people who used the word were "not actually dispossessed people in their social and economic standing, but they now felt marginal in reputation, essentially powerless to influence national religious life, morals, education, and public affairs." He goes on to say that these conservative Protestants could recall a time when their faith had exercised a "near-hegemony" and that that memory "made their current status even more painful."[7]

Neither Carpenter nor I see the concept of hegemony as the master key which unlocks all the secrets of evangelical history. When historians become overly fascinated with hegemony, they tend to forget that culture is not just about power; they are thus in constant danger of lapsing into reductionism. Historians who talk about hegemony often end up leaving their readers with the impression that they have forgotten that there are forms of domination—physical force and economic exploitation, for instance—other than cultural. Then, too, hegemony can sometimes obscure the diffuse nature of cultural authority. It is better to think in terms of a variety of dominant cultures, not about a single dominant culture. The difference is important. Using the plural emphasizes that in twentieth-century America no single group monopolizes cultural authority. T. J. Jackson Lears is helpful here. "To resort to the concept of cultural hegemony is," Lears says, "to take a banal question—'who has power?'—and deepen it at both ends." "Power" is deepened by looking at things other than politics and economics, narrowly defined. "Who" is deepened because it can no longer mean simply who has capital or who has control of the state. Rather "who" will have to include a heterogeneous aggregate: "parents, preachers, teachers, journalists, literati, 'experts' of all sorts, as well as advertising executives, entertainment promoters, popular musicians, sports figures, and 'celebrities'—all of whom are involved (albeit often unwittingly) in shaping the values and attitudes of a society." I am not sure that "deepen" is precisely the right word; "broaden" might be better. And "banal" is one of the last adjectives in the world I would use to describe the question "who has power?" But the thrust of Lears's argument is correct. Here, as in so many other places, the plural is preferable to the singular.[8]

Even when we are not seduced into thinking in the singular, the concept does not, of course, explain everything. One of the things that became increasingly clear to me as my 3×5 notecards mounted was that dominant cultures did not produce all the changes that I was thinking about. Evangelicals' changing ideas about "the proper role of women" were rooted, for example, in their own changing lifestyles as well as in their interaction with feminists. Similarly, the increasing politicization of evangelicals in the 1960s and 1970s cannot be explained merely in terms of their interaction with dominant cultures. It had a lot to do, too, with their increasing economic achievement and rising social status.

LIMITATIONS

Although it is the result of several years of research in the primary sources of evangelical history, this book does not contain "proof" that its assertions are true. Many quotations from evangelical sources have been incorporated into the text. I hope these quotations reassure readers that my conclusions were not cut from whole cloth. But I have not tried to force readers into accepting my arguments by smothering them with quotation after quotation or example after example.

This book explores ideas and attitudes, not practice. That bothers me a little, for I am closer to being a materialist than an idealist and I am deeply impressed by the work of historians such as Timothy Weber and Martin Marty who investigate how religious beliefs influence behavior. But the sources I worked with are fairly reliable guides to ideas and attitudes and fairly unreliable ones to behavior. And I am unwilling to privilege "society" and "base" over "culture" and "superstructure." The latter are no less fundamental than the former.

I have not tried to describe all varieties of evangelicalism in the United States. Rather I have focused almost exclusively on what is sometimes called the "evangelical denomination." (It is of course, a metaphorical, not a literal denomination.) The appendix of this book contains a brief description of that denomination. Most readers will want to read the appendix long before they get through the main text—most probably after they have finished reading chapter two and before they go on to chapter three. For right now, let me just say that I think of the evangelical denomination as a network of born-again Protestants associated with organizations such as the National Association of Evangelicals, the Billy Graham Evangelistic Association, and Campus Crusade; magazines such as *Christianity Today*, *Eternity*, and *Moody Monthly*; schools such as Wheaton College and the Moody Bible Institute; and publishing firms such as Eerdmans and Zondervan. The evangelical denomination is related to conservative Protestantism as a whole in roughly the same way that New England is related to the entire United States. Anyone who read a history of New England and thought that she or he knew the history of the United States would be making a serious mistake. I hope that as you read this book you will continually remind yourself that it is, so to speak, about New England rather than about America.

This study is primarily based, quite deliberately, on the *popular* literature produced by the evangelical denomination. But I am well aware that my sources did not give me direct access to the attitudes of all evangelical Christians. So I want to emphasize that in this book "evangelical" usually serves as no more than a shorthand for "those evangelicals who possessed enough prominence and/or good fortune to get their ideas into widely-circulating books and periodicals associated with the evangelical mainstream." The generalizations I advance are applicable, strictly speaking, only to those evangelical leaders whose ideas I have been able to examine directly. I suspect that there are significant correlations between the history of that elite and the history of the broader evangelical denomination. But that is still, given how much work remains to be done on the history of American evangelicalism, an open question—a hypothesis not a presupposition.

STRUCTURE

The book opens with an unabashedly impressionistic chapter on what is probably the most widely circulating of all the texts produced by the evangelical mainstream: a short pamphlet, written by Bill Bright, called "The Four Spiritual Laws." I use that document as a peg on which to hang a series of reflections about American evangelicalism in the 1960s and 1970s. My reflections are intended primarily for readers who need a basic and general introduction to the ethos of popular evangelicalism. Readers who do not need that sort of introduction or who have little patience for impressionistic essays should probably skip Chapter 1.[9]

The next chapter describes the fundamentalist controversies of the 1920s and their aftermath, paying particular attention to matters of cultural authority. Although the controversies have traditionally been interpreted as unequivocal defeats for the fundamentalists, recent studies imply that the controversies must have been victories of a sort, for they preceded and paved the way for the tremendous vitality conservative Protestantism displayed in the 1930s, 1940s, 1950s.[10] Those decades saw dramatic increases in the membership rolls of conservative churches, the expansion of evangelical schools and colleges, the maturation of evangelical publishing, and the launching of a number of important new evangelical endeavors such as Youth for Christ, the National Association of Evangelicals, and the Billy Graham Evangelistic Association. The controversies are, I argue, best interpreted as neither a victory nor a defeat for the fundamentalists but rather as events which demonstrated evangelicalism's transformation from the dominant religious ideology of America—a status it enjoyed throughout much of the nineteenth century—into a subordinate culture. Conservative Protestants responded to their loss of cultural authority in two distinct manners. Some— the so-called "fundamentalists" of the 1940s and 1950s— adopted an adversarial stance toward the dominant cultures of modern America. A more influential group of conservative Protestants—themselves the heirs of the fundamentalists of the 1920s and 1930s—adopted a less hostile and more flexible attitude toward the various dominant cultures of modern America. They played a crucial role in shaping the network which became the "evangelical mainstream" upon which this book focuses.

The third chapter of this book is concerned with politics. In the 1970s, conservative Protestants played a more prominent role in American political life than they had in any previous decade in the century. That prominence was, according to most observers, largely the result of the increasing politicization of laywomen and laymen, that is, of the laity's increased interest in public affairs and increased determination to affect public policy. This chapter traces the ideological roots of the politization of the evangelical mainstream. It argues that the evangelicals of the 1940s and 1950s did not depart far at all from the political and social ideals of their fundamentalist predecessors and that the evangelical mainstream thus moved into the 1960s and 1970s with a set of political and social views which were quite close to fundamentalists'. The evangelicals of the 1960s, no less than the fundamentalists of the 1930s, were prone to rely on conspiratorial interpretations of public events, convinced that healthy families were the cure to most social ills, suspicious of most efforts to use the government to produce a better society, inclined to believe that America was a Christian nation, and determined not to let the state fall into the hands of the enemies of the gospel. Those were not the sort of views that could produce an equanimous interpretation of the events of the 1960s and 1970s. Developments in those decades convinced evangelicals that the Christian way of life and the Christian family were both being attacked by a group of men and women—"secular humanists"— who were determined to use the agencies of the government to undermine Christianity and to destroy the family. Evangelicals became convinced that unless the secular humanists' attempts to gain control of the government were beaten back, the way of life to which they were attached and the private sphere in which they placed so much hope would be destroyed.

The next chapter is concerned in part with the question of why this attachment to the family was so strong. What I try to show is that it may be regarded as a new form of a very traditional outlook for conservative Protestants, as a way of finding private hope in a hopeless world. Whereas the literature produced by the fundamentalists of the 1920s and 1930s was largely devoted to the hopes offered by the Second Coming of Christ, much of the literature produced by the evangelicals of the 1940s, 1950s, 1960s, and 1970s focused on hopes associated with the family. In this essay I consider those two distinct sorts of hopes in tandem because I want to suggest that despite obvious and important differences between evangelical attitudes toward the family and fundamentalist attitudes toward the second coming of Christ, the way the two groups discussed the family and the Second Advent often converged. Those discussions presented a view of the world which was not purely hopeful nor purely despairing and which did not picture humans as either totally powerful nor as completely impotent. Rather, they melded elements of hope and despair and of power and powerlessness. The hope and the sense of power were focused primarily on believers' private fates; the despair and the sense of powerlessness were concentrated largely on the public sphere.

The fifth and sixth chapters explore the way that the evangelical mainstream responded to the changing role of women in American society. The fundamentalists of the 1920s and 1930s were generally hostile to those changes and to feminism. The attitude of the evangelicals of the 1940s and 1950s was considerably more flexible. In the 1960s and 1970s many evangelicals forthrightly embraced feminism: indeed, some evangelicals were so eager to embrace feminism that they moved away from the doctrine of biblical inerrancy—a doctrine that had been one of the hallmarks of fundamentalism. The 1960s and 1970s also saw, as is well-known, the emergence an evangelical counterfeminist movement. But those evangelical attacks upon feminism were more complex than they first appeared, for when closely examined they turned out to include several crucial accommodations to feminism and to involve the adoption of fairly elastic notions concerning "the proper role of women."

The final chapter of the book is concerned with the way that the rise of "modern psychology"—a phrase that the evangelical mainstream associated with figures ranging from Sigmund Freud to Norman Vincent Peale—affected the evangelical mainstream. The fundamentalists of the 1920s and 1930s were extremely suspicious of modern psychology. But in the 1940s and 1950s evangelicals adopted a different, less hostile approach; they made a series of quiet compromises with those therapeutic outlooks that their predecessors had viewed with such suspicion. In the 1960s and 1970s the evangelical mainstream was infused with themes and practices that were rooted in modern psychology. Those themes and practices were, moreover, evident in the more conservative wings of the mainstream, as well as in those that were relatively liberal.

In the main body of the book this last point is, I am afraid, slightly overargued. That is because I want to dramatically juxtapose my account of evangelicalism with one of the standard approaches to the study of evangelicalism: that which empha-sizes how much freedom and power subcultures such as evan-gelicalism have in modern America. Of course, such subcultures have many options at their disposal other than simple accom-modation. But what seems most striking in the final analysis is the remarkable power of the various dominant cultures of twen-tieth-century America to mold a subordinate culture like the one this book is about. Evangelical spirituality was, as the chapter on the four spiritual laws suggests, increasingly commodified. The political battles that evangelicals won did not really move the United States much closer to being the holy commonwealth they desired. Their private hopes were pushed in a more secular di-rection. They increasingly came to see the role of women through lenses that had been fashioned by secular feminists. Their view of the world came increasingly to rely on ideas and attitudes drawn from modern psychology. So the portrait of the evangelical mainstream that emerges from this book makes it look less and less like a disciplined and charging army that is trying to drastically reform American society and more and more like a group of Americans that are trying—quite successfully—to fit in.

1

THE FOUR
SPIRITUAL LAWS

ON A PARTICULARLY BLEAK DAY in 1955, a tall, nervous Texas oil-
man named Keith Miller pulled his company car to the side of
the road and began to sob. Lately he had been unaccountably
breaking into cold sweats, drifting into periodic depressions,
and wondering if he were not on the verge of losing his mind. At
the side of that East Texas road he realized that there was nothing he wanted to do with his life.[1]

His life had begun to unravel ten years before when he was an
athletic and affable high school senior. It was nothing as grand as
the onset of the Atomic Age that had disrupted his adolescent
complacency, but rather a series of the sort of personal adversities that have always troubled women and men: his brother's
sudden death, his mother's nervous breakdown, his father's
heart attack and eventual death. Under these pressures, Miller
came to see his family in a new and distressing light. He began to
see that a great emotional gap had always existed between his
mother and his father and that they had inadvertently, but con-
tinuously, wounded one another.

These adversities did not, of course, deprive Miller of all happiness. In the next few years he fell in love, got married, and
fathered two children. And when his job took him on long, soli-
tary drives, Miller occasionally experienced moments of intense

joy. At such times he felt certain that God was trying to show him the peace that he could give his creatures and teach him something of his own divine majesty and power. Ironically, such sharp joys made the rest of Miller's life all the more unendurable, for they were brief and transitory, and he could not count on them happening again. And when Miller enrolled in a prestigious Eastern seminary so that he could learn how to know God, he found only intellectual excitement, not spiritual succor. A little crestfallen, he made his way back to Texas and back to a career in the oil industry. That was how he ended up crying at the side of the East Texas road.

Much to his surprise, he found God there. He exclaimed that if there was anything that God wanted out of his "stinking soul," then he was welcome to it. Even years after he uttered that prayer Miller was certain that God had taken him up on that slightly vulgar offer. It was, he insisted, like being born again. "I realized then that God does not want a man's money, nor does He primarily want his time," Miller later recalled. "He wants your *will* and if you give him your will, He'll begin to show you life as you've never seen it before." What Miller discovered on that road was the hope that ordinary persons can live extraordinary lives.[2]

The evangelical affirmation of the tremendous importance of personal conversion is one of the most significant differences between evangelicals and liberal Christians. Conversion experiences are fairly common in modern America: one-third of the respondents in a 1976 survey of the American people reported that they had been born again.[3] It is not difficult to compile a large number of such stories; they can be readily extracted from interviews with evangelicals or from the literature published by evangelicals. And stories such as Miller's unquestionably communicate some facets of the evangelical view of the world that might otherwise remain obscure. It is tempting, therefore, to simply collect, compare, and ponder as many of these stories as one can.[4]

There are, however, fundamental flaws inherent in such a procedure. Interviews subtly distort the evangelical view of conversion, for they yield transcripts that reflect the interests, concerns, and preconceptions of the interviewer as well as those of the convert. Furthermore, oral history can produce relatively little evidence concerning how evangelicals thought about conversion in previous decades of this century. The stories that have made their way into print consistently overrepresent the dramatic and underrepresent the mundane. The conversion experiences that tend to be recorded in evangelical literature are the most dramatic ones: a well-to-do graduate of Yale Law School who was suddenly overwhelmed by the meaninglessness of his life, a strapping youth whose conversion led to martyrdom at the hands of a tribe of South American Indians, a Southern farm boy whose faith pushed him into the civil rights movement and then into an antagonistic but loving chaplaincy with the Ku Klux Klan.[5] Nor are such accounts presented in a way that inspires complete confidence in their veracity. Biographies of evangelical leaders tend toward hagiography. Autobiographies and reminiscences usually record experiences that took place years—often decades—earlier.

Furthermore, even the most cursory reading of conversion accounts suggests that the experiences that evangelicals interpret as "conversion" could be interpreted in many other ways. They could be seen, for instance, as signs of psychic disturbance, products of social maladjustment, mystical contacts with some pantheistic deity, or even the onset of demonic possession. How these protean experiences are interpreted is as important as the experiences themselves.

Literature intended to provoke conversion, such as Bill Bright's *Have You Heard of the Four Spiritual Laws?*, provides a promising starting point for an investigation of how evangelicals interpret conversion.[6] The pamphlet's preface indicates its basic message: "Just as there are physical laws that govern the physical universe so are there spiritual laws which govern your relationship with God." It explains clearly and concisely what those laws are and how a person can begin to live in harmony with them. The pamphlet eventually became one of the most widely circulated works ever written by an American evangelical: over 250 million copies of *The Four Spiritual Laws* have been printed and distributed. It has also been frequently imitated. Evangelical groups such as the Navigators and the Billy Graham Evangelistic

Association produced their own versions of it. Indeed the pamphlet proved so effective that at least one mainline Protestant denomination developed its own modified rendering of the four spiritual laws.[7] Next to the Bible it is the work that contemporary evangelicals are most likely to have encountered. Whether it is *the* representative document of popular evangelicalism in postwar America can be debated. It would, however, be hard to argue that it is not *a* representative document.

A close reading of Bright's pamphlet discloses some central themes of popular evangelicalism. It also reveals popular evangelicalism's close ties to the advertising ethos of American commercial culture and its emphasis on the this-worldly rewards of Christianity. It suggests some subtle but important modifications that evangelicals have made in their traditional message. It suggests as well the care with which they came to avoid giving unnecessary offense to nonevangelicals and their simultaneous refusal to fully embrace pluralism. Most interestingly, it points toward an important tension in the message of popular evangelicalism. On one level that message seems to offer only comfort and no challenge to its auditors. On another it presents a rigorous, if somewhat circumscribed, call to discipleship.

Bill Bright, its author, accepted Christ in the mid-1940s, a few years after he had graduated from Oklahoma's Northeastern State College and moved to southern California. Bright's conversion was not nearly as dramatic as was Miller's; it was certainly not the sort of event that would have interested William James. Indeed, Bright's biographer did not bother to record the exact date of the conversion. Nevertheless, it changed Bright's life.

It changed the lives of others as well, for though Bright was not a charismatic figure and though his face never became as familiar as those of Billy Graham, Oral Roberts, or Jerry Falwell, he eventually became one of the most important promoters of aggressive Christian evangelism in postwar America. According to Richard Quebedeaux, a knowledgeable student of contemporary evangelicalism, by the 1970s Bright was spending and raising more money to spread the gospel than any other American.[8]

Bright was instrumental in founding Athletes in Action, an

organization that used sports exhibitions as a means of evangelism; Agape, a world service organization modeled after the Peace Corps; and the Christian World Liberation Front, which sought to evangelize those affected by California's counterculture. Campus Crusade for Christ, which he founded in 1951, later grew into a huge international organization with an annual budget of over $42 million, 6,500 employees, and representatives in ninety-seven nations. Some of the sessions of Explo '72, another of Bright's ideas, were attended by 180,000 participants. Police estimated that two of the sessions of Explo '74, held in Seoul, South Korea, attracted more than 1.3 million people. The "Here's Life, America" and "Here's Life, World" campaigns were even more ambitious. Constructed around the often-parodied slogan "I Found It," the campaigns used volunteers from local churches, billboards, bumper stickers, newspaper ads, radio spots, and television specials (starring Pearl Bailey, Roy Rogers, Pat Boone, and other Christian celebrities) to blitz selected cities with the gospel.[9] In 1981, Nelson Bunker Hunt announced that he had raised $225 million for the "Here's Life, World" campaign.[10]

The campaigns that Bright marshaled and the institutions that he founded linked several generations of important evangelical leaders. Henrietta Mears, who taught Bright the rudiments of Christian discipleship and steered him toward work with college students, had herself been influenced by W. B. Riley, the man who had done as much as any other to assemble the fundamentalist coalition of the 1920s. At Fuller Theological Seminary in Pasadena, California, where Bright prepared for his ministry, his classmates included David Hubbard, who eventually became president of that school, and Dan Fuller (son of the seminary's founder), who studied with Karl Barth at Basel before returning to Pasadena to teach hermeneutics. Dan Fuller was on Campus Crusade's original board of directors. So were Mears, Wilbur Smith (a professor at Fuller), noted evangelists such as J. Edwin Orr and Billy Graham, and Dawson Trotman, the founder of the Navigators.[11]

Prominent evangelicals in the generation that came to maturity in the 1960s were also involved in Bright's ministry. Hal

Lindsey, author of *The Late Great Planet Earth*, spent most of the 1960s directing Campus Crusade's flagship chapter at the University of California at Los Angeles. Pete Gillquist, Jon Braun, and Dick Ballew, all noted evangelical spokesman, were also deeply influenced by their association with Bright. Marabel Morgan worked for Campus Crusade before writing *The Total Woman*. Josh McDowell, author of *Evidence That Demands a Verdict* and perhaps the best-known evangelical apologist, was also a member of the Campus Crusade staff.[12]

In spite of his position near the center of the postwar evangelical mainstream, Bright was never ordained, and in many respects he seemed to have less in common with conventional clerics than he did with the successful, ambitious businessmen whose ranks he had once hoped to join. He had, in fact, originally been drawn to the church largely because it gave him a chance to meet so many ambitious and successful men and women of the world. After his conversion he dramatically renounced the materialistic ambitions that had once driven him, but he continued to work extraordinarily long days, to take few vacations, and to make only a minimal effort to sustain friendships that could not help him in his work. From the earliest days of Campus Crusade, Bright often turned to business executives for advice; in the late 1960s he restructured the entire organization along lines proposed by four students from the Harvard Business School. His campaigns were generously supported by businessmen such as Richard DeVos and Nelson Bunker Hunt.[13] Bright's political views were also similar to those of many American businessmen: he was deeply concerned about the Communist threat to America, and he sometimes presented the Christian faith as a way of meeting that threat, but he was also quite willing to travel to the Soviet Union and to praise some features of Russian society.[14] Finally, Bright had a sophisticated grasp of the techniques of modern advertising and few scruples about using them to interest the public in his wares.

It was only natural, then, that in 1957, when Campus Crusade sponsored its first summer retreat on the shores of Minnesota's Lake Minnetonka, Bright scheduled a talk by a layman who made a living as a sales consultant. The consultant argued that witnessing for Christ was in most respects like selling a product and that though they usually did not recognize it, most Christians had a standard sales pitch they used when trying to win converts. He issued a challenge: "Bill Bright, who works with students and professors and outstanding business executives, as well as with men on Skid Row, thinks that he has a special message for each of them, but . . . I would be willing to wager that he tells them all the same thing."[15]

Writing years later, Bright recalled finding many of the points in the consultant's speech "repugnant and offensive." But even before the talk was over, he began wondering if there was not, after all, some truth in it and upon reflection he decided that he did indeed have a uniform sales pitch for Christ. He wrote it out as a twenty-minute presentation, directed his staff to use it in their evangelical efforts, and found it was extremely effective. In succeeding years, the presentation was condensed, revised, and put into print (to insure "faithfulness to the content and uniformity of presentation"). That printed version was known as *The Four Spiritual Laws*.[16]

In the pamphlet's early drafts, the first of the four laws boldly proclaimed: "You are a sinner and separated from God." That was a traditional starting point for the proclamation of the gospel, one that John Calvin and Jonathan Edwards surely would have approved. That tradition was cherished by evangelicals well into the twentieth century; popular books published in the postwar era insisted that "the first fact that every person must face as he ponders his spiritual relationship to God is that of SIN."[17]

But just before the pamphlet went to press Bright decided on a very different point of departure. In its final form—"God *loves* you and offers a wonderful *plan* for your life"—the first law implicitly rejected the notion that God has predestined some humans to damnation.[18] Many born-again Christians were quick to spot—and to pillory—Bright's deviation from tradition. Indeed

Bright's own daughter wept when she first heard of the proposed change, for she feared that her father had begun to dilute the gospel.[19]

In the final draft, the four laws were first asserted baldly, and then supported with quotations drawn from the New Testament, and finally elaborated and explicated. The crucial citation for the first law was John 10:10, in which Christ said, "I came that they might have life, and might have it abundantly." As Bright elaborated that theme, he posed a question vaguely reminiscent of Jean Jacques Rousseau's investigation of how it came to be that man, born free, is everywhere in chains. Why is it, Bright asked, that human beings, whom Christ loves and came to earth to save, frequently die without ever having tasted the abundant life that he came to give man?

Law Two, essentially a less personally accusatory version of the first draft of the first law, provided the answer. "Man is," it asserted, "*sinful* and *separated* from God. Therefore he cannot know and experience God's love and plan for his life."[20] Human beings are all too slow to recognize the enormity of their own sin or the vastness of the gulf that divides them from God. They try to find abundant life by following a moral code, by studying philosophy, or by immersing themselves in religion. Those are not ignoble pursuits, but none of them, not even religion, can bridge the gap between God and man. All such efforts are thus bound to end in disaster.

Though the second law presented a fairly bleak assessment of human affairs, it was far less harsh than many earlier evangelical presentations of the gospel, for it was carefully phrased to avoid any mention of hell. Indeed hell was not mentioned anywhere in the pamphlet. Though it is difficult to imagine what sense, if any, a fundamentalist such as Billy Sunday could have made of it, that lacuna was actually entirely consistent with Bright's general approach to presenting the gospel. At every point his pamphlet put less emphasis on what the gospel can do for human beings in the afterlife than on what it can do for them here and now. Rather than offering a mere fire insurance plan against the terrors of hell, it offered abundance on earth. To be sure, in Bright's view, the abundant life is eternal, but it does not begin when one dies. Its genesis and first fruits are firmly rooted in this world. Bright had far more to say about those fruits than he did about the rewards that the saints will enjoy in heaven.

Law Three asserted that "Jesus Christ is God's only provision for man's sin. Through him you can know and experience God's love and plan for your life."[21] It was buttressed by three scriptural references: one from Romans, one from First Corinthians, and—to clinch the argument—John 14:6, in which Jesus said, "I am the way, and the truth, and the life; no one comes to the Father but through Me." This last passage played a crucial role in the pamphlet's text and indeed in the whole evangelical subculture. Significantly, it was this passage to which the familiar "one way" sign—usually made by smiling, outgoing, and joyous youth like those who attended events sponsored by Campus Crusade—alluded.[22] Just beneath the smiles of those who flashed the one way sign and the careful, smooth phrases of Bright's pamphlet, lurked a resolute refusal to join in the general postwar celebration of religious pluralism. Despite all the important and obvious differences between the outgoing temperament of mainstream postwar evangelicalism and the ghetto mentality of fundamentalism in the 1930s, there was then at least one fundamental similarity: an insistence that Jesus Christ was the only route to salvation.

That insistence was arguably one of the greatest strengths of postwar evangelicalism. Christians, unlike Hindus, for example, have traditionally found it difficult to combine a lively devotion to their own tradition with a recognition of the validity of other faiths. The fact that evangelicalism has chosen not to wrestle with that problem may account for some of its striking vitality.

But its rejection of pluralism was also one of the greatest liabilities of postwar evangelicalism. It predisposed evangelicals to view all those whose way of life differed significantly from their own with deep suspicion, and it tempted them to engage in smug celebrations of the innumerable benefits that come from discovering the only route to salvation. One evangelical author claimed that some of his coreligionists honestly believed that born-again Christians had "fewer cavities, shinier floors, less headaches, less constipation, softer hands, and, of course, more sex appeal" than nonevangelicals.[23] And even when it did not lead to smugness, evangelicals' insistence that there was only one route to an abundant life and that they were on it was an implicit—and, to many, deeply offensive—denunciation of those who were following some other route to salvation. The evangelicals' rejection of pluralism thus no doubt accounted for much of the hostility that many Americans felt toward them.

The Fourth Law asserted that "we must individually receive Jesus Christ as Savior and Lord; then we can know and experience God's love and plan for our lives."[24] The pamphlet explained that neither a mere intellectual familiarity with the spiritual principles nor a simple emotional response to them could produce an abundant life. Receiving Christ was essentially an act of the will, a decision to turn from self to God.

As Bright presented it, that act did not necessarily rest upon a thorough acquaintance with or acceptance of fundamentalist dogma. The pamphlet did not require potential converts to subscribe to such standard fundamentalist tenets as the inerrancy of the Scriptures, the virgin birth, Christ's substitutionary atonement, his bodily resurrection, or the authenticity of miracles. Indeed, the pamphlet did not explicitly demand that potential converts affirm such basic Christian doctrines as the Trinity, the existence of Satan, or even the divinity of Christ.

Of course, Bright himself was thoroughly orthodox on all those points. If a potential convert voiced deep skepticism concerning any of them, Bright no doubt would have been deeply concerned. But dogma was not at the heart of his message. In the scores of his other, longer writings as well as in the *Four Spiritual Laws* he deemphasized dogma and stressed the techniques of holy living.[25]

Bright's relative lack of dogmatism suggested the remarkable degree to which recent evangelical history has been shaped by those who view Christianity primarily as a way of life rather than as a body of belief and by those who stress orthopraxy over orthodoxy. To them being a Christian is largely a matter of living a holy life, that is, living a life in accord with the spiritual principles by which God governs his affairs with mankind. C. S. Lewis, an Oxford don whose popular expositions of Christianity deeply influenced Bright[26] and many other prominent American evangelicals, summed up this view of Christianity. Borrowing his terminology from the religious traditions of the Orient, Lewis wrote at length about the Tao, the mystic way that the universe progresses, arguing that "every man should tread in imitation of that cosmic and supercosmic progression, conforming all activities to that great exemplar."[27]

Of course, some postwar evangelicals did stress the need for converts to affirm explicitly the full orb of orthodox dogma, but even those who stressed dogma more than Bright emphasized that Christianity was more than a set of doctrines to be affirmed. Thus Carl Henry, postwar evangelicalism's most influential theologian, challenged his coreligionists to develop "a fresh and pervading conception of the Christian life."[28] Francis A. Schaeffer, who for a time had more young and reflective admirers than any other American evangelical author, wrote volume after volume addressing a single basic question: "How shall we then live?"[29]

One of the greatest of the theological controversies in the recent history of evangelicalism, the so-called "Battle for the Bible," was occasioned largely by the publication of a book devoted to the very practical issue of whether or not evangelical women should conform to traditional gender roles.[30] Even spokespersons for the Moral Majority, the most prominent of the organizations arrayed under the "fundamentalist" banner, sometimes hinted that one could disavow one of the major tenets of the faith and still be a Christian.[31] And most of the Moral Majority's campaigns were directed at defending not orthodox dogma but a particular vision of the Christian way of life.

Nor were conservative Protestants particularly interested in reading books about purely doctrinal issues. Fewer than 19 percent of the classifiable titles in one scholar's carefully selected sample of conservative Protestant works actually dealt primarily with theological or doctrinal concerns. On the other hand, fully 57 percent of them were concerned with "spirituality," "lifestyle," or emotional and psychological well-being.[32]

A group of evangelicals—persons generally far less impressed with the ethos of American business and far more influenced by that of American academics than was Bright—presented a set of diverse but overlapping critiques of the popular evangelicalism Bright exemplified. They argued that his interpretation of the gospel offered too little challenge to the self-interests of the converted. They worried that his formulas oversimplified the great Pauline and Augustinian traditions upon which they were based. They accused Bright of presenting a faith that resembled authentic Christianity only as closely as fast food resembled home cooking.[33]

They spoke pointedly of the need to distinguish between proclaiming and selling the gospel.[34] In more exasperated moods they resorted to satire. One issue of the *Wittenberg Door*, a publication halfway between the *National Lampoon* and *Christianity Today*, carried both a sophomoric account of how "the last known pagan was finally broken down and brought to repentance following late-night intensive 'Four Lawing' by Dr. Bill Bright" and a biting representation of dialogue between Jesus of Nazareth and one "Richard Y. Ruler":

> **R:** I was wondering what one had to do to get it. Eternal Life that is.
>
> **J:** Well, it's quite simple. . . . You see, just as there are physical laws that govern the universe, so there are spiritual principles that govern our relationship with my Father.

Jesus went on to explain that the answer to all the young man's problems was "Principle Three, Me," and told him that all he had to do to be saved was "simply pray this little prayer which I'll give you here." The young man—who had somehow gotten the notion that he might have to go and sell all that he owned and who repeatedly asked Jesus if conversion might involve some sort of sacrifice—was greatly relieved to find out that eternal life did not cost anything and that he could go right on being a rich young ruler.[35]

What made Bright's message particularly troubling to such

writers was its typicality: such apparent offers of cheap grace abounded in postwar American evangelicalism. Billy Graham's *Peace with God*, published in 1953, two years after Bright had founded Campus Crusade, emphasized the consolations Christianity offered and downplayed the more challenging and disturbing elements of the faith. "Contrary to worldly belief," wrote Graham, "being a Christian does not mean the forfeiting of all real pleasure. Christ's way of life does not require that a man renounce any legitimate interests or ambitions."[36] Though Graham's assertion was not logically incompatible with Jesus's demand that his disciples take up their crosses and follow him, Graham's book could not be easily harmonized with that invitation nor with a great many other of the notoriously difficult demands of Jesus.

Evangelical intellectuals concluded that there was something dreadfully wrong with popular evangelicalism. From their perspective it offered "velvety comfort," "smooth promises," and "kindergarten Christianity." It had produced an era of "small happenings, of Pygmy spirituality."[37]

There was often an elitist strain in such critiques, but there was more to evangelical criticism of Bright than simple cultural snobbery. Even those who saw some sort of vulgarization as an inevitable and not unhealthy by-product of ensuring that Christianity was a religion of the people and not simply a faith of theologians and clerics were concerned about the particular form that Bright's vulgarization took. They worried that many of the men and women who read his pamphlet believed that an abundant life was a happy life, a life without much pain, suffering, or sacrifice. "Take a few moments to scan these pages and pray this prayer," the pamphlet might plausibly have been interpreted as saying, "and you will receive God's blessing and be happy." Bright seemed to have forgotten, in other words, that the Bible included the Book of Job.

Little wonder, then, that some evangelicals concluded that the primary appeal of evangelicalism to modern Americans was its willingness to preach a gospel without the cross. While leaders in mainline churches asked their members to support struggles for political freedom and economic justice, evangelicals seemed content to rely upon denunciations of the evils of tobacco and alcohol. Mainline leaders asked their flocks to wrestle with the challenges that modern thinkers such as Darwin, Freud, and Marx posed for reflective Christians; evangelical leaders dismissed those challenges and offered their followers simplistic, formulaic summaries of truth.[38] Naturally, many Americans found the evangelical message appealing. But evangelicalism's remarkable statistical strength was, according to some of its critics, the result of its failure to preach a challenging message. As they saw it, it was a simple matter of cheap, easy grace selling better than costly discipleship.

There was undoubtedly much truth in that explanation of evangelicalism's appeal. As it was presented in the *Four Spiritual Laws*, conversion was not troubling or difficult. Bright assured his readers that salvation could be obtained by simply reciting the model prayer he included the pamphlet:

Lord Jesus, I need You. Thank You for dying on the cross for my sins. I open the door of my life and receive You as my Savior and Lord. Thank You for forgiving my sins and giving me eternal life. Take control of the throne of my life. Make me the kind of person You want me to be.[39]

The pamphlet noted that conversion might not be accompanied by any external signs of the inner change that had been brought about. A new convert might not then feel any different than he had before reciting the prayer, and there might well be no dramatic alterations whatsoever in outward behavior. Surely it is safe to assume that the seeming ease of being born again helps explain at least some of the tremendous statistical strength that born-again Christianity possessed in postwar America: if all Americans thought that being born again was necessarily a dramatic, gut-wrenching experience, then fewer of them would have told pollsters that it had happened to them.

There was, however, more to conservative Protestantism's surprising vitality than that. Although the sort of popular evangelicalism associated with Bright did not routinely place rigorous intellectual demands upon its adherents and though it rarely impelled them to join the struggles of the oppressed, there were other respects in which it called for a fairly high degree of religious commitment. A closer look at the *Four Spiritual Laws* suggests the form that that challenge took. The pamphlet concluded with some suggestions intended to help new converts to continue to grow spiritually. It advised them to "go to God daily in prayer," to "read God's Word daily," and to "witness for Christ" by their life and words. It directed converts to affiliate immediately with a nearby church "where Christ is honored and His Word preached" and to attend that church regularly.[40] No doubt many converts simply ignored that advice. On average, however, American evangelicals really did read their Bibles more often, pray more consistently, attend church more regularly, and give a larger proportion of their income to the church than did either Roman Catholics or nonevangelical Protestants. Depth of religious commitment is obviously difficult to quantify, but the statistical evidence that scholars have thus far unearthed makes it hard to argue that evangelicals were any less committed to their faith than were other religious Americans.[41]

The pamphlet advised new converts to trust God for every detail of their lives, to allow the Holy Spirit to "control and empower" their daily living, and to "obey God moment by moment." It presented these instructions in a vivid diagram:[42]

SELF-DIRECTED LIFE
S — Self is on the throne
† — Christ is outside the life
• — Interests are directed
   by self, often resulting in
   discord and frustration

CHRIST-DIRECTED LIFE
† — Christ is in the life
   and on the throne
S — Self is yielding to Christ
• — Interests are directed
   by Christ, resulting in
   harmony with God's plan

Such advice was not an afterthought; it was embedded in the text of the pamphlet's model prayer. That prayer stressed the lordship of Christ. In it the convert asked Christ to "make me the kind of person You want me to be" and to "take control of the throne of my life."

Bright realized that when the average convert accepted Christ she or he would probably not understand the full implications of that decision or all the sacrifices that it might eventually entail. He admitted that his pamphlet was a drastic oversimplification of the Christian faith, and he knew that attempts to use it to instantly convert persons with absolutely no exposure to Christianity would never succeed. But that was not, he insisted, the pamphlet's purpose. It was addressed, rather, to men and women who already possessed a basic acquaintance with the gospel but who had never directly responded to its challenge. It was designed to induce such a response and so help its readers take the first crucial steps in a very long process.[43]

Bright wrote prolifically on the more advanced steps of a Christian's spiritual development, carefully distinguishing between "spiritual" and "carnal" Christians. He applied the latter term to those who had once genuinely accepted Christ as their Lord and Savior but who had since lapsed into robbing him of the lordship of their lives as they once again put self on the throne.[44] Evangelicals who followed Bright made a special point of denigrating the life of a carnal Christian, sometimes implying that it was in many respects a less honorable position than that of one who had never accepted Christ.

Beyond that, evangelical literature suggests that there was a sense in which its overall message was too challenging. Historians examining the effects that ideas like Bright's had on previous generations of American evangelicals have found a people obsessed by attempts to annihilate and abase their own sense of selfhood and self-worth so that they could conform unhesitatingly to the will of God: men and women always at war with the self and yet never able to escape it.[45]

An even-handed survey of the twentieth-century evangelical mainstream produces less evidence for the pathological effects of a strenuous effort to govern self-will than in earlier centuries. Evangelical preachers and writers consistently stressed that the Christian was not called upon to annihilate the self but rather to forget it and to concentrate on what were, in the ultimate scheme of things, more important matters.[46] In the diagrams that Bright drew to represent the spiritual conditions of the ideal Christian, the self had not been eradicated: it had simply assumed its rightful place at the foot of God's throne.[47] Bright and his fellow evangelicals were certainly not deliberately inculcating the morbid, obsessive spirituality that afflicted previous generations of evangelicals.

But that sort of pattern nevertheless did appear, sometimes with startling clarity, within postwar evangelicalism. Evangelicals who wrote about the cure of souls themselves diagnosed this condition and wrote of its pernicious effects. And although their works reveal a widespread understanding of how easy it is to misapply the principles of self-denial and a realization of how damaging such a misapplication could be, evangelicals such as Bright nevertheless insisted that a life lived without reference to those principles was hopelessly out of harmony with the spiritual realities of the universe. In his talks and books Bright exhorted his fellow believers to submit every detail of their lives to the lordship of Christ. Committed evangelicals were expected, he said, to organize their families, rear their children, manage their time, regulate their sexual activity, and prepare for death in accord with that principle. Some of them surely did so. What Bright's critics interpreted as nothing more than an offer of cheap grace could also be interpreted as a serious call to a devout and holy life. That call was, however, delivered in a way that embodied rather than questioned the commodification of the Christian tradition. The spirituality fostered by the Four Spritiual Laws was not always unstrenuous. The strenuousness it called for was, however, usually entirely congruent with a thoroughly commodified culture.

2

THE FUNDAMENTALIST CONTROVERSIES AND THEIR AFTERMATH

WHAT WAS THE RESULT of the fundamentalist controversies of the 1920s? Observers have traditionally interpreted them as an unequivocal defeat for the fundamentalists. Many have seen them as the time when the old-fashioned religion was put on its way to a gradual, but inevitable, extinction.

Contemporary accounts assumed, more often than not, that the fundamentalists had been dealt a terrible blow in the controversies. Before the controversies reached their peak, fundamentalism's opponents, frightened by its strength, had penned many passionate denunciations of the movement, replete with extravagant estimates of its power. Such accounts surfaced far less frequently in the late 1920s than in the first half of that decade. They were even less common in the 1930s. A movement that once seemed potent and terrifying to its enemies now moved to the periphery of their vision, nearly dropping completely from sight.

Whatever victories the fundamentalists had won in the anti-evolution campaign now seemed "Pyrrhic."[1] The campaign had provoked "laughter among the thoughtful of the earth from London to Peking,"[2] horrifying Christians and warming the hearts of "all who sneer at religion."³ In 1926, the *Nation* confidently announced that "the fundamentalist menace" was now a thing of the past.⁴ In the same year the *Christian Century* observed that fundamentalism was "vanishing": the fundamentalists had suffered "decisive" defeats in recent struggles; the routs had snapped fundamentalism's "backbone." Henceforth it would be "a disappearing quantity in American religious life."⁵

A few historians—Richard Hofstadter and George Marsden, for example—have presented alternative interpretations.⁶ But for the most part scholars have been content to describe the controversy as a conservative debacle. Accounts of the 1920s assert that the Scopes trial in Dayton, Tennessee, exposed the fundamentalists' "pitiful ignorance";⁷ textbooks report that the ridicule the trial engendered "lost them their cause."⁸ Recent essays on twentieth-century evangelicalism report that within a year of Bryan's "last stand," it was clear that fundamentalists had met defeat "on all fronts": fundamentalism was "in eccentric disarray."⁹ Earlier studies maintain that by the late 1920s fundamentalism "had run its course."¹⁰ Sociological studies note that the 1920s were a time when a significant portion of the American populace "consciously repudiated the beliefs of conservative Protestantism."¹¹ From now on, asserts the most authoritative account of American religious history, evangelical Protestants "would occupy an increasingly restricted place in the nation's life . . . . [T]hey would never again be able to alter the content of scientific education. . . . Hereafter fundamentalism was in retreat."¹²

Subsequent developments reveal how misleading it is to describe the fundamentalist controversies as simple fundamentalist defeats. The controversies were followed by a string of impressive evangelical accomplishments.

Signs of conservative Protestantism's recent vitality have been noted so frequently that their recitation has nearly hardened into a litany. Public opinion research suggests that by the 1970s there were at least 30 million and perhaps as many as 50 million born-again American Christians. Enrollment in evangelical schools and colleges was burgeoning and in an era when the mainline churches were losing members membership in conservative Protestant denominations was still climbing. Political leaders eagerly vied for evangelical support. Evangelical television programs attracted huge audiences. Books written, read, and published by evangelicals regularly headed best-seller lists, selling millions and sometimes tens of millions of copies.

Of course the current vitality of conservative Protestantism does not by itself demonstrate that the fundamentalists were not routed in the battles of the 1920s. The fundamentalist controversy conceivably could have been followed by dramatic decline; a deep trough might separate recent evangelical vitality from the vitality evangelicalism displayed before the controversy. Observers have sometimes assumed that the evangelical renaissance is a recent phenomenon and that the decades immediately succeeding the controversy were years of fundamentalist decline; they have maintained that fundamentalists were engulfed by despair in the 1930s and that this state of affairs prevailed until the late 1950s. Then, after decades of contraction, evangelicalism began to "mushroom" in the 1960s.[13] But there is little evidence to support that hypothesis. For example, membership in conservative denominations did not decline sharply after the controversy. Nor did it spurt upward in the 1960s and 1970s. The pattern is rather one of sustained steady growth. And in each decade since the fundamentalist controversies conservative Protestants displayed considerable strength.

The 1930s were years of effervescence rather than of decline. The circulation of fundamentalist periodicals such as the *Moody Bible Institute Monthly* increased dramatically: the journal's circulation rose from 27,000 to 40,000 in the course of the decade. The enrollment at Wheaton College, an important conservative Protestant school in Illinois, went from 400 in 1926 to 1,100 in 1941. Fundamentalist foreign mission agencies throve in the 1930s, raising more funds and attracting more volunteers than in any previous decade. Fundamentalist preachers such as Martin

R. DeHaan, Donald Grey Barnhouse, and Charles Fuller carved out huge radio audiences. Fuller's "Old-Fashioned Revival Hour" was the most popular religious radio program.[14]

The heirs of fundamentalism displayed, if anything, more energy after 1940 than before. The 1940s and 1950s saw the organization of the National Association of Evangelicals, the founding of new evangelical publishing houses, magazines and schools, the advent of dramatic youth rallies in every major city in the nation, a dramatic expansion of evangelical outreach to secular colleges, and the emergence of Billy Graham. Two decades after it had spoken so confidently of "vanishing fundamentalism," the *Christian Century* was running articles that pondered the continuing strength of the old-time religion.[15] By 1957 it was trying to fathom the "fundamentalist revival" that had touched the lives of so many Americans.[16]

Evangelical Protestantism—that branch of Christianity which stresses the importance of personal conversion and which emphasizes the inspiration and authority of the Bible—was the most powerful religious ideology of pre–Civil War America.[17] Many Americans celebrated its power; a substantial number lamented it; very few indeed denied its reality. Robert Baird—a Presbyterian minister and the author of *Religion in America* (1844)—noted that dozens of different sects could be found in America and that not all of them faithfully preached the saving truths of the evangelical faith, but he noted with satisfaction that the bewildering profusion of sects and denominations America possessed was undergirded by evangelical hegemony. The saving gospel of Christ, he asserted, was preached effectually through out the land.[18] John Hughes, the Roman Catholic bishop of New York, fought to circumscribe evangelical power and prestige and pointed with pride to the cracks in evangelical hegemony, but he also acknowledged its reality, bewailing for example the fact that Catholics' religious and civil rights were "abridged and injuriously affected" by Protestants' power.[19]

THE FUNDAMENTALIST CONTROVERSIES

Recent historical investigations confirm the importance of evangelicalism in early nineteenth-century America. Whether scholars set out to explore its intellectual, social, or political history, they are ineluctably drawn into a study of evangelicalism. Evangelicalism infused the world view of America's educated classes. It molded the way Americans lived their private lives and the way they thought about their nation's destiny; fueled crucial reform movements such as temperance and abolitionism; and helped produce the American two-party system—the first full-blown party system in the world. William G. McLoughlin's well-known assessment—"the story of American Evangelicalism is the story of America itself in the years 1800–1900"—is hyperbolic and more applicable to the first half of the century than the second, but nevertheless essentially accurate—simply a stark expression of a historian's commonplace.[20]

Evangelical dominance was, of course, never absolute. Even in the second quarter of the nineteenth-century—when evangelical cultural prestige was probably at its height—a few of the nation's colleges had turned away from orthodoxy and a few of the nation's finest intellects had questioned its verities. Even then, nonevangelical voters, their ranks swelled by immigrants, challenged evangelical political power. Freethinkers were scattered throughout the nation. A few of the nation's manifold sects and denominations were not evangelical.

During the five decades after the Civil War, evangelicalism's power was greatly eroded. By 1910 America possessed a political system in which most specifically evangelical concerns were far less important than they had been earlier, a bold and articulate intelligentsia who thought that the fundamentals of the faith were not only untrue but also uninteresting, and scores of colleges that were more likely to undermine than inculcate the evangelical faith. The character of the leading Protestant denominations had also changed dramatically in these decades. Their seminaries, councils, and boards gradually came under the influence of persons who eschewed literal interpretation of scriptures, de-emphasized the importance of personal conversion, and advocated modifying the doctrines of the church to meet the changing social and intellectual situation in which it found itself.

Many, though by no means all, evangelicals were aware of—and horrified by—the old-time religion's loosening grip on American culture. They saw themselves confronted by a hydra-headed monster, satanic in origin and worldwide in scope, that threatened all that they held dear.[21] Fundamentalism, an inter-denominational movement that coalesced in the second decade of the twentieth century, was a militantly antimodernist variety of evangelicalism. It was not, as the stereotype would have it, an exclusively rural or an exclusively Southern movement. Its strongholds were in the cities and in the North. Most of its leaders were committed to the doctrine of biblical inerrancy—a precise if somewhat brittle understanding of the nature of revelation that had been formulated most fully by professors at Princeton Seminary. Most of them subscribed as well to dispensationalist premillennialism—a method of scriptural interpretation that originated in Britain in the 1830s, spread to America in the 1850s, and received its classic expression in the notes of the Scofield Reference Bible (1909).[22]

In the 1920s fundamentalists, determined to regain the ground that evangelicalism had lost since the Civil War, launched concerted drives to recapture control of the nation's public schools and of its most influential denominations.

Their attempts to prevent evolution from being taught in the nation's schools produced the famous Scopes trial of July 1925. The events that led up to the trial, the trial itself, and its aftermath are among the most familiar episodes in American religious history. They were front page news for months; eventually they were transformed into a Broadway show and a highly successful motion picture. Some of the details of what happened in Dayton, Tennessee, are, therefore, inscribed in the American imagination: almost everyone can picture the cardboard fans, beating rhythmically and ineffectually against the summer heat, Darrow's witty and devastating attacks on orthodoxy, and Bryan's confused defense of the faith. Almost everyone remembers as well that the Scopes trial hardly produced the outcome the fundamentalists desired. Scopes was found guilty, but the fine was disappointingly small, and at the end of the trial the crowd surged to congratulate Darrow.

The other facet of the fundamentalist controversy—the conflicts between conservatives and liberals that erupted in a number of American denominations in the early and middle 1920s—is not so familiar, but no less significant. Pitched battles between conservatives and liberals broke out in two of the nation's largest denominations: the Northern Baptists and the Presbyterian Church in the USA (the Northern Presbyterians). Lesser conflicts affected Methodists, Disciples, Episcopalians, Southern Baptists, and Southern Presbyterians.

An attenuated but still substantial evangelical hegemony was within the living memory of the generation of the 1920s, and many conservative Protestants presented their case in a way that reflected that heritage. They presented themselves not as outsiders besieging the establishment but as insiders politely but firmly insisting that the modernists quit the premises.

That was how Professor J. Gresham Machen of Princeton Seminary, a central figure in the fundamentalist controversy among Northern Presbyterians, stated his case. Machen, the son of a prosperous and erudite Baltimore attorney, had studied at Johns Hopkins, Princeton, Marburg, and Göttingen. His goals, as he beguilingly presented them, did not seem outlandish. There was a time, he argued, when men who could not accept orthodox Christianity did not try to become ministers of the gospel. In the previous century, he said, a man who did not believe in the doctrines of the Presbyterian church would not have attempted to administer its affairs, preach from its pulpits, or teach in its seminaries.

Machen, who had himself been plagued by religious doubts as a young man, professed sympathy for all (and great admiration for some) men who could not accept the orthodox position.[23] He urged no draconian measures against the heterodox. He simply asked them to withdraw from the orthodox denominations whose creeds they doubted and attach themselves to religious organizations, Unitarian meeting houses for instance, that did not pretend to be evangelical. They would be more comfortable in such organizations, and there they could express their views more honestly; after their withdrawal the Presbyterian church would once again be what it should be—a bastion of orthodoxy.[24]

Fundamentalism's opponents presented their case in an equally beguiling manner. They did not suggest that mainline denominations repudiate the doctrines conservatives considered the fundamentals of the faith, nor did they demand that those denominations endorse the doctrinal formulation of the liberals. They simply pleaded for tolerance. Harry Emerson Fosdick, whose 1922 sermon "Shall the Fundamentalists Win?" fanned the flames of controversy among both Northern Baptists and Northern Presbyterians, neatly stated the basic argument: all the liberals wanted was "a church inclusive enough to take in both liberals and conservatives without either trying to drive the other out."[25]

Denominational battles did not pit all conservatives in a given denomination against all its liberals. Rather, the battle lines were drawn in a way that put the conservatives at an extreme disadvantage. On the one side were those who possessed both an allegiance to the fundamentals of the faith and a conviction that devotion to those fundamentals necessitated an attack upon the modernists. Of course, those who believed that traditional dogmas needed to be abandoned or revised were on the other side of the battle. They were joined by a sizable body of men and women who did not share the liberals' dissatisfaction with the old dogmas or their enthusiasm for the new but who believed in tolerance—men and women who, for instance, disagreed with Fosdick on many issues but who nevertheless saw no reason why his views as well as those of conservatives like Machen should not be propounded from Presbyterian pulpits. These circumstances made it impossible for the fundamentalists to force the liberals from the mainline denominations. Instead, conservatives fared so poorly in the denominational contests of the 1920s that many of them felt that they had no choice but to withdraw from the mainline denominations and establish their own separate and thoroughly orthodox organizations.

THE FUNDAMENTALIST CONTROVERSIES

By 1930, Fosdick's question, "Shall the fundamentalists win?" seemed as dated as the celebrations of American prosperity that had accompanied it. The dramatic, well-publicized confrontations between fundamentalists and their opponents were at an end; the fundamentalist counteroffensive had been met with stiff and effective resistance. Rooted in the efforts of a party within evangelicalism to reverse evangelicalism's declining power and prestige, the fundamentalist controversies had instead dramatized and certified that decline. The outcome of the battles in the denominations showed that evangelicalism's power had so diminished that it could no longer control what had once been its most important bastions. The taunting press reports of the Scopes trial demonstrated that evangelicalism was in the eyes of many educated Americans no longer respectable. Many educated Americans had been convinced, as a Methodist fundamentalist put it, that every fundamentalist had a "greasy nose, dirty fingernails [and] baggy pants."[26]

When we glimpse the smiles on the reporters' faces in Dayton, or see the distinguished editor of the *Sunday School Times* attending a church peopled by what his son called "the white socks crowd,"[27] or see Machen leaving the church in which he had been reared and the seminary in which he had been educated and organizing a new denomination and seminary, finally dying amid a handful of supporters in Bismarck, North Dakota, when we see these things, we are watching a culture that had once been dominant becoming undeniably subordinate.

That transformation was of course a serious setback, but the magnitude of the setback should not be exaggerated. There were many hollows in the cultural landscape not controlled by America's dominant cultures. There were other places where their influence was felt, resented, and resisted. While dominant cultures, once established, are not easily overthrown, neither are subordinate cultures easily extinguished. And the evangelical subculture had considerable resources at its disposal.

There were, after all, millions of conservative Protestants—members of various holiness groups, Missouri Synod Lutherans, Southern Baptists, Pentecostals, Campbellites, Anabaptists,

Mennonites, and German Pietists—outside the mainline denominations. Then too there were still millions of conservative
Protestants in the mainline denominations. The Northern Presbyterians and the Northern Baptists had not, for instance, embraced the views of the modernists nor had they rejected those of
the conservatives. The Presbyterian General Assembly and the
Baptist Convention had simply affirmed, after heated debate,
that there was room in those denominations for theological liberals so long as those liberals did not express their doubts about
traditional dogma in too extreme or too explicit a manner.[28] Even
liberals admitted that the fundamentalist defeat in the denominational battles was not a victory for theological modernism. "It
was a tolerationist victory."[29] For the most part, laypersons in
those denominations that the fundamentalists could not control
still felt at least as much affinity for the gospel preached by fundamentalists as for that preached by liberals.

In short, the outcome of the controversies of the 1920s did not
necessitate conservative Protestant capitulation. It had, rather,
raised the question that would dominate much of the history of
conservative Protestants in twentieth-century America: now that
evangelicalism was clearly a subculture, how should evangelicals orient themselves toward America's dominant cultures?

Between the conclusion of the fundamentalist controversy and
the Second World War, fundamentalists wrestled with that question, producing nearly as many individual responses to the new
situation as there were individual fundamentalists. But with the
founding of the American Council of Christian Churches in 1941
and the National Association of Evangelicals in 1942—national,
interdenominational associations of conservative Protestants—
two distinct responses emerged.

The first approach was associated with men and women who
called themselves fundamentalists. It was exemplified by the
American Council and by the council's founder, Carl McIntire.
The second response, formulated by Christians who generally

chose to describe themselves as evangelicals, was associated with church leaders such as Harold John Ockenga, Billy Graham, and Carl Henry; with schools such as Wheaton College, Moody Bible Institute, and Fuller Theological Seminary; with magazines such as *Moody Monthly*, *Eternity*, and *Christianity Today*; and with the National Association of Evangelicals.[30]

Fundamentalists and evangelicals had much in common. Both were, when compared with, say, the leadership of the Federal Council of Churches, politically "conservative": skeptical of big government, deeply impressed by the virtues of the free enterprise system, and keenly aware of the vices of socialism.[31] Both were, of course, committed to the fundamentals of the evangelical faith, and deeply opposed to modernism. Both had been strongly influenced by the fundamentalists of the 1920s: Ockenga and McIntire had studied together under Machen; most of the leaders of both the American Council and the National Association of Evangelicals came from fundamentalist backgrounds.[32]

They had similar views of the situation in which conservative Protestants found themselves in the wake of the fundamentalist controversy. They believed that in the preceding decades their cause had suffered a series of potentially disastrous setbacks,[33] but that the prospects for the future were bright. The vitality of fundamentalist magazines, schools, and mission agencies was an encouraging sign. Bible-believing Christians were, they believed, a very large minority—perhaps even an actual majority—in America.[34]

Evangelicals and fundamentalists both viewed the denominational boundaries that existed in the 1940s with some distaste. Those boundaries limited contact between Bible-believing Christians and forced them into unnatural alliances with the heterodox. More real fellowship could be found in a "good Rotary club" than in many of the presently existing denominations.[35] They hoped therefore for the creation of a single national association that would bring Bible-believing Christians into closer contact with one another and that would challenge the right of the Federal Council to speak for all of American Protestantism.

But the creation of such an association proved impossible. The convention that launched the National Association of Evangelicals opened with speeches that, without mentioning the American Council by name, assailed its policies and called for its dissolution. The public statements of convention leaders gave the secular press the impression that their position was closer in some respects to the Federal Council (which many fundamentalists regarded as the citadel of modernist unbelief) than to the American Council (which was, whatever its failings, clearly committed to the fundamentals of the faith). While the leaders of the evangelical convention limited their criticism of the Federal Council to the rather mild observation that it vitiated evangelistic efforts, they said that they "abhor[red] the destructive methods" of the American Council.[36]

Fundamentalists' attempts to present their case before the convention produced hours of parliamentary maneuver and bitter debate. McIntire's paper, the *Christian Beacon*, carried hostile accounts of the convention[37] and crowed over its failure to garner much attention in the secular press; his association published venomous parodies of the evangelicals' position.[38]

The passage of time aggravated rather than eased the tension; fundamentalists like McIntire eventually seemed to devote as much energy to attacking evangelicals as to exposing the errors of modernism. Evangelicals, for their part, came to regard fundamentalist journals as "smear sheets"[39] and fundamentalist leaders as embarrassing atavisms.

A closer look at the differing strategies fundamentalists and evangelicals adopted reveals why cooperation between the two groups proved impossible.

Carl McIntire, who did as much as any other man to shape the fundamentalist response,[40] was embroiled in bitter controversy for most of his adult life. He was a pugnacious man who loved truth and hated error—a man who did not mind, and perhaps even relished, being in the middle of a good fight. During his three years of study at Southeastern State in Durant, Oklahoma, and another at Park College in Parkville, Missouri, he fashioned a reputation as a fine college debater. He arrived at Princeton Seminary in the fall of 1928 and immediately involved himself in the controversy that was raging between Machen and the less conservative members of the faculty. He followed Machen from Princeton to Westminster Seminary, aided him in the fight to keep modernists out of Presbyterian foreign missions, and shared with him the bitter fate of ejection from the Presbyterian church.[41]

The strategy McIntire advocated was one of combative separatism. "Destroying every means of retreat, and abandoning all compromise," exhorted his newspaper, "let us unfaltering stand with God against an unbelieving world."[42]

McIntire continually stressed the sinister nature of the forces against which conservative Protestants struggled and the folly of seeking to appease one's adversaries. Modernism, for instance, was anti-Christian, a false gospel that daily sent deceived men and women, boys and girls, to hell. It was an intolerant faith, bent on the suppression of the true gospel and determined to win complete dominance. It therefore had to be attacked at every opportunity.[43]

McIntire stressed as well the importance of conservative Protestants isolating themselves from the heterodox. Separation, he asserted, was "the way of . . . purity and holiness, blessing and power." Every municipality seeks to keep its citizens isolated from garbage and "every hospital . . . fights to keep corrupted, diseased flesh separate from the good." It was just as important for Bible-believing Christians to keep themselves free from entanglement with a godless world.[44]

He admitted that the drastic curtailment of intercourse with the nonfundamentalist world that he proposed would involve sacrifice. But that was, he insisted, the only logical response to the situation in which conservative Protestants found themselves. Having, so to speak, lost control of the finest boulevards of the city, conservative Protestants must now regroup in a humbler but safer neighborhood. In effect, he proposed the deliberate creation of a ghetto into which all true Christians would make their way.

Membership standards for the ghetto were relatively strict. Conservative Protestants who refused to support actively McIntire's campaigns against nonfundamentalists were not allowed to enter. Neither were those conservative Protestants who did not accept the doctrine of biblical inerrancy or those who spoke in tongues.

McIntire's strategy made a good deal of sense. It is a commonplace among social scientists that a worldview that conflicts with those of a society's dominant cultures is most easily preserved in isolation.[45] Historians know of innumerable examples of isolated subcultures that have survived intact for decades and even centuries. Faithfully pursued, McIntire's strategy would have safeguarded the purity of the faith and hectored the mainline denominations.

In some respects, however, it was a sharp departure from evangelical tradition. For over a century American evangelicals had readily adapted to their environment. They had long been accustomed to thinking of themselves as insiders, and it was not an easy view to jettison.

McIntire's strategy seemed to preclude the possibility of conservative Protestants recapturing the cultural prominence they had formerly enjoyed. Seemingly more concerned with winning martyrdom than victory, he started fights that he could not possibly win. His strategy might well have consigned conservative Protestantism to an ever more peripheral role in the cultural life of the nation. Unceasing opposition to mainstream America might have produced impotency.[46]

The actual influence of McIntirean fundamentalism may, in fact, easily be exaggerated. A sympathetic, well-informed student of fundamentalism (writing in the early 1970s, when there were approximately 50 million born-again Christians in America) estimated that there were at that time only about four million separatist fundamentalists in America.[47]

The mid-century evangelical program was developed by men determined to avoid what they saw as the "errors" of fundamentalism. Their descriptions of those errors make it clear that the fundamentalism they were defining themselves against was for the most part McIntirean fundamentalism. At the same time they were seeking to distance themselves from the fundamentalists of the 1920s. All of the evangelicals of the 1940s would have said that the fundamentalists of the 1920s had been great Christians. Still, the tactics they had adopted in defending the faith had not, perhaps, been wisely chosen, for they had inadvertently brought the cause of Christ into disrepute. In any case, the America of the 1940s was very different from the America of the 1920s. One could not assume that the ideas and practices of the fundamentalists were sure guides in the present situation.

The evangelicals of the 1940s had no intention of forsaking the fundamentals of the faith, but they adopted a fairly constricted notion of what those fundamentals were. They believed that the exigencies of the situation required that conservative Protestants downplay doctrinal differences and eschew attempts to define truth in all its phases. The doctrinal statement upon which they eventually settled was, as they acknowledged, little more than a sort of "least common denominator" statement of faith.[48]

They wanted to build a broad coalition that included conservative Protestants from a wide variety of backgrounds and denominations. They made determined efforts to bring into their ranks varieties of conservative Protestants—Pentecostals, for instance—with whom their fundamentalist forebears had often refused to mingle.

They were determined not to cut themselves off from the rest of American society. To do so might preserve the purity of the elect, but it would also deprive those outside the wall of the saving truth of the faith.

Evangelicals adopted a far less hostile stance to nonevangelicals than had McIntire. They saw nothing wrong with mounting evangelistic crusades under the auspices of groups dominated by liberals,[49] or with inviting nonevangelicals to speak at their seminaries.[50] They did not think of themselves as compromisers or as accommodationists, but they were moderate men of irenic temper

who studiously avoided "fanaticism."[51] They refused to expend
time and energy on "warlike" maneuvers designed to destroy the
Federal Council.[52] They treated the epithets that fundamentalists
wore proudly—"fighting," "militant," even "uncompromising"—
with derision.[53]

Of course, their goal was to make the rest of America more like
the evangelical community. But the possibility that the give-and-
take would affect the evangelicals themselves could not be ruled
out. So the evangelical strategy was a risky one. It opened up the
evangelical community to secular and liberal influences which
could well have ended up corrupting—or even destroying—the
conservative Protestant subculture. But it paid rich dividends. In
sharp contrast to fundamentalists like McIntire the evangelicals
won considerable cultural influence in the postwar decades.
They never regained the prestige and power enjoyed by nineteenth-century evangelicals. They did however obtain a number
of important victories, winning for themselves a prominent role
in American culture, flourishing rather than merely surviving.

3

POLITICS

IN THE 1960S AND 1970S A NUMBER of prominent evangelicals adopted moderate, liberal, and even leftist political stances.[1] The emergence within evangelicalism of these voices, which I will for the sake of convenience call "progressive," was a development of real significance—of more significance than most non-evangelicals suppose. The progressives were not lonely prophets crying in the wilderness: some of the progressives taught at the most widely respected evangelical colleges and seminaries; others were closely associated with Billy Graham. Articles written by progressives were published by leading evangelical magazines such as *Moody Monthly*, *Eternity*, and *Christianity Today*; books written by progressives were printed and distributed by leading evangelical publishing houses. There is good reason to suppose that the political views of the progressive spokespersons were representative of a sizable minority of women and men within the evangelical subculture. Moderate and liberal political stances are furthermore particularly common among that group of women and men likely to become leaders of the evangelical mainstream in the next generation.[2]

But the significance of these evangelical progressives has often been exaggerated.[3] The progressives were always a minority voice within the evangelical mainstream and they themselves recognized that their political views diverged sharply from those of most other conservative Protestants. Their public pronouncements often took the form of confessions of evangelicals' political "blindness" or passionate denunciations of the alliance between evangelical Protestantism and political conservatism.[4] "More often than not," conceded an evangelical progressive in 1970, "those who hold conservative religious positions also hold conservative political positions."[5]

By the late 1970s these progressives, who by then had been trying for a decade to prod evangelicals to adopt a less passive and more liberal approach to politics, were forced to acknowledge that their co-religionists had become more politicized in directions not to their liking—indeed, in directions which they found appallingly reactionary. Thus in the 1970s the evangelical left found that its efforts were in large part confined, as *Christianity Today* observed, to "stacking sandbags against a conservative flood."[6]

The wellsprings of that flood are not easily discovered. This chapter does not pretend to examine them all. It is confined rather to the more modest, but still daunting, task of attempting to trace the ideological roots of evangelical Protestants' political mobilization behind conservative causes and candidates in the 1970s. Most students of evangelicalism who have considered this matter have focused, understandably, on developments that took place in the 1960s and 1970s. If, however, one focuses on the views of fundamentalists of the 1930s and evangelicals of the 1940s and 1950s, the recent politicization of American evangelicals loses some of its mystery.

The social and political views of the fundamentalists of the 1930s were hardly monolithic. Never embedded in a public declaration comparable to, say, the platform adopted by the Republicans who met together in 1928 in Kansas City, Missouri, to nominate Herbert Hoover for the presidency or to the so-called "social creed" adopted by the Federal Council of Churches in 1908, they are perhaps best thought of as a set of mental habits.

Those habits turned out to be of immense importance. Passed on, with several significant modifications, by evangelical leaders of the 1940s and 1950s to those of the 1960s and the 1970s, they became the ideological filter through which evangelicals interpreted the turmoils of the 1960s and 1970s. Those turmoils, thus interpreted, pushed evangelicals toward a more political outlook.

Fundamentalists steadfastly refused to equate the cause of Christ with either business or labor and from time to time they denounced America's business leaders with great ferocity. On the whole, however, fundamentalists were generally more sympathetic to business leaders than to labor organizers. Donald Grey Barnhouse was willing to admit that in the past labor had been "much sinned against," but he also believed that labor, not business, was now doing the most sinning. Unions had already won too much power in shaping American society; the tactics they used as they tried to obtain more control were outrageous and unconstitutional.[7] Fundamentalist magazines such as the *Sunday School Times*, apparently finding it difficult to imagine how a commitment to labor organization and a commitment to Christ could be reconciled, ran stories that detailed miraculous conversions of "labor agitators" into preachers of the gospel.[8]

Fundamentalists did not like to get directly involved in partisan politics and they rarely endorsed candidates for office. But most fundamentalist leaders seem to have believed that the Democratic party was less trustworthy than the Republican party. To be sure, there were Southern fundamentalists, and they naturally enough tended to support Democrats. But fundamentalists rarely had much praise for Democratic politicians from outside the South: they associated such politicians with bossism, corruption, and Roman Catholicism.[9] Fundamentalists could not help but notice, to pick a minor but revealing point, that President Roosevelt's son bade farewell to Prohibition with an unseemly enthusiasm. President Roosevelt himself seemed to have a poor grip on the doctrines of the church: his Christmas message of 1933 was, in *Revelation's* judgment, shot through with heresy.[10] President Coolidge, on the other hand, had a firm grasp of the essentials of the faith: the *Moody Monthly* noted that his holiday pronouncements had been full of reassuring wisdom,[11] and that his comments on ecclesiastical affairs had been sane and sensible.[12]

In part because they believed that there was a close relationship between political and religious liberalism, fundamentalists often assumed that political conservatives were more trustworthy than political liberals. On the whole, fundamentalist rhetoric throughout the 1930s had more in common with that of political conservatives than with that of the political liberals of their day.[13] But fundamentalists' generally conservative outlook did not lead to a celebratory chauvinism. To be sure the fundamentalists loved their country and they scorned those who sought to bring about the "death of patriotism."[14] But the variety of patriotism that predominated in fundamentalist circles was neither celebratory nor complacent. Fundamentalists were keenly aware of the nation's shortcomings—its lawlessness, its godlessness, its immorality—and those shortcomings disgusted them.[15] "The Parable of the Favored Land," an article written by a Pennsylvania fundamentalist named E. B. Dwyer, epitomized the attitude of many. It began with a paean to America's past greatness and concluded with a hope that in the future the nation would be "the lightbearer among the nations of the world." Nevertheless, a note of deep anxiety ran through the piece. America, Dwyer argued, was at present intoxicated with power, mad with wealth, unmindful of God, and in "covenant with evil."[16] Fundamentalists loved their country in about the same way that a man might love an adulterous wife.

Nor did the fundamentalists' generally conservative outlook include an unbridled enthusiasm for the economic system under which they lived. Not surprisingly, many fundamentalists were as impressed with the virtues as with the vices of the American economic system. They noted, for instance, that American society was still a fluid one; there was no reason, they argued, that a poor man could not, through hard work, enjoy rather than merely envy the life of the wealthy.[17] However, fundamentalists regularly displayed considerable uneasiness about modern economic life. They wondered if some of the practices that modern economic thinkers took for granted, such as the lending of money for interest, were not unbiblical.[18] They wondered too if many forms of employment offered by the American economy—working for railroads whose trains ran on Sundays[19] or for large corporations tainted by involvement in the tobacco industry,[20] for instance—were not ungodly.

Indeed, fundamentalists sometimes voiced remarkably strong denunciations of the economic system under which they lived. Donald Grey Barnhouse commented frequently and passionately upon the poverty that surrounded him, and he did not shrink from asserting that it was rooted in economic injustice.[21] I. M. Haldeman, pastor of the First Baptist Church in New York City, described the economic conditions he observed in terms that seemed to echo the rhetoric of the radical left. Control of natural resources, he explained in a 1933 pamphlet that *Revelation* praised, was in the hands of a tiny minority. Those same men and women controlled the labor force. The members of that powerful elite used their influence not to promote the good of the commonwealth but for their own selfish ends and were, therefore, able to live like kings. Two classes lived in the shadow of these lords. The first managed to avoid sinking into outright penury only by constantly ignoring their desires and minimizing their needs. The second, much larger, class led far more desperate lives, comparable in some respects to the lives of slaves; the conditions under which they labored made them into a sort of machinery which their employers would use up and then cast aside as scrap metal.[22]

That sort of economic analysis impelled some fundamentalists to call for drastic changes in American life. A California fundamentalist named William F. E. Hitt, outraged at the behavior of America's "ruling class" and convinced that injustice and evil would reign in America if "our system is not changed," called for breaking the government's alliance with "the capitalist" and cementing a new one between the state and "the workers."[23] F. W. Haberer, a Virginia pastor, frankly averred that "capitalism is antichristian" and explained at some length and with considerable force why socialism was, from the Christian's point of view, a superior economic system.[24] Such prophets did not have to do all of their proclaiming in the wilderness: magazines such as the

Moody Bible Institute Monthly expressed their esteem for them, willingly printed their articles, and commented upon those articles with respect.

But the editors of the *Monthly*—and most other fundamentalist leaders—viewed such drastic experimentation with considerable skepticism, for they thought that hopes of obtaining economic equality in the present dispensation were chimerical. Socialism, most fundamentalists thought, was unworkable, an attempt to impose Christian ethics on a non-Christian world.[25] Communism horrified them. Its spirit, a writer in the *Sunday School Times* typically asserted, was precisely the same as that of the awful beast whose appearance was predicted in Revelation.[26]

Fundamentalists were convinced, in any case, that economic suffering and economic injustice were less calamitous than spiritual disease and that spiritual disease was what the gospel was supposed to cure. Thus, in the same pamphlet in which he sketched such a dismal picture of economic conditions, Haldeman warned Christians against devoting any of their energy to trying to ameliorate them. Jesus Christ had encountered countless evils—governmental corruption, war, slavery, drinking, poverty—and steadfastly refused to attack them head on. Christ regarded the world as a sinking ship, said Haldeman (using a metaphor that was already beginning to be worn smooth by continual use in fundamentalist circles) and Jesus had not tried to right it, but simply to prevent those on board from being pulled into the vortex.[27]

As recent scholarly investigation has demonstrated, not all fundamentalists were so willing to let the ship of civilization sink without a struggle.[28] But even those fundamentalists who did embrace social reform believed that "no reform will be effectual that does not begin with the heart."[29] They therefore believed that the best way to solve the social problems of the nation was not to attack them directly but rather to attack the spiritual disease of which they were symptomatic; the fundamentalists' approach to social issues thus veered toward a sort of spiritual determinism. Cartoons by E. J. Pace, an illustrator whose works circulated throughout the fundamentalist subculture, drew pointed comparisons between man's misguided attempts to make a better world through socialism or fiscal policy and God's approach to social problems, which involved spiritual regeneration instead.[30] In the midst of the Depression, A. J. Nesbit, a banker and a trustee of the Moody Bible Institute, wrote to a number of North American newspapers explaining that the real solution to the world's economic crisis did not involve any dangerous economic experiments. Rather, the moment the nation turned back to God, the fear, distrust, and hate now so prevalent would disappear, replaced by faith, hope, and love. Industry would improve, and prosperity and peace would prevail.[31] The *Sunday School Times* asserted similarly that statistics demonstrated that business depressions were caused by "dissipation" and "disobedience to God's will." They were cured—and again statistics demonstrated this—by "moral awakening, spiritual revival, and the rehabilitation of righteousness."[32]

Deeply intertwined with their emphasis on the role that religion and morality played in determining the health of a society was another theme to which fundamentalists returned again and again: the importance of the family and of the home. Those institutions in large measure determined, fundamentalists were sure, the quality of a nation's social life: strong families produced strong societies; families in disarray produced social decay. Walter A. Maier insisted in his national radio broadcasts that no country was stronger than its homes.[33] Writers in fundamentalist magazines asserted that family life was the soul of the social structure,[34] and that the homes of the world were "the great tributaries of the river of social trends."[35] Arno C. Gaebelein painted the same picture in darker hues: the decline of a nation, he warned in *Hopeless—Yet There Is Hope*, sprang from the disintegration of family life.[36]

Fundamentalists' attitudes toward civil governments were more ambivalent than their attitudes toward the family. On the one hand, fundamentalists viewed all governments and all those who ran them with considerable suspicion. The manner in which other nations were ruled convinced them that too strong a government could quickly transform itself into a "bureaucratic dictatorship." A Russian, the *Moody Bible Institute Monthly* observed, could not obtain a place to sleep, a job, or the right to buy food or clothes without permission from the government. The old-age pensions, free hospital care, unemployment benefits, child support, and tuition-free education the Soviet government promised to its subjects dramatically increased the state's control of its citizens, for they could be withdrawn at any time and they surely would be withdrawn whenever a subject opposed the will of the rulers. Russia thus embodied "paternal government to the last degree, skillfully designed to enforce discipline."[37] Fundamentalists were comforted by the fact that the American government was not similarly designed, but they were not convinced that it could not itself become an agent of oppression. Maud Howe, writing in the *Sunday School Times*, warned that even in America the state seemed determined to invade household and family life. Unless its encroachments were resisted, the American people might well soon become "slaves of Bureaucracy."[38]

On the other hand, fundamentalists were convinced that no government could exist without God's permission, and they thought that the American government was in most respects superior to all others in the world. And fundamentalists did not believe that the best government was the one that did the least governing: nearly all fundamentalists thought that the state had a duty to do whatever it could to suppress lawlessness, disorder, and open immorality. Indeed many fundamentalists expressed a hope that the American government and its agencies might still be used to help promote a virtuous—even a pious—citizenry. Few of the fundamentalists of the 1930s were willing, for instance, to see prayer or Bible reading excluded from the nation's public schools. On the contrary they reported with great satisfaction on schools in which such exercises were still practiced,[39] and they warned of the dire consequences that had been produced by other schools' abandonment of them.[40]

Nearly all fundamentalists were committed to doing whatever they could to prevent the American state from falling into the hands of persons who did not have a proper respect for the religious liberties of Bible-believing Christians, for they were determined not to let the government be used to eradicate, suppress, eviscerate, or hem in the gospel. Fundamentalists were, of course, determined to prevent modernists from exercising undue influence upon the American government, and they found, to their distress, that such persons were profoundly affecting the way the country was being run.

The influence of Roman Catholicism was an equally grave concern to the fundamentalists. To be sure, fundamentalists said from time to time that Roman Catholicism was closer to true Christianity than were any of the modernist varieties of Protestantism. And fundamentalists did find themselves involved in a few battles—against new standards of sexual morality, for instance—in which Roman Catholics seemed like valuable co-belligerents.[41] But fundamentalists regarded Catholicism as a perverted form of Christianity and they were seldom inclined to minimize the enormity of those perversions.[42] They regularly warned that the American people must not allow their government to fall into the hands of Roman Catholics.[43]

Occasionally fundamentalists excoriated atheists' attempts to influence government officials. In 1930, for instance, the *Sunday School Times* indignantly noted that a group of atheists had asked President Hoover not to issue the usual presidential Thanksgiving proclamation. The atheists argued that in light of the deprivations then suffered by so many Americans such a proclamation was inappropriate, even callous. They argued too that such a proclamation was wrong in principle. The president, they said, had no business directing the "religious exercises" of the American people. Hoover, unsurprisingly, paid them no mind. The *Sunday School Times* was gratified. "It is," the journal said, "a cause for devout thanksgiving that our President declined to be influenced by those who believe that there is no God."[44]

In part, no doubt, because of the mental habits produced by days of meditation upon premillennialist eschatology—which, as one recent exemplary study has noted, was itself in a sense "a conspiracy theory of cosmic proportions"—fundamentalists were fascinated by secret plots and designs and devoted much energy to trying to uncover them.[45] Sometimes the conspirators they feared were Communists. The *Moody Bible Institute*

Monthly acknowledged numerous proximate causes for a Harlem riot that produced more than a million dollars worth of damage, 121 arrests, 34 injuries, and 1 death. The Depression, unemployment, poor housing, poverty, racial prejudice—all of these, it admitted, had helped pave the way for the riot. But it was clear that "at bottom" Communist scheming had been its cause.[46]

Sometimes the conspirators were Jewish. Fundamentalists such as Billy Graham's mentor, William B. Riley, were convinced of the authenticity of the *Protocols of Zion*; Riley thought it was a trustworthy guide to future events.[47] The *Moody Bible Institute Monthly* thought of itself as a friend of the Jews and a foe of anti-Semitism; that self-description was, as scholars have recently argued[48] and as the magazine's columns demonstrate, not groundless.[49] Yet the *Monthly* too was fascinated by the *Protocols* and it defended their authenticity. As late as January 1934, it was willing to grant the possibility that the Nazis might be right in suspecting that some German Jews were "plotting against their lawful rulers."[50]

Sometimes, as in the writings of Gaebelein, the conspiracy that fundamentalists feared had a mixed constituency, including Jews, Communists, and the Illuminati.[51] In other instances the conspiracy was even more diffuse and thus all the more sinister. In 1931, the *Moody Bible Institute Monthly* published "An Open Letter from Patriots to Christians" signed by, among others, J. Elwin Wright, the New England fundamentalist who would later play a crucial role in the organization of the National Association of Evangelicals. It described the efforts of a far-flung network of conspirators to establish an empire built on atheistic principles, political and economic slavery, and the moral degradation of "our mothers, wives and daughters." The empire seemed perilously close to creation. Already signs of the conspirators' handiwork were all too visible. They had produced hostility among the races and antagonism between poor and rich. Educational systems and press outlets throughout the world had been transformed into "propagandizing agencies." Brazenly atheistic organizations were beginning to gain recognition from the judiciary. It might not be too late simply to "locate the responsible parties and discover ways of countering their devices." But if worst came to worst, the letter warned, the conspiracy might have to be put down by force of arms.[52]

Secondary accounts of evangelical history differ sharply in their analysis of the relationship between the political and social views of the evangelicals and those of the fundamentalists. Some, such as William McLoughlin's *Billy Graham*[53] and George Marsden's "From Fundamentalism to Evangelicalism,"[54] have emphasized the similarities between the two groups. But other works emphasize the differences. One standard account of evangelicalism says that during this era conservative Protestants became markedly more sensitive to the necessity of alleviating human suffering in this world, that they strove in a new way to apply the gospel in the sphere of social welfare, and that these developments constitute one of the most important developments in recent evangelical history.[55] Another work argues that the 1940s and 1950s were pivotal in bringing about the emergence of "evangelical social concern."[56] A recently published reference work on American religious history lists a rejection of fundamentalism's lack of a social ethic as one of the hallmarks of the evangelical outlook.[57] Another recent book devotes a chapter to explaining how the work of one of the most prominent evangelical leaders, Carl Henry, helped pave the way for the emergence of liberal and leftist evangelical voices in the 1960s and 1970s.[58] On the face of it, those scholars most struck by discontinuities would seem to have the better case.

It is clear, first of all, that in these years evangelicals made their way into the American political mainstream. The popular press diligently sought out evangelical leaders' views on the important questions facing the country. More intellectually inclined journals—*Christian Century, Library Journal,* and *Yale Review,* for example—commented with interest and even respect on the views of the more scholarly evangelicals. And throughout the 1940s and 1950s, government officials courted evangelicals with great assiduity: during the Eisenhower years evangelicals obtained more visibility in government circles and had more access to government officials than they had at any time since the days of Woodrow Wilson.[59] Politicians at every level of government flocked to prayer breakfasts presided over by evangelicals. Mayors and governors took pride in taking seats on the podium at evangelistic crusades. Observers from the State Department attended—and then commended—conferences sponsored by the National Association of Evangelicals;[60] the director of the Federal Bureau of Investigation became a frequent and enthusiastic contributor to the evangelical press.[61] Congressmen and senators invited evangelical leaders to preach and pray from the steps of the Capitol.[62] President Truman invited Billy Graham to the White House; President Eisenhower asked Graham for advice concerning inaugural arrangements and invited a delegation from the National Association of Evangelicals to the White House.[63]

We know that the evangelicals abandoned the stance of militant opposition to America's dominant cultures that had been a hallmark of the fundamentalists of the 1920s and 1930s. We know, too, that on a whole range of matters—dispensationalism, modern psychology, the proper role of women in society—the evangelicals were innovative and flexible. The evangelicals' own pronouncements suggest that they approached political and social questions with a similar flexibility, for they frequently expressed dissatisfaction with the social and political views they had inherited from the fundamentalists, and they often emphasized how sharply they had departed from that inheritance.[64]

In fact, however, the similarities between the views of evangelicals and those of fundamentalists were at least as remarkable as the differences. The important point for our purposes is that to a remarkable degree evangelicals of the 1940s and 1950s found that the social ideals they had inherited served them quite well in the political climate of postwar America. Here the story is not, as elsewhere, one of evangelicals' accommodation. That it was not so was a matter of great consequence: it meant that the evangelical mainstream would move into the 1960s with a set of political and social views which were quite close to those of the fundamentalists. They were not the sort of views that could produce equanimous reactions to the turbulent events of the 1960s and 1970s: from the evangelical perspective, as from so many other vantage points, all hell broke loose in the 1960s.

The extent of evangelical commitment to, or even interest in, social issues may easily be exaggerated. Evangelicals clearly smarted under the charge that orthodox Christianity necessarily entailed a lack of social concern: in their private councils they complained of their adversaries' attempts to "discredit" orthodox Christian endeavors by claiming that they were marked by "a fundamentalist indifference to social problems."[65] A number of evangelicals did emphasize, more often than fundamentalists did, the importance of Christians taking an interest in the social problems of the day. That emphasis was most pronounced in the writings of evangelical intellectuals such as Carl Henry. But it surfaced, too, in conventions of the National Association of Evangelicals, in the public statements of Billy Graham, and in the columns of evangelical magazines such as *Moody Monthly* and *Eternity*. William Ward Ayer, pastor of Calvary Baptist Church in New York City, told the readers of *Moody Monthly* that it was essential that the church "concern itself with society's problems";[66] editorials in *Eternity* called upon orthodox Christians to address forthrightly "the social problems of our day."[67] Sometimes, however, evangelicals seemed at least as concerned with disproving what they called the "embarrassing" accusation that they lacked a social conscience as with actually promoting social justice or solving social problems.[68] Surely they came up with few concrete proposals to improve social conditions, and surely the amount of money they expended on direct efforts to improve social conditions seems paltry indeed when compared to the amount they spent on evangelistic efforts. Their calls for increased attention to social problems were, in any case, hemmed in by warnings about the dangers of paying too much attention to those problems. Thus in the same article in which he called for a new concern with social problems, Ayer warned against Christians adopting any sort of "emasculated 'social gospel' program."[69]

Evangelicals were moral-spiritual determinists just as their predecessors had been. They regularly proclaimed that social evils were rooted in the weaknesses of families and that strength-ening the nation's families would improve American society. Ayer said, for instance, that Christian homes were the only last-ing solution to the problems of juvenile delinquency.[70] Graham told his national radio audience in 1955 that broken homes were the nation's most pressing "social problem" and that that prob-lem was "eating away at the heart and core of the American structure." When the home—"the basic unit of any society"—began to break down, society was on its way to "disintegration."[71] Social problems, evangelicals insisted, were rooted ultimately in spiritual maladies and therefore best combated by attacking the underlying spiritual sickness that caused them. Henry's much-discussed *The Uneasy Conscience of Modern Fundamentalism*, published in 1947, said that Christianity's prime task in the twentieth century was preaching the gospel "in the interests of individual regeneration by the supernatural grace of God, in such a way that divine redemption can be recognized as the best solution to our problems, individual and social."[72] In a 1960 ser-mon called "The Mystery of Conversion," Graham noted that "Marx said, 'All the problems come from without. You remove the social problems, the economic problems from society and you'll solve the problems of society.' Jesus said, 'No you won't—the problem comes from within.'"[73]

The evangelicals' view of the state was close to that of the fun-damentalists'. They wanted the state to suppress lawlessness and disorder and to make sure that God's commandments con-cerning personal morality were not flouted. Few evangelicals could see any reason for excluding Bible readings or devotions from the classrooms of the public schools. Sometimes they seemed to argue that the state should favor orthodox Chris-tianity, quoting with warm approval, for instance, the senti-ments of nineteenth-century jurists who had commented that all those who believed in the truth of Christian revelation would naturally believe that their government had a special duty to fos-ter and encourage the faith among its citizens.[74] Always they evinced a determination not to let the state become a tool of the adversaries of the faith.

Evangelicals were, almost without exception, hostile to big

government and to government-sponsored "social engineering." They thought that the United States was on the verge of transforming itself into a welfare state and they found that transformation deeply objectionable. The National Association of Evangelicals adopted resolutions warning against the usurpations of the "omnipresent state" and denouncing one of President Truman's proposals on the grounds that it would give America's "political bureaucracy" yet another "instrument of terror."[75] Evangelical journals argued that it was high time that Christians consider the possibility that "state welfare programs are inherently anti-Christian."[76]

Evangelicals generally refused to equate the cause of Christ with the goals of either capital or labor, conservatives or liberals, or Republicans or Democrats. Their sympathies were, however, generally clear enough. The politicians with whom evangelical spokesmen felt the most affinity were generally either Republicans or Southern Democrats. And evangelicals had little sympathy for political liberals. In the late 1950s, the catalog of Wheaton College assured prospective students and their parents that Wheaton was "conservative" on political and economic questions as well as on purely religious ones.[77] Although Henry's social views were among the most innovative and flexible of those of any leading evangelical, his outlook was in fact consistently conservative. Although a chief financial supporter of the magazine Henry edited suspected him of having dangerous socialist tendencies,[78] Henry was a great admirer of Richard Nixon, deeply suspicious of rapid social change, an avid supporter of free enterprise, and an open critic of the goals of organized labor. In his private correspondence Henry carefully corrected the misapprehension that his social philosophy included any politically liberal elements.[79]

Most evangelicals shared Henry's suspicion of organized labor. In his more reflective moments Graham wistfully noted that his efforts to get to know the nation's labor leaders had not thus far brought forth much fruit: everywhere he went there were businessmen with whom he could easily mix, but labor leaders were far harder to get to know.[80] At other times, carried away by his own rhetoric, Graham proclaimed that there had been no snakes, no disease, no union dues, and no labor leaders in the Garden of Eden.[81] A. Herman Armerding, like Graham, strove to demonstrate his impartiality to management and labor. But, explaining in the *Moody Monthly* why American factories should be staffed by industrial chaplains, Armerding expressed both keen admiration for the businessmen who were willing to pay the chaplains' wages and confidence that such chaplains would reduce labor unrest and insure that employees would follow management's directions more conscientiously. He had contempt for "the goal of the average modern industrial worker today": to enjoy both the carefree security the Southern slaves had possessed *and* the freedom of a hobo.[82]

Evangelicals sometimes interpreted national and international events as the outward and visible signs of a vast conspiracy. Graham, for instance, seems to have adhered to an essentially conspiratorial interpretation of John F. Kennedy's campaign successes in the early months of 1960. He wrote to J. Howard Pew from Europe in July to report that there was a general impression among European writers that there was a "mysterious something" behind Kennedy's candidacy. That mysterious something was, Graham told Pew, far more sinister than most observers dreamed. The Roman Catholic Church, having lost ground in its traditional strongholds such as Latin America and Europe, had determined "to capture the United States at all cost." That determination was what was behind Kennedy's success: the Roman Catholic Church, carrying out a strategy that had been carefully worked out over the course of many years, was now perilously close to taking over the nation.[83]

Were there then *no* significant changes whatsoever in the social and political views of conservative Protestants between 1930 and 1960? By no means. But it would be a mistake, and a serious one, to interpret the changes that took place primarily in terms of increased "social concern" or a drift to the left of the political spectrum.

Evangelicals were more likely than fundamentalists to believe that America's elected officials were treating the Christian faith with the respect it deserved. In the late 1940s, for instance, Wilbur M. Smith noted with some surprise and considerable satisfaction that there now seemed to be a powerful Christian element in the United States Congress. It was far more powerful than Smith had previously suspected.[84] And evangelical leaders were no less likely than fundamentalists to believe that Americanism and orthodox Christianity were closely linked. To be sure, in their minds Americanism and orthodox Christianity were not equivalent terms. There were many Christians in other nations; an African who converted to Christianity was obviously under no obligation to embrace Americanism. True Christians who lived in America were, however, all loyal and enthusiastic patriots, and the best patriots were, evangelical rhetoric assumed, orthodox Christians.[85]

Another important change concerned conservative Protestants' views of the economic system under which they lived. Evangelicals frequently protested that American society was too materialistic. They occasionally implied that its economic life was somehow askew, arguing, for instance, that the low salaries upon which missionaries had to live, when compared to the incredible sums paid to motion picture stars, demonstrated that "Satan [had] switched the price tags" in American society.[86] But explicitly economic issues, unsurprisingly, were not nearly so burning for the evangelicals as they had been for the fundamentalists. Surely such issues were addressed less frequently in the columns of the conservative Protestant magazines of the 1940s and 1950s than in the magazine columns of the 1930s. Most evangelicals seem to have been generally satisfied with the American economy. They celebrated the prosperity it had produced and defended it against its critics. Although there was some decidedly one-sided debate upon the matter within its councils, the National Association of Evangelicals explicitly endorsed "competitive free enterprise and private ownership." The Association was convinced that whatever un-Christian elements surfaced from time to time in economic life under the free enterprise system resulted not from the system itself but from man's innate sinfulness. Socialism was, on the other hand, anti-Christian by its very nature.[87]

A final change—one concerning the group of adversaries whose influence upon the American government conservative

Protestants found most worrisome—is worth noting. Throughout the 1940s and 1950s, evangelicals continued to denounce Roman Catholicism's undue influence on the American government. The National Association of Evangelicals regularly denounced Roman Catholicism's "interference" in government affairs and its "militant and aggressive" efforts to bend local, state, and national governments to its will.[88] The Roman Catholic threat was so palpable to some evangelicals that they even refused to consider themselves co-belligerents with Catholics in the struggle against godless Communism. Indeed, some evangelicals—such as Clyde W. Taylor, a leading figure in the National Association of Evangelicals—saw no essential difference between Roman Catholicism and Communism. Both were at base "political"; both aimed at "world domination." Roman Catholics, just like Communists, persecuted evangelical Christians. Evangelicals, Taylor vowed, were not about to cooperate with an institution which "slaughters our people."[89] But by the early 1960s many evangelicals had adopted a new and less hostile attitude toward Roman Catholics. *Eternity*, for instance, took to chiding authors whose polemics against Catholics were too harsh.[90] And despite their fears about the dangers of a Catholic president, evangelicals accepted Kennedy's 1960 triumph with surprising grace. Within months after the election, Graham—apparently abandoning his conspiratorial interpretation of the election—had played a round of golf with the President-elect and lauded Kennedy's victory as a sign that relations between Catholics and Protestants were improving.[91]

Throughout the 1940s and 1950s evangelicals also devoted increasing attention to another traditional nemesis, outright atheism, whose influence upon agencies and institutions supported by the American government seemed to be waxing. The National Association of Evangelicals declared that many of the textbooks and teachers in America's schools were presenting an anti-Christian view of the world. It called for a nationwide, grassroots protest against these outrages, and it called upon the Un-American Activities Committee of the House of Representatives to investigate the situation and to draw up proposals for rectifying it.

Wilbur Smith devoted a very short book with a long title—*The Increasing Peril of Permitting the Dissemination of Atheistic Doctrines on the Part of Some Agencies of the United States Government*—to the atheistic menace. The book focused on atheism's victories in the nation's universities, in the agencies of the United Nations, and in cases argued before the Federal Communications Commission, but Smith clearly envisioned a much broader struggle. His work ended by warmly endorsing the sentiments of a Mississippi congressman who had noted that in the present confrontation between America and godless Communism there was an urgent need to drive undesirables from labor unions, from educational institutions, from every branch of the government, and indeed "from every phase of American life." The congressman seems to have had in mind primarily a struggle against Communism; Smith was primarily concerned with godlessness. Neither man displayed a whit of interest in compromising with the foe.[92]

In the early 1960s, evangelicals began to comment frequently and anxiously on a series of developments that they found profoundly disturbing. Although those developments ranged from the increasing "lawlessness" of American society (by which evangelicals meant chiefly racial riots in the cities and antiwar demonstrations on college campuses) to a general decline in America's power and prestige in the international realm,[93] evangelicals' concerns about the society in which they lived centered on three closely related problems: the decline of the American family, America's rejection of family values, and America's drift away from its Christian moorings. To most evangelicals those three maladies were not simply signs that their society was in deep trouble. Those maladies were, rather, the wellsprings from which all the other difficulties of American society flowed. Thus the sorts of developments they found most disturbing were ones such as a new openness in the national media concerning sexual matters, increases in the divorce rate and in the ratio of illegitimate to legitimate births, young Americans' lack of respect for parental authority and their eagerness to consider values and life styles that differed from their parents', and Americans' willingness to listen to, and even admire, the views of those involved in various non-Christian cults and sects and the views of those who were hostile to organized religion.[94]

Distress does not always produce political mobilization; religious women and men, especially, do not have to respond politically to a perceived social crisis.[95] Yet it does seem clear that as the 1960s and 1970s wore on, evangelicals did indeed devote a larger share of their energy to political matters than they had in previous decades, and that among the evangelical laity especially, the conviction grew that the time for the passing of resolutions and the wringing of hands was past. It was time now for political action.[96] Why?

Part of the answer to that question is that evangelicals were convinced in the 1970s, in a way that they were not in the 1930s, that they were not doomed to political impotence. That conviction was rooted in their sense that although practicing Christians were a minority in America, that minority was a growing one, and that nominal Christians, who made up the vast majority of the American population, might join forces with them in some battles. It was rooted too in their awareness that men and women schooled in the arts of political organization were eager to show evangelicals how to increase their political clout and that many politicians were sympathetic to their outlook and eager to win their support.

The other part of the answer has to do with evangelicals' understanding of what had caused the decline of the family and the increase in the impiety of the American people. In the 1960s and 1970s, a large proportion of the evangelical community became convinced that those phenomena were rooted not in impersonal social forces but in the deliberate efforts of a group of women and men who were dedicated to undermining the family and to destroying religion. It was that group of women and men that they eventually took to calling "secular humanists."[97] (This was of course a modern version of a theme with deep roots in the evangelical tradition. Evangelicals had habitually assumed that social disorder was produced by a secret group of ungodly persons working to accomplish evil ends.)

It became increasingly clear to evangelicals in those decades, furthermore, that the American state was the battleground on which those adversaries had to be met. Evangelicals devoted more attention to politics largely because they believed that if they did not the actions of the government would make creating strong families, maintaining traditional family values, and propagating the Christian gospel unnecessarily difficult—in the long run, perhaps, even impossible. To them it seemed clear that one could not draw a clear line between the realm of politics and the realm of the family and religion. Rather, a concern for the latter meant that one had to be concerned with the former.[98]

Evangelicals had traditionally been suspicious of big government, and throughout the 1960s and 1970s they frequently commented on the American government's assumption of new duties and responsibilities. Many found the federal government's expansion a disturbing development in and of itself; and many evangelicals sensed that its expansion made it, potentially at least, a more dangerous foe than ever before.[99] And as the 1960s and 1970s wore on they became more and more disposed to believe that the enemies of the faith had succeeded in harnessing the power of the state to serve their own ends. As they surveyed the world in which they lived, evangelicals were left with a distinct impression that the American government was not checking America's drift away from its Christian moorings or its move away from the family, but rather was legitimating those changes in thousands of subtle but terribly significant ways.[100] Secular humanists were actively seeking to keep the government from enforcing laws against pornography, homosexuality, and prostitution. They were trying to use the state to put into effect programs and policies drawn up by radical feminists. They were attempting to use the public schools to inculcate their beliefs and to induce students to question their parents' beliefs. All these campaigns were, in the evangelicals' eyes, shockingly successful.

Three Supreme Court decisions came to symbolize for evangelicals the secularists' capture of the state. The school prayer decisions of 1962 and 1963 were greeted with outrage by many evangelical leaders and by most of the evangelical rank and file. They became in subsequent years an especially powerful symbol of the American government's wrong-headedness. We had taken God out of our classrooms, Graham observed, and put sex in.[101] The Court's ruling in *Roe v. Wade* (1973) convinced many in the evangelical mainstream, including the editors of the *Moody Monthly*, that biblical moral standards, once the heart of America's legal system, had been expelled from that system.[102] *Christianity Today* concluded that the decision demonstrated that "the American state no longer supports, in any meaningful sense, the laws of God."[103] By the middle 1970s, evangelical leaders were proclaiming that there was a pitched, worldwide conflict between Christianity and the modern nation state.[104]

It is not at all clear that evangelicals' counteroffensive against secular humanists insulated family values or the family itself from the acids that were eating away at them. Nor is it clear that it actually promoted the propagation of the gospel. Indeed, if one suspects that the changes which evangelicals interpreted as declensions were caused by impersonal social forces rather than by the actions of secular humanists, then one will suspect that the counteroffensive will, in the long run, not have the effects that those who launched it hoped for.

It did, however, help change quite concretely the shape of American politics. Most political scientists agree that the American political system was beginning to undergo an important transformation in the middle 1970s. Some interpret that transformation as a party realignment similar to the one that occurred in the late 1920s and early 1930s; others see it as a move away from traditional partisan politics toward a new sort of political system dominated by interest groups rather than parties. In either case, evangelicals had by 1975 put themselves in a position to play an important role in shaping American political life. The evangelicals, together with their allies, were able to make their influence felt on several important political issues. If they were not in a position to put prayer back in the schools or to pass a constitutional amendment to overturn *Roe v. Wade*, they were obviously in a position to put those issues on the political agenda. So if what was beginning to take shape in the 1970s was a move from partisan to interest group politics, then the evangelical right was surely one of the more important of those interest groups. And evangelicals were one of the constituencies from which the Republican party began to draw heavily in the late 1970s. If what was happening was a political realignment, then the evangelicals were surely one of the crucial elements that went into the creation of one of the two partisan coalitions. Not yet one of the dominant cultures in America and still not yet, certainly, able to control the broader society of which it was a part, evangelicalism was by 1975 a movement that no American who desired political power could safely ignore.

4

THE PRIVATE
AND PUBLIC SPHERES

MANY FUNDAMENTALISTS OF THE 1930s had been profoundly influenced by the doctrine of Darbyite dispensationalism. Named after John Nelson Darby (1800-1882), that form of chiliasm had originated in the British Isles in the 1830s among a small group of religious dissenters called the Plymouth Brethren. It had begun to be disseminated in the United States before the Civil War, but did not gain wide acceptance until afterwards. A series of turn-of-the-century interdenominational prophetic conferences greatly expanded its influence; the notes of the famous Scofield Reference Bible, published in 1909, gave dispensationalism its classic American expression.

Dispensationalists believed that the second coming of the Lord would have two distinct phases. The first of these would come at the end of the era—or to use the more technical term, the "dispensation"—in which we are now living. In this first phase of Christ's second coming, all of the world's true Christians would be caught up from the earth to meet their master in the air. They would then be taken to heaven to dwell with him. After this "rapture of the saints" another dispensation would commence on earth.

During this new dispensation, Jews would play a central role in God's dealing with the human race. Huge numbers of them would make their way to Palestine. Many Jews would accept Christ as the messiah; others would revive the religious practices Israel had followed during the Old Testament era. This dispensation would also see ferocious persecution of Jews. But not all of the many dramas to be played out during the tribulation focused on Jews. A perverted ecclesiastic called the "Antichrist," or the false prophet, would win the allegiance of millions and thus play a crucial role in many of the dramas that would take place after the Rapture. And "the beast," a political leader who would create a new version of the ancient Roman Empire and install himself as its head, would also strut across the stage of world history.

All of the events of this new dispensation would occur in quick succession, for the sway of these two emissaries of Satan— indeed the entire period of tribulation—would be relatively brief. Christ himself would put an end to the tribulation by returning once again to the earthly realm and waging a bloody battle against the forces of wickedness. During this second phase of Christ's second coming the wicked would be absolutely crushed after which the earth would be ruled for a thousand years by Christ and his saints.[1]

Dispensationalism bulked large in the fundamentalist movement. Students at fundamentalist schools such as the Moody Bible Institute were taught the tenets of dispensationalism and tested to make sure they knew those tenets by heart.[2] Many fundamentalist journals carried titles such as *Our Hope* or *Revelation* with chiliastic connotations; the columns of most of the leading fundamentalist magazines brimmed with dispensationalist discussions. Fundamentalists published hundreds of books and pamphlets and preached innumerable sermons that propounded dispensationalism. When they explicated the Scriptures, fundamentalists focused on chiliastic themes with startling regularity—often discussing the Second Coming of Christ more often than they discussed any other topic. Those fundamentalists who commented with any frequency on national and international events saw them, more often than not, as ultimately important only insofar as they related to the second coming. Moreover, fundamentalists boldly speculated on the connections between current events and the events the prophets foretold. Was Mussolini the Antichrist?[3] Did the New Deal's Blue Eagle emblem prefigure "the mark of the beast" to which the prophets had referred?[4] The laity were apparently no less fascinated by the second coming than were clerics: they deluged evangelical publications with chiliastic poems, pored over the notes in the Scofield Bible with an impressive assiduity, and discussed arcane points of the dispensationalist scheme with erudition. Collectively, laypersons in the fundamentalist subculture must have spent millions of hours mastering the intricacies of dispensationalism and millions more meditating upon dispensationalism's implications for their lives.[5]

Those meditations produced many different conclusions: conclusions on subjects ranging from the role of Judaism in the modern world to the need for personal holiness, and from the nature of the Christian church to the proper way to face the prospects of one's own death. The inferences that I want to emphasize were rooted in dispensationalism's characteristic conjunction of hope and despair. Fundamentalists' reflections on that conjunction seemed to have followed these lines.

After surveying world history (in this paragraph and in the next five I am paraphrasing fundamentalists) we cannot believe in progress. History is largely the story of things that have gone wrong: in each and every dispensation mankind has failed to meet the challenges the Lord set before us.[6] And we are, at this present juncture, undoubtedly nearer the nadir than the apex of human civilization. Political, economic, moral, and spiritual conditions are all retrogressing. Impiety is rampant everywhere—even, perhaps especially, in the churches. Lawlessness is on the increase, and the world's civil governments are on the verge of collapse. We can be certain, moreover, that world civilization will soon be in even worse shape than it is now.[7]

It is no surprise therefore that so many clear-sighted persons who once confidently put their faith in human efforts to bring about a better world are now quaking with fear.[8] Those persons still sanguinely relying on human initiative to improve the world are blind, pathetic fools.

For in fact there is very little that human beings can do to influence the course of world history; the Scriptures clearly show that human agency plays only a very minor role in shaping world history and that God long ago determined the future course of world history. The broad outlines—and indeed many of the details—of what the future holds are plainly recorded in the Bible.[9] Those versed in the Scriptures know what the future course of civilization will be, and that human wills are not going to change that course. God fixed it. Men cannot change it.

But the knowledge we glean from the Scriptures does not by any means plunge us into despair. Although world civilization is far beyond our control, we nevertheless can find a limited, but terribly significant, degree of personal power. In the midst of a world situation that appears completely hopeless we can find genuine hope.[10]

The future fate of individual believers is, the Bible assures us, as bright as the fate of world civilization is bleak. Individual believers will not be touched by the famines, wars, persecution, tyranny, and apostasy that will come during the tribulation. That is one of the reasons that the doctrine of the Rapture is so comforting: we believers who are still alive in the last days will be removed from the earth before human civilization is shaken to its foundations.[11]

And though there is an obvious sense in which our private fates are beyond our control, determined ultimately by God's will, there is another sense—and in some respects this the more important point—in which our private fates are in our own hands. Whether we are raptured out of the world before the tribulation begins or left to suffer through the time of trials will be determined by whether or not we decide to accept Christ as our Lord. So though world history is beyond our control, our place in the cosmic drama is not. Will we be ground under the wheels of history? Or will we watch the disintegration of the present world from a safe haven? The matter will be settled, in a fundamental sense, by our own actions. Our inability to change world civilization for the better is counterbalanced by our capacity to determine our private destiny.[12]

———————————

Dispensationalism was not an ideology of pure hope or one of pure despair. Nor did it picture humans as purely powerful nor as completely impotent. Rather, the dispensationalist vision melded elements of hope and despair, and of power and powerlessness. The hope and the sense of power were focused primarily on believers' private fates; the despair and the sense of powerlessness were concentrated largely on the public sphere.

Similar assessments of the public and private spheres appeared in many forms of fundamentalist discourse. Such assessments were often present, for instance, in fundamentalist discussions of what they called the victorious life. Those discussions held out the possibility that born-again Christians could live a life free from all known sin: a life of individual perfection, lived in the midst of a sinful world.[13] Analogous assessments were also, naturally enough, embedded in a large proportion of fundamentalists' comments on national and international events.[14] Interestingly enough, however, the fundamentalists of the 1930s devoted surprising little systematic attention to the private hopes offered by family life.

That is a surprising lacuna, for in a number of different eras of American history those troubled by the state of the broader society of which they were a part did place a great deal of hope in the family.[15] Moreover, the comfort and joys of family life have been a staple of Protestant discourse for as long as there has been such a thing as Protestantism, and those joys and comforts were stressed with great regularity by a variety of nineteenth-century American Protestants.[16] One would naturally expect, then, fundamentalists to devote a good deal of attention to the family. Indeed, the fundamentalists did sometimes describe their family life in roseate terms, and did, from time to time, implicitly emphasize the power they had in the home and their relative impotence in the broader society. But the fundamentalists of the

——————— **77** ———————

1930s devoted surprisingly little systematic attention to the private hopes proffered by family life. They did not write nor preach about the family very often at all, and even when they did do so, they seldom dwelt either explicitly or implicitly on the theme of private hopes and public despair. Private familial hopes were, when compared to private chiliastic hopes, a quite minor theme in their rhetoric.[17]

The chiliastic hopes that infused the fundamentalist subculture were not killed off by the evangelical movement's emergence in the 1940s. There are a good many indications that just the reverse happened. One specialist has concluded that dispensationalism achieved a wider hearing in the decades that followed the Second World War than it did in the decades that preceded it, winning the allegiance of at least 8 million and as many as 16 million Americans. Of course not all of those dispensationalists were part of the evangelical mainstream: fundamentalists made up a large proportion of dispensationalism's constituency; dispensationalists could be found in many conservative Protestant groups such as the Southern Baptist Convention that were never brought into the mainstream. But many evangelicals were wholeheartedly committed to some variety of premillennialism. In some segments of the evangelical community, moreover, the doctrine of the second coming of Christ was no less fascinating a hope than it had been for the fundamentalists of the 1930s.[18]

Signs of evangelicals' continuing fascination with eschatology were particularly easy to spot in the 1970s. In that decade, evangelical film makers eagerly explored the cinematic possibilities of eschatology, and evangelical singing groups took to concluding their concerts with melancholic tunes about the fate of those left behind after the Rapture. In that decade, evangelicals produced scores of books on the Endtimes: readers who happened to ask clerks in evangelical bookstores to see the books in stock concerned with the Second Advent were likely, evangelical editors observed, to be trapped in the store for the better part of a day.[19] Some of these books, such as Hal Lindsey's *The Late Great Planet Earth*—a remarkably breezy account of the events leading up to the destruction of the present world—sold millions of copies.

The 1970s were, however, by no means the only decade in which chiliasm in general and dispensationalism in particular showed signs of vitality. Throughout the postwar years, evangelicals continued to interpret national and international events largely in terms of what they could tell believers about the nearness of Christ's return. Many of the developments so interpreted took place, naturally, in the Middle East. The establishment of the nation of Israel in 1948 lent new plausibility to dispensationalists' traditional insistence that the prophecies concerning the last days were not to be fulfilled figuratively by the Christian Church but rather by a literal Jewish state. Similarly, the Israelis' capture of Jerusalem in the Six Day War of 1967 made it more conceivable that the rebuilding of the Temple and the restoration of the Old Testament sacrifices, which the dispensationalists had long expected, might soon come to pass. Writing in the *Moody Monthly*, Wilbur Smith noted "for the first time since 597 B.C. the Jews have sovereignty over the old city of Jerusalem. . . . If they can keep it, we are very close to the end of the age."[20]

Middle Eastern events were hardly the only ones that evangelicals interpreted in light of prophecy. The dropping of atomic bombs on Hiroshima and Nagasaki, the outbreak of the Cold War, the twists and turns of the national and international economies, the creation of the European Common Market, the unrest in America's inner cities and on campuses in the 1960s and 1970s—all of these developments and many other besides were viewed through the lens of biblical prophecy. Each, many evangelicals concluded, pointed toward one unmistakable conclusion. They were living in the last days.

In the postwar years magazines such as *Sunday School Times*, *Moody Monthly*, and *Eternity* regularly published articles that focused on the Second Advent. *Eternity* continued to publish a column in its January issues that set forth its editors' predictions, based on biblical prophecies, about the events that would occur in the coming twelve months. The *Monthly* published prophecy quizzes similar in spirit to the puzzles that might appear in a secular newspaper's Sunday supplement, and it often featured prophetic themes on its cover. The Scofield Reference Bible enjoyed good sales throughout the postwar years; interest in it was so great that a revised edition was brought out in 1967. Faculty members at schools such as Wheaton were required throughout the postwar years to declare their allegiance to premillennialism; the faculty at schools such as the Moody Bible Institute and Dallas Theological Seminary remained fully committed to dispensationalism. Throughout the postwar years scholars such as Lewis Sperry Chafer, Charles Ryrie, and John Walvoord devoted their considerable intellectual gifts to developing scholarly presentations of the dispensationalist position. The body of works they produced gave dispensationalism a more systematic, fully-orbed exposition and defense than it had ever before received. In short, there can be no doubt that throughout the postwar years millions of American evangelicals found the promised coming of their Lord to be—as John Walvoord put it—a "blessed," and "comforting hope, . . . a ray of light in a dark world."[21]

———————

The continuing vitality of the chiliastic tradition suggests the limitations of one standard scholarly approach to evangelicalism: hypothesizing that modernity poses a "quandary" for evangelicals and then picturing the recent history of American evangelicalism as a series of responses to that quandary. That approach has been adopted at points in the present study; it has been pursued, too, by the sociologist who has done as much as any other to illuminate the evangelical world, James Davison Hunter.[22]

Modernity is a notoriously difficult term to define. Students of religion sometimes use it as a virtual synonym for a modern world view: a world view, that is, which sees all human ideas—including human ideas about God—as having been decisively shaped by the social circumstances in which they arose, or, alter-

THE PRIVATE AND PUBLIC SPHERES

natively, a world view in harmony with the assumptions, methods, and discoveries of modern scientific investigations.[23]

Few students of twentieth-century American society would be entirely comfortable with that understanding of modernity. For them modernity is likely to conjure up reflections about the rise of governmental structures far more elaborate, expansive, and bureaucratic than those that had existed in earlier eras of American history and reflections on the development of an economic system of exceeding complexity, whose inner workings were to most Americans incomprehensible, and which was capable of producing astounding prosperity.[24]

And when historians of twentieth-century America think about what a modern American world view is, they are likely to have in mind the sort of attitudes fostered by those social realities. The attitudes that would first occur to them might well include: your life is shaped by shadowy forces and institutions beyond your control; there is little you can do to produce any fundamental positive changes in the nation's political or economic structures, and, therefore, it seems wise to concentrate your energy on achieving satisfaction in your private life, either through attaining psychic health or through the acquisition of consumer goods.[25]

If one adopts this second understanding of modernity, then it is far from obvious that modernity poses a quandary for evangelicals. Indeed there is good reason to suppose that its characteristic insistence that one's hopes should be private rather than public was likely to make a good deal of sense to many Americans. In some respects, evangelicalism in general and dispensationalism in particular were remarkably compatible with some of the central features of modern American society.

The continuing vitality of eschatological hopes was, however, at most half of the story. The eschatological tradition that the evangelical movement inherited from the fundamentalists was subjected to tremendous pressures in the postwar years. The leaders of the evangelical movement, determined to build coalitions with other sorts of conservative Protestants, were well aware that dispensationalism could stand in the way of such coalitions, for it had never won general acceptance in many of the communities from which they hoped to draw allies. Evangelicals, determined not to let nonessentials prevent lost men and women from coming to Christ, suspected that many potential converts were confused, or even repelled, by a full, passionate explication of the elaborate dispensational scheme. Evangelicals liked to think of themselves, with much justification, as more committed to the Scriptures and to the broader traditions of Protestant orthodoxy than to the tenets of the fundamentalist movement per se; they were far from sure that dispensationalism was in complete accord with either the broader Protestant tradition or with the Scriptures themselves. Determined to buttress the respectability of their faith, they could not help but notice that an odor of disrepute surrounded the eschatological traditions they had inherited from the fundamentalists.[26] Those pressures had a palpable effect on the way that evangelicals living in the postwar years viewed the Second Coming. In several distinct ways they moved away from their eschatological heritage.

A handful of evangelicals became postmillennialists. They came to believe, in other words, that the millennium would not be preceded by dramatic, supernatural intervention in human history; it would, rather, be brought about by God's use of human beings and their actions. A few evangelicals became amillennialists: that is, they became convinced that the prophecies concerning the millennial kingdom should be interpreted figuratively rather than literally.[27]

Many evangelicals remained within the general premillennial framework but explicitly rejected some of the distinctive tenets of dispensationalism in which the fundamentalists had found so much spiritual sustenance. Carl Henry, for instance, described his own views concerning prophecy as premillennial. But he was careful to attach the adjective "broadly" to that description, and he displayed a marked coolness toward dispensationalism in general and the rapture theory in particular.[28] George E. Ladd—a graduate of Gordon College, Gordon Seminary, and Harvard University, and one of the most widely-respected of the evangelical students of prophecy—adopted a similar position. Ladd was a premillennialist who advanced vigorous attacks upon postmillennialism and amillennialism, but he was also an indefatigable critic of dispensationalism. In his writing he consistently argued that dispensationalism's distinctive doctrines could not be adduced from a clearheaded reading of Scripture.[29]

Another more common path was followed by Billy Graham. Graham remained a premillennialist and he did not directly question any of the distinctive doctrines of dispensationalism. He often asserted that he and his listeners were living in an age of crisis, and that the world was teetering on the verge of catastrophe. He emphasized the hope and comfort to be found in the Bible's prophetic promises. But in the postwar years he rarely preached overtly dispensationalist sermons. And he generally refused to equate unequivocally the contemporary world situation with the events that dispensationalists said would immediately precede Christ's return.[30]

Many evangelicals displayed a great deal of unease concerning any sort of chiliastic specificity—a leeriness which went far beyond the fundamentalists' eschewal of date setting. As early as 1945 Wilbur Smith confessed that he had never been able to deduce from the Scriptures which way the latest war in Africa was going to turn out or whether the temporal power of a given nation in the Middle East was about to wax or wane. In the 1970s, *Eternity* ran a scornfilled cover story concerning Christians' efforts to determine which of the world's contemporary leaders might turn out to be the Antichrist. At about the same time, the *Wittenberg Door* published parodies of dispensational charts that marked the precise moment when the expensive automobiles purchased by Hal Lindsey's royalties would be raptured.[31]

And, Lindsey's sales figures notwithstanding, it seems clear that eschatological hopes have not bulked as large in the evangelical subculture as they did in the fundamentalist movement. Postwar evangelicals have not abandoned the doctrine of the Second Advent—but not many evangelicals have meditated on it day and night. Evangelicals were themselves aware of this move toward peripherality. Some confessed puzzlement at why their spiritual forefathers had been so fascinated by eschatology.[32] Others, to whom eschatology was still important, bitterly protested their contemporaries' lack of interest in the Second Advent.[33]

Evangelical periodical literature gives a particularly clear indication of how far eschatology drifted from the heart of evangelicals' concerns. In the postwar years publications such as *Our Hope* and the *Sunday School Times*, whose columns had brimmed with eschatological fervor, folded. Those magazines such as *Christianity Today* which began publishing in the postwar era tended to devote comparatively little attention to the Second Advent. *Revelation* published twenty-five major articles on eschatology in the year 1935; in 1975 *Eternity*, its direct successor, published only one article on eschatology, warning of the danger of Christians focusing too much attention on the Second Coming.[34]

As evangelicals began to question the distinctive tenets of dispensationalism, as their hopes for the Second Advent became hazier and less concrete, as eschatology moved out from the center of their vision, as all that was happening, they focused their attention on the hope and comfort offered by the Christian family.

The family was given much more systematic, sustained attention in the 1940s and 1950s than it had been given in the 1930s. In those decades, evangelical intellectuals such as Frank Gaebelein asserted that no task in the world was more important than nurturing one's offspring, and argued that even if every school in the land were required to cease inculcating all forms of piety, and even if every church in America were forced to close its doors, a vibrant evangelical Christianity could survive, so long as evangelicals maintained truly Christian homes.[35]

Evangelical leaders frequently asserted that making sure

America's homes were strong was the most important task facing the American people—more important than fighting poverty, or crime, or Communism. Their lists of the most positive words in the language were dominated by family-centered words like home and mother, and their attitudes towards those who elected to live outside of families oscillated between pity and suspicion.[36]

The family was a central theme in Billy Graham's postwar ministry. He returned to the topic time and time again on his radio broadcasts and in the sermons he preached in his great city-wide crusades. It was, apparently, a topic in which his listeners were particularly interested: over half of the mail the Billy Graham Evangelistic Association received concerned family matters. And evangelical lay people possessed, as informed evangelicals noted, a remarkable appetite for books and articles on the family.[37] It was an appetite that evangelical writers strove to satiate: they wrote enough books on the family in the 1940s and 1950s to make some of the more reflective members of the evangelical community wonder if the subject was not receiving too much attention.[38] Evangelical periodicals editorialized frequently upon the family and devoted regular columns to its joys.

The importance evangelicals attached to the family in the 1960s and 1970s can scarcely be exaggerated. In those decades evangelicals talked about the family with about the same regularity and with nearly the same passion with which the fundamentalists had discussed the Second Advent.

In the 1960s and 1970s, the proportion of evangelical articles and books devoted to the family grew still larger. In a single fairly typical year, the *Moody Monthly* ran two dozen stories that treated the family. By then it had made two revealing changes in its subtitle: The first, in 1960, from "The Christian Service Magazine" to "The Christian Magazine for All the Family"; the second, in 1975, to "The Christian Family Magazine."[39]

There was a marked tendency in these years for evangelicals to subordinate even the church to the family. Evangelical leaders such as Graham repeatedly reminded their followers that God had created the institution of the human family before he had created the church.[40] The writings of other evangelicals suggest that they found that it was the family, rather than the church, that most clearly demonstrated how supernatural grace could transform human existence.[41] Evangelical leaders often noted that the programs of the local church and the duties associated with them made it difficult for families to spend a great deal of time alone together. And they responded to that tension, more often than not, by asserting that in such situations the family had to come before the church.[42]

Throughout the 1960s and early 1970s evangelicals flocked to week-long seminars which used diagrams similar to those traditionally used to illustrate God's prophetic timetable, to illustrate the principles that should govern the Christian home. By the end of the era, evangelicals had begun to sponsor well-publicized "congresses on the family" where delegates from throughout the nation considered "the best ways to share God's family concern with our generation." Few if any evangelicals seem to have noticed it at the time, but those conventions were, in a way, reminiscent of the great prophetic conferences that had figured so prominently in the life of conservative Protestantism in the decades that preceded the fundamentalist controversy.[43]

Little wonder, then, that historians of American religion who have surveyed recent developments within American evangelicalism have been struck by how much of that community's energy focused on the family, or that political scientists who have studied the political attitudes of evangelicals argue that a devotion to family and family values was the central hallmark of those ideals.[44]

The increasing emphasis on the family was, as many observers have argued, rooted partly in evangelicals' opposition to the changing role of women in American society and to Americans' increasing acceptance of sexual relations outside of heterosexual marriage. But it would be a mistake to assume that that was *all* there was to evangelicals' emphasis on the family. For one thing, even those evangelicals who were sympathetic to the feminist movement and who were not particularly flustered by the nation's changing sexual mores often focused much of their attention on the family. The evangelical "left," as well as the evangelical "right" was solicitous of the family.[45] Moreover when one reads through evangelicals' discussions of the family one cannot help but notice how much they are concerned with a theme that shot through the dispensationalist literature: how to find hope in a hopeless world.

There is no reason to suppose that any evangelical, anywhere, at any time, consciously substituted familial hopes for chiliastic ones. It would be putting the case too strongly to say that the vitiation of eschatological hopes paved the way for an increasing focus on the family. It is after all entirely possible to find hope simultaneously in the family and the Second Advent. But it is only against the eschatological backdrop that the increasingly prominent role the family has played in postwar evangelical discourse can be fully understood. By focusing on the joy and comfort of family life, evangelicals found a new language in which to express a traditional message: Christians can find hope in a world careening wildly out of control.

When we leave our homes, evangelicals said, we enter a world full of competition and anonymity, one where we are not likely to find much respect or affection. It is a world in which we must assume roles rather than be our real selves and in which we are forced to keep our emotional distance from those with whom we come in contact. Our work in that outside world enables us to accumulate many material possessions—possessions that we are not really willing to give up. But those possessions seldom give us lasting satisfaction and the jobs that enable us to buy them are not in themselves terribly rewarding. The public institutions of the world outside our homes—the schools and courts especially—are not at all what they should be. Indeed they sometimes seem to be in the hands of women and men who are unsympathetic to us, hostile to our values, and scornful of the faith that gives our lives meaning. And it is, sad to say, not at all certain that we will be able to do anything to change those social realities.

It makes sense to place our hopes on the families in which we live, for our homes are more subject to our control than is the outside world. Our homes can be safe places, havens from the competition and struggle that shape our life in the outside world. Within their walls we can find refreshment, encouragement, and fellowship. In our homes we are apt to be treated with respect and kindness. We are more likely to find acceptance there than anywhere else in the world. There, as nowhere else, we are free to be our real selves.[46]

Thus far I have stressed the similarities between evangelicals' familial hopes and their chiliastic convictions. In so doing, I have perhaps given the impression that all of the differences between the two sorts of hope were unimportant. In fact, however, some of the differences were of immense importance. For one thing, that evangelical hopes came to focus increasingly on the family rather than on the Second Advent of Christ decreased the tension between the evangelical faith and the broader culture with which it was intertwined. Sociologists, journalists, politicians, and jurists who would have been repelled by an insistence that one could find hope in the midst of a hopeless world by clinging to the apocalyptic promises found evangelicals' emphasis on the family entirely praiseworthy. Neighbors who would have been mystified by evangelicals talking about the Rapture found evangelicals' insistence on the value of the family comprehensible and laudable.

Evangelicals' fundamental assumptions about what a family was and how a family ought to be run were not markedly different from those of their neighbors. Most evangelical discussions of the family asserted that God was the head of the family. Most stressed the importance of a family attending worship services together. Most said—though there was actually some disagreement on this point—that families should set aside some time each day for devotions in the home. Most said a healthy family life was only possible in homes which were deeply religious. But of course there was nothing distinctively evangelical about those assertions: Roman Catholics, Jews, and liberal Protestants would have echoed them. Billboards throughout the nation said that families that prayed together stayed together. And much of the advice evangelicals gave one another about how to have strong families was of a sort that men and women who had no religious beliefs whatsoever, or even those who were violently opposed to religion, would have found unobjectionable. Indeed evangelicals seeking advice on how to build strong families were frequently told that they could profit from reading books written by non-evangelicals and from visits to non-Christian counselors.[47]

Thus considered, the changed locus of evangelicals' private hopes looks like an accommodation of their faith to the values of the broader culture in which evangelicals lived. But if it was an accommodation, then it was surely a complex one, for even as they staked more and more of their hope on the family evangelicals were becoming increasingly certain that they were living in an age in which the family was being subjected to terrible pressures.

This brings us to a second difference between familial and chiliastic hopes: the former were more vulnerable. Evangelicals' awareness of that vulnerability was embedded in nearly all of their discussions of the family. It was almost as if evangelicals found it impossible to point out how important building strong families was, or how much hope and comfort could be found in strong families, without pointing out at the same time how hard it was to create healthy families in twentieth-century America. Evangelicals of every stripe told anecdotes about disintegrating families, used statistics to show that they were not being alarmists when they argued that the family was in trouble but simply stating a plain fact, and drew up extensive lists of the various social changes that were weakening the foundations of the American family.[48]

Naturally, evangelicals liked to believe that Christians were better equipped than non-Christians to fend off the attacks to which modern families were subject. Distinguished evangelical educators such as S. Maxwell Coder emphasized that the Bible contained answers to all the family problems that a Christian would ever confront.[49] Widely circulating discussions of the family, such as Larry Christenson's *The Christian Family*, often exhibited an impressive confidence that if one lived one's life in accord with the deep spiritual principles that govern human relations, then one's family would necessarily be the blessing that God intended it to be.[50] Billy Graham used statistics to demonstrate the resiliency of the Christian family: in America as a whole, Graham said, one in three marriages ended in divorce; among practicing Christians the figure was one in four hundred. Indeed Graham and other preachers sometimes presented conversion as a remedy to the ills that beset non-Christian families.[51]

But there was another side to the story. One cannot read through even a small proportion of the evangelical literature on the family without realizing that for many born-again Americans familial hopes turned out to be chimerical. Most of that literature was directed, quite consciously, at an audience that was assumed to have been missing the satisfaction that evangelicals were supposed to find in the private sphere. And that literature was made up to a remarkable degree of stories—drawn from the experience of the authors themselves or from the lives of those that had come to them for help—about Christian families that were not working. Those stories presented, of course, a skewed picture of the evangelical family, but they revealed that evangelicals knew on one level that simply accepting Christ as one's savior did not give one immunity from divorce, from infidelity, from loneliness in the midst of family, or from the sadness of seeing one's offspring repudiate one's own values.[52]

Little wonder, then, that as early as 1965 evangelicals were speaking of the disintegration of the Christian family and the failure of the Christian home as though these were phenomena with which all born-again Christians were familiar. Evangelicals such as Tim and Beverly LaHaye lamented that the forces that were producing a general breakdown of the family were making serious inroads into the born-again community.[53] In the middle 1970s, evangelical periodicals were admitting that there did not appear to be any qualitative difference between the health of Christian families in America and the health of non-Christian ones.[54] By then speculation on precisely why Christian families were in such terrible shape absorbed a significant portion of the intellectual energies of the evangelical community.

There is one other noteworthy difference between the two hopes. Familial hopes are more likely to lead to direct and sustained involvement in politics. If you have staked your hopes on your family, if you are convinced that your family is in peril, and if you conclude that your government's actions are what imperil it, then your private hopes can, paradoxically, push you into political action. That is, as I have suggested, precisely what happened to some evangelicals in the 1960s and 1970s.

5

FEMINISM

In the early 1970s, it sometimes seemed as if the history of women in twentieth-century America was in essence the story of the emergence and triumph of the feminist movement. There were many battles still to be fought, but it appeared certain that the tide of history was running with the feminists and against their adversaries. Women had won access to educational institutions and careers from which they had previously been barred. Alternative divisions of labor between wives and husbands and between mothers and fathers had gained new legitimacy. Women who chose not to marry or have children had gained a measure of respect not accorded to them in previous centuries. Women had won the right to vote and had played a prominent role in shaping both the Progressive Movement and the New Deal. The Civil Rights Act of 1964 explicitly prohibited discrimination on the basis of sex. Legal restrictions upon women's access to birth control and abortion were relaxed. And in 1972 the Equal Rights Amendment (ERA), stalled in Congress for half a century, was finally approved and sent to the states for ratification.

But the middle 1970s saw the development of a powerful backlash against the feminist movement: the struggle for ratification of the Equal Rights Amendment proved to be divisive, protracted, and unsuccessful, and the relaxation of abortion laws that feminists favored was stoutly resisted by the "right to life" movement. Since the feminist movement was in large part a struggle to eliminate the exclusive rights and prerogatives of men, it was not surprising that many men strenuously opposed it. There had been a similar backlash against the civil rights movement. But, as Susan Harding has noted, feminists were "largely unprepared for the extensive mobilization of *women*" against the reforms they proposed.[1]

So in the late 1970s and early 1980s scholars concluded that previous accounts of the recent history of women had focused too exclusively on the transformations associated with the feminist movement. A full history of the women in twentieth-century America would have to illuminate not only the emergence of feminism but also the roots of women's opposition to that movement.[2]

What made the crystallization of this counterfeminist movement all the more intriguing was that it drew its support from segments of American society that rarely became deeply involved in the political process. Political scientists determined, for instance, that anti-ERA activists had social backgrounds, educational levels, and political attitudes that generally inhibit political activism. Poorer, less well educated, and more estranged from the American political system than feminist activists, these counterfeminists nevertheless mobilized remarkably powerful coalitions.[3] Scholarly investigation confirmed what feminists and counterfeminists had suspected: religion played a crucial role in the crystallization of the counterfeminist constituency. Quantitative analysis demonstrated the strong correlation between counterfeminist activity and conservative religion, and suggested that the religious fervor of the counterfeminists overrode the demographic traits that inhibited other forms of activism. Study after study concluded that one could not understand women's opposition to feminism without understanding their religion. "Their political beliefs," as one study of counterfeminists concluded, "may be viewed as extensions of their religious beliefs."[4]

Conservative Protestants played an especially critical role in the most dramatic expression of the potency of the counterfeminist coalitions: the thwarting of the expected ratification of the Equal Rights Amendment. Anti-ERA coalitions included, of course, Catholics and Mormons as well as conservative Protestants. But the Mormon population, decisive in Utah, could not determine the outcome of ratification battles in other states. The Roman Catholic population was actually concentrated in regions where there was strong support for the ERA. Even in those states, such as Texas, where the amendment faced stiff opposition and where Roman Catholics made up a sizable proportion of the population, Catholics did not play a prominent role in mobilizing opposition to the amendment. Catholics made up a quarter of the population of Texas, yet a careful analysis of the ratification battle in that state found that only 5 percent of the anti-ERA activists were Catholics. Many of those activists were Southern Baptists; over 60 percent of them were adherents of some other variety of conservative Protestantism.[5]

But a survey of the history of evangelical attitudes toward gender shows that the significance of evangelical counterfeminism must be assessed with care. Though nearly all evangelicals sensed that the increasing acceptance of feminism within the mainstream of American culture posed a particularly sharp threat to the survival of the evangelical faith, the evangelical response to that threat was not monolithic. Some evangelicals responded to it not by attacking feminism but by modifying the evangelical tradition. It is upon this group of evangelicals that this chapter focuses.

In 1924, the year before the Scopes trial in Dayton, Tennessee, the *Baltimore Sun* reported on a sermon entitled "Husbands and Wives, Their Respective Places in the Home," which was preached by Wilbur M. Smith, then the pastor of a Baltimore church and later a mentor of Bill Bright and Billy Graham and a professor at the Moody Bible Institute and the Fuller Theological Seminary. Although the *Sun* confessed that it found Smith's insistence that "man is made to rule" and woman to obey as

obsolete as the dodo, it observed that if one really did believe
that the New Testament should be taken as a binding rule of
conduct, then Smith's views were absolutely "flawless."[6]

If the *Sun* was correct, then John R. Rice's *The Home—Courtship, Marriage and Children* (1945), his *Bobbed Hair, Bossy
Wives and Women Preachers* (1941), and the 1939 edition of
Walter A. Maier's *For Better Not For Worse* each possessed the
same sort of flawlessness. Neither author's influence was limited
to the battle over woman's proper role in society, for both were
major figures in the conservative Protestant world. Rice, a Baptist evangelist, editor, and writer, published over 120 books with
total sales of 36 million. The magazine which he founded in
1934, *The Sword of the Lord*, reached a circulation of 250,000.[7]
Maier was a professor at Concordia Theological Seminary, a pro-
lific author, and a noted radio preacher. His weekly radio show,
"The Lutheran Hour," attracted a huge national audience for
twenty years; at the time of Maier's death in 1950 it was heard on
1,200 stations, attracting perhaps as many 20 million listeners.[8]

Neither Maier nor Rice was truly in the evangelical mainstream. Rice was to its right on most theological and social issues. He published warnings concerning the dangerous liberalism
of Bill Bright's Campus Crusade for Christ[9] and denounced Billy
Graham's fraternization with liberals.[10] In the early 1970s his
sympathetic explanation of the segregationist policies at Bob
Jones University in Greenville, South Carolina, forced Moody Bible Institute, one of the most conservative of the mainstream institutions, to distance itself from him publicly.[11] Since Maier was
a member of the Missouri Synod of the Lutheran Church—a
synod with great sensitivity to denominational distinctions—he
scrupulously avoided identifying himself too closely with the
interdenominational evangelical mainstream.

There were however many links between the two authors and
the evangelical mainstream. Maier received an honorary doc-
torate in 1945 from Houghton College. His radio show was the
direct inspiration for Billy Graham's "Hour of Decision." Evangelical magazines spoke of his ministry with great enthusiasm[12]
and printed glowing notices of his books.[13] Rice enjoyed a similar

relationship with prominent evangelical journals. Indeed, *Moody Monthly* held up Rice's family as an example for its readers to follow.[14] The doctrinal differences between Rice and Graham can easily be exaggerated: Rice occasionally expressed warm praise for Graham's ministry, comparing his preaching to that of Moody and Sunday.[15] Indeed, it was largely because Graham and Rice had so much in common that Graham was hurt and confused by Rice's criticism.[16]

Maier and Rice believed that the much-discussed question of the proper role of women in modern society presented no real quandary for Bible-believing Christians: the Bible contained a clear, practical, and conservative guide to the proper relations between men and women. It presented a hierarchical vision of human society: citizens must be subject to rulers, servants to masters, children to parents, and wives to husbands. Since rebellion against the hierarchy was rebellion against its architect, women who did not defer to their husbands were, in the final analysis, rebelling against God and His authority.[17]

A woman's happiness depended, in the traditionalists' scheme, upon her following sound Christian tradition. She had to marry; not to do so would show that she was "subnormal in social instincts" and "misanthropic."[18] Once married, she had to conform wholly to her husband's will. Rice presented a sweeping enumeration of a wife's duties to her husband that could have passed for a feminist's caricature of traditional notions of the relationship between women and men. Should a wife obey her husband? Unquestionably. Should a husband have the same authority over his wife as parents have over their children? Of course. Should a wife "reverence" her husband? Yes, she should. Should she call him lord? The scriptures show that she should. "Should she submit to him as if he were a god?" That is what the Bible teaches her to do.[19]

In Rice's view, such injunctions had nothing to do with the relative intelligence or spiritual maturity of wives and husbands. To be sure, most women were "less mature spiritually" than men. But that fact was not the basis for female submission, which was based on the divine order and not on the individual traits of a particular husband or wife. Women with more native intelligence and better education than their husbands nevertheless had to be subject to them. Christian women who were married to unregenerate and even anti-Christian men were still required to give them the full devotion outlined in the Scriptures. Such husbands must be obeyed even if they demanded, for instance, that their wives give no money or time to church work. "God expects," Rice insisted, "women to feel their duty to obey their husbands, good or bad, saved or unsaved."[20]

It was just as immoral for women to become leaders outside of the home—even if the outside activities in which they were engaged were in and of themselves unobjectionable—as it was for them to usurp their husbands' authority within the domestic sphere. Even leadership in the church was unscriptural. In Rice's mind women preachers, like "bobbed hair" and "bossy women," were a sign of modern decadence.[21] Maier similarly advised his readers that working wives transgressed "God's ordinances."[22]

So did the programs of women such as Margaret Sanger, who linked a devotion to the advancement of women to advocacy of birth control.[23] The practice of birth control was an "outrage against nature,"[24] morally "wrong for the individual and dangerous to society as a whole";[25] it was the sort of practice advocated, logically enough, by atheists, modernists, and Communists.[26] From the biblical perspective it was clear that "abortion is murder."[27]

In Rice's mind feminism was closely associated with "spinsters" and "frustrated divorcees."[28] He professed pity for "modern women."[29] Maier denounced the "rabid, overbalanced emphasis on women's rights" which had emerged in recent decades[30] and read the growing prevalence of "female domination" in American homes as a symptom of national decline.[31]

That same interpretation surfaced in the sermons Billy Graham preached on the eve of America's entry into the Second World War. Modern women, complained Graham, seemed "determined to usurp the ways and sins" of men.[32] Graham was still resisting innovation two and a half decades later: in 1964 he insisted that the husband was the "master of the house" and preached that a woman's primary duty in life was to be a good homemaker;[33] in 1968 he reaffirmed that God's word taught that a man should be the head of the house and the breadwinner for the family and warned that America was veering toward matriarchy.[34]

Many other evangelical leaders voiced similar views throughout the 1940s, 1950s, and 1960s, warning, for instance, that a wife's working outside the home had to be considered an emergency measure and that such jobs might lead to sexual frigidity.[35] The Christian Home, published by Moody Press in 1952, quoted with approval lengthy passages from Shakespeare's Taming of the Shrew, devoted a chapter to explicating the "Christian Wife's Responsibility of Subjection," and told women that Ephesians 5: 22–25, 5:33—a passage dealing with a wife's subjection to her husband—was the "divine key" to becoming "a happy, faithful, and successful wife."[36] Six years later, C. C. Ryrie's careful and scholarly The Place of Women in the Church, based on research undertaken at the University of Edinburgh, concluded that a Christian woman's "special sphere of activity" must be the home, and that even in that sphere she must serve as a "subordinate help meet" to her husband. In the church she must be silent.[37]

———

The traditionalists' writings could plausibly be read as the literary expression of an entrenched patriarchy that was secure in its prerogatives, unbending in its opposition to the winds of change, and self-confident in its defense of the old ways and in its dismissal of the new. That reading suggests an appealingly simple interpretation of the relationship between feminism and evangelicalism: evangelical leaders have always opposed the goals of the feminists; evangelical women have always followed their advice and found it met their needs; the counterfeminist drive of the 1970s was mounted, therefore, by contented conservatives.

But when carefully examined the traditionalists' writings suggest the need for another interpretation, for they do not prove to be the work of an entrenched and confident patriarchy. Apparently aware that they were sailing against the prevailing winds, the traditionalists carefully avoided presenting themselves as foes of the cause of women. Rice could not hide his doubts about granting women the vote, but he carefully avoided expressing outright opposition to women's suffrage.[38] He also recounted stories of women who had found that a willingness to admit in the abstract that their husbands had unlimited authority over them brought in practice the freedom to do anything they pleased.[39] Graham said that the Bible did not call for reducing women to powerlessness; on the contrary, it was full of examples of women who had changed history.[40] Smith told his congregation that Christianity had dramatically advanced the cause of women: it had found her in subjection and elevated her to spiritual equality.[41] Maier even suggested that the women's movement was responsible for some of humanity's greatest recent achievements.[42]

In fact, the story of evangelical attitudes toward women's proper role was in large part the story of the evangelicals' departures from the traditionalists' ideals. In the postwar era, the conservatives' advice was frequently ignored and their assessments of the relative merits of working outside the home and of the life of the housewife were tested and found inaccurate. There was, furthermore, a gradual change in the sort of advice evangelical leaders gave women; that advice became, on the whole, less conservative between 1940 and 1970.

None of those developments was the direct result of feminist agitation, and until 1970 few evangelicals thought of themselves as feminists. But many evangelical women acted in ways that feminists could approve and that thoroughgoing traditionalists would decry. They interpreted their experiences in ways that resembled the world view of secular feminists at least as closely as they resembled that of the traditionalists. In the early 1970s, when evangelicals began systematically to consider the ideas of secular feminists, the pattern of unobtrusive departure from tradition was disrupted. Many prominent evangelicals forthrightly embraced feminism. Others noisily attacked the feminist movement while at the same time making significant concessions to it.

In the 1940s and 1950s some evangelical women may have

scrupulously conformed their behavior to the traditionalists' advice; even in the 1960s and 1970s traditional notions had a palpable effect upon evangelicals' reactions to changing gender roles, dampening their enthusiasm for such changes and making their acceptance of them somewhat hesitant and tentative. (We know, for instance, that even in the late 1970s two-thirds of the men and women in a community inhabited largely by conservative Protestants believed that women should bear the primary responsibility for housework and that in nearly half of the households in the community women actually did all the housework.)[43] But the traditionalists' advice was not always followed. Rice admitted that many devout women did not conform their behavior to his views,[44] and Maier noted how many American husbands lived in a "desert of female dominion."[45] Secular newspapers assumed that the silence with which women sometimes received the traditionalists' advice indicated a quiet determination to ignore such counsel rather than a willingness to follow it.[46] Sometimes the resistance to traditionalists' demands was not so passive: preachers occasionally found, to their mortification, that their own wives flouted their admonitions concerning the proper behavior of women.[47]

Some evangelical households were organized in ways that would have appalled the traditionalists. Writing in the 1970s, an evangelical journalist named Sharon Gallagher recalled that she and her father had seen her mother paint the house, lay linoleum, and handle all of the family's driving.[48] Another evangelical writer recalled her father taking care of the family grocery shopping and helping with the cooking.[49] Women exercised such power in some conservative Protestant households that their sons were haunted for the rest of their lives by the possibility that they would somehow allow a woman to dominate them the way their mothers had dominated their fathers.[50]

Popular evangelical books and magazine articles written in the 1960s and 1970s suggested that such departures from the traditionalists' ideals rarely brought evangelical women contentment. Those books and articles generally presented a bleak interpretation of the actual lot of the housewife; indeed, they often gave the impression that in the 1960s and early 1970s there were very few evangelical housewives who were not profoundly dissatisfied. That impression was rooted partly in the intentions of the authors who described the housewife's lot. Most of them were presenting prescriptions to improve her condition and so, like social physicians everywhere, they tended to portray the problems they addressed in the bleakest possible terms. But though their presentation was tendentious, and though the evidence it yields was admittedly fragmentary and impressionistic, its main outlines seem plausible and convincing. The widespread disenchantment reflected in the literature of evangelicalism eventually led many evangelical women to look for new, less traditional, and more egalitarian, ways of organizing their family life. It also led many women to wonder if working outside the home might not help them achieve some of the satisfactions that were lacking in their homes.

Most of the blessings in the world evoked by this literature were decidedly mixed. Frozen foods, "miracle fabrics," and a host of household appliances had made women's lives less harsh than those of their forebears, and the televisions and radios they possessed meant that they were less isolated from the outside world than their mothers and grandmothers had been. But television and radio were full of threats to their faith,[51] and the conveniences that they enjoyed seemed to put family finances under a constant strain. In fact, many evangelical women felt guilty about using such products: their mothers had baked fresh cookies for them; why, they wondered, couldn't they bake fresh cookies for their own children?[52] They also felt that "the time we are given by labor-saving devices . . . too often becomes empty time, without meaning or sense of accomplishment."[53] If housekeeping did not seem quite so demanding as it once was, it still had its drudgery and it was no more glamorous than it had been in previous decades. The labor was still taxing enough to leave many women feeling bone-tired; it still seemed disproportionate to the tangible results it produced.[54] Many evangelical women felt that their monotonous rounds of dishes and diapers were pushing them into a rut. They feared that they were losing their earlier "spark and charm" and sinking into a life in which the only diversion was self-pity. They remembered displaying great promise in school and recalled that they had often seemed brighter than the male students in their classes.[55] But their daily routine in the house seemed to them to have dulled their wits and limited their mental horizons. Aware that Christian bookstores were "bulging" with books "longing to be read," they nevertheless found it hard to find time to read.[56] When they did, they often lacked the energy to read anything more demanding than *Real Confessions* or *True Love*.[57] They were left, then, with the uncomfortable feeling that they would never be able to keep up with the rapid increase in the world's knowledge and that they were cut off from "new trends" and "new ideas."[58]

Popular evangelical literature evoked a world where marriages were full of awful moments: anger always lurked just beneath the surface of the day-to-day relations between husbands and wives; frequently it flashed out in biting words or humiliating jokes.[59] In that world it was not uncommon for brides to realize within hours of the wedding ceremony that they had just made a terrible mistake with which they would have to live the rest of their lives.[60] Women found that after six months of marriage they and their husbands no longer talked to each other or made love, and they expressed their unhappiness in tones that suggested that they had always expected their marriages to end up that way. Their only surprise was that their marriages had turned sour so soon.[61] Women believed a marriage must eventually slump and drag along, becoming "a dull monotony." Wives, they assumed, could either "hate" or "endure" their husbands.[62]

Evangelical women were dependent to a large degree on their husbands for their financial security, status, and fulfillment; however, they often felt that their husbands could not be relied on to meet those needs. They sometimes complained that their husbands failed to provide for their financial needs or to win the promotions that would bring the family more status;[63] they complained more frequently that their husbands failed to meet their emotional needs. Women reported, for instance, that men who had been wonderfully talkative and entertaining before marriage lapsed into glum silence after the wedding ceremony, going for hours or even days without speaking to their wives.[64] Husbands routinely came home two hours late for dinner without bothering to call to let their wives know where they were. Women reported that even churchgoing men would not be trusted to be faithful to their wives, for they were unable to resist the "soft, easy, and available" women who surrounded them. "Wherever you live," one housewife warned, "'out there' is some little sexpot, looking wide-eyed at your husband."[65]

Largely because they needed money, but also because they found traditional roles so stultifying, evangelical women frequently ignored the traditionalists' warnings about the danger of their working outside the home. In 1940 over a fourth of the women in one conservative Protestant community were working outside the home; by 1970 four out of every ten of that community's women did so.[66] Traditionalists advised evangelical women that their happiness depended upon their staying in the home; the message evangelical women passed on to their daughters was often precisely the reverse. Mothers, determined that their daughters not be housewives, refused on principle to let them join 4H homemaking clubs and encouraged them to get an education and pursue a career.[67]

To be sure, evangelicals generally viewed working outside of the home as an ameliorative measure rather than as a panacea. Such work might, after all, snare them in what they called the "worldly rat race" or have a pernicious effect upon their family life. "I always give my best hours, my best disposition to someone other than my husband and my children," said one woman. "By the time I get home," she lamented, "I'm like a dishrag, and I'm afraid I'm as cranky as a witch." She found that her job, together with her housework, left her "almost no time for the Lord."[68] Another evangelical woman, a college professor, complained of having to come home from draining days at work to prepare dinner, clean the house, and look after the children while her husband loafed.[69]

Evangelical women, like their nonevangelical neighbors, knew that their opportunities in the work place were restricted. Hypothetically free to pursue a wide range of careers, evangelical women actually tended to choose their occupations from a fairly narrow range of jobs: indeed in some evangelical circles teaching school was thought to be the only career to which women could legitimately aspire.[70] Women often concluded that their opportunities for advancement were meager, for they frequently saw men less qualified than they being given positions of responsibility that they themselves deserved.[71] When evangelical women did manage to gain positions of responsibility, they often found that the employees they supervised took their directions less seriously than those given by men.[72]

To some evangelical women, opportunities within the church seemed even more circumscribed than prospects in the secular world. They noted, for instance, that evangelicals generally viewed female assertiveness in the religious realm with even greater skepticism than assertiveness in the secular world,[73] and that even those churches that allowed women to assume positions of authority seemed to prefer hiring men rather than women whenever possible.[74] Even those women with remarkable and widely recognized preaching talents sometimes thought it wise to disarm potential critics by insisting that they were not ministers or preachers but only "teachers."[75]

But in spite of such obstacles, in the postwar decades women did in fact hold important positions in institutions at the heart of the evangelical mainstream. They staffed foreign mission outposts, held *de facto* pastorates that influenced men such as Bill Bright and Billy Graham,[76] helped administer schools such as the Moody Bible Institute, and helped produce magazines such as *Christianity Today* and *Eternity*.[77] Not surprisingly, then, many evangelical women found church work liberating rather than confining. One reported that the church had if anything been too quick to push her into a responsibility: she had been urged to share her insights into the Christian faith while the baptismal water was, so to speak, still in her ears.[78]

Evangelical women found that working outside of the home, whether in the church or not, acted as an antidote to the deadening routine of housework, made them feel needed, and improved their family's finances. Some women found that the money they earned made for a more equal partnership with their husbands. One reported how much she enjoyed finally being in a position "to tell my husband off." So while the problems housewives faced impelled many evangelical women to pursue careers outside the home, the obstacles faced by women who worked outside the home seldom pushed them back into the role of homemaker. More often the problems left evangelical women with a determination to work for the removal of the restrictions they had encountered. Evangelical women told evangelical leaders that they "wouldn't give up working for anything in the world."[79]

Such determination apparently had an effect on evangelical psychologists, authors, editors, and preachers, for as the middle decades of the century wore on, the advice which they dispensed and the views they expressed on the proper role of women drifted away from those of men like Smith, Rice, and Maier. The movement away from the traditionalists was uneven, and resistance to innovation never disappeared, but between 1940 and 1970 expressions of thoroughgoing traditionalism became rarer and rarer in evangelical literature while departures from traditionalism occurred with ever-greater frequency.

Even in the 1940s articles in conservative Protestant magazines were begining to make light of some traditional notions. The *Christian Herald*, for instance, compared the belief that higher education was unsuitable for women to the equally "picturesque" belief that women could not swim.[80] In the 1950s evangelical periodicals published interpretations of marriage that contrasted sharply with Rice's views. Dwight Small, for example, writing in *Eternity*, warned women not to engage in "husband worship"[81] and remarked upon the "intolerable tyranny" that resulted from a husband who had not died to self trying to act as the head of the family.[82]

Joe Burton's *Tomorrow You Marry*, first published in 1950 by the Southern Baptist Convention, departed even more dramatically from the traditionalists' position by celebrating the decline of "the old patriarchy" that the traditionalists sought to prop up. The old regime had, according to Burton, virtually reduced women to slavery. As he presented it, modern Christian marriage was based less on submission than on "mutual respect" and a willingness to see one's mate as "an equal" and "a comrade." In such a union questions such as who should be the breadwinner, who should prepare the family's meals, and who should clean the house were decided not by any immutable decree of nature but rather by two "interacting . . . personalities."[83]

Clyde Narramore's *A Woman's World*, published in 1963, gave further evidence of the erosion of traditionalism.[84] It advised women to balance their duties to their husbands against their duties to God, praised households in which men did a large share of the housework, carefully enumerated the advantages of women working outside of the home, and assured women who decided to pursue careers that there was no reason in the world why God could not bless their decision. Narramore also presented a new view of the life of single women. In his view, the greatest disadvantage of such a life was the continual bother of having to explain to conventional minds why one had chosen not to marry. Such a decision needed no elaborate explanation, for its advantages were obvious: single women had, for instance, more independence and "more freedom to carry out their ambitions" than did married women.[85]

Evangelicals' quiet acceptance of changing gender roles continued throughout the 1960s and into the 1970s. In the early 1960s, *Christianity Today* reported, with only a hint that it had any qualms about the matter, the moves underway in many denominations to ordain women.[86] In the early 1970s it noted with enthusiasm calls for developing Sunday School materials that presented new, nonstereotypical gender roles,[87] denounced the stupidity of congressmen who resisted the passage of the Equal Rights Amendment,[88] called for giving women more responsibility in church work, and noted the inconsistency of letting women preach in foreign missions (a practice that enjoyed nearly universal approbation) while not allowing them to preach in the pulpits of America.[89] By the middle 1970s, Billy Graham, finding meanings in Scripture that had previously eluded him, had begun to tell husbands that they had a duty to submit to their wives.[90]

By then self-conscious feminists had already begun to elaborate their position in articles printed in leading evangelical magazines and in books published by major evangelical firms. In
1971 *Christianity Today* published Ruth Schmidt's "Second-
Class Citizenship in the Kingdom of God";[91] in that same year
Nancy Hardesty's "Women: Second Class Citizens?" appeared in
Eternity.[92] More articles by evangelical feminists appeared regularly in succeeding years, and in 1975 evangelical feminists even
established their own journal, *Daughters of Sarah*. In 1974 Letha
Scanzoni and Nancy Hardesty presented a book-length explication of evangelical feminism called *All We're Meant To Be*,[93] and
a year later Paul K. Jewett of Fuller Seminary published his *Man
as Male and Female*.[94]

Though these articles and books did not provoke unanimous
assent, their importance was universally conceded. *Eternity*
named *All We're Meant To Be* the most important book of 1974;
other periodicals asked panels of experts for their evaluations of
the writings, and some magazines even devoted entire issues to
the questions raised by evangelical feminists. Readers who
found the feminists' arguments convincing responded to these
writings with great enthusiasm. They recalled that after ten years
of simply having to ignore the Pauline Epistles, they could—
after learning the lessons that evangelical feminists had to
teach—read those letters with "appreciation" rather than "heart-
ache."[95] They reported that they came to books like *All We're
Meant To Be* feeling miserable, guilty, alienated, rebellious, and
angry, but read it with tears of "relief and joy at being reconciled
with God"[96] and that reading Jewett's book made them feel like
the witnesses to the resurrection of Christ.[97]

A similar sense of excitement shot through the well-attended
and well-publicized conferences sponsored by a group called the
Evangelical Women's Caucus. The closing address of the first
conference, held in the autumn of 1975, summed up the hope
and excitement which filled evangelical feminists in the middle
1970s: God was at work; new wine was bursting the old wineskins, and a whole new world was opening up for women.[98]

By the end of the decade, when evangelical seminaries wished
to debate whether or not it was permissible to ordain women,

they sometimes discovered that they could find no one in the seminary willing to take the negative side of the question.[99] Nor was a widespread acceptance of changing gender roles limited to the writers and teachers in the evangelical camp: national surveys showed that more evangelicals supported than opposed the passage of the Equal Rights Amendment.[100] In short, feminist sentiment had a strong presence within the evangelical subculture—far stronger than most commentators outside of the evangelical community have realized.

The precise relationship between evangelical and secular feminism caused great controversy within the evangelical community. Conservative evangelicals charged that evangelical feminists were simply parroting an ideology whose origins were purely secular. That assertion was vociferously denied by evangelical feminists. They insisted that it was precisely their faith that had impelled them into the feminist movement.[101] Both the conservatives' charge and the feminists' response contained grains of truth; neither was wholly accurate. It is more helpful to see the evangelical feminist movement as a sustained effort to disprove a proposition whose truth seemed self-evident to many conservative evangelicals and to many secular feminists: namely, that a thoroughgoing commitment to the evangelical faith and an allegiance to feminism were simply incompatible. Evangelical feminists refused to choose between the faith that gave meaning to their lives and a cause whose justice was to them undeniable. They took a fresh look at the history of evangelicalism and at the Bible itself, trusting that when correctly interpreted it would prove a source of hope and succor rather than of oppression. At the same time, they carefully evaluated secular feminism, appropriating those facets of its ideology that seemed most congenial and rejecting those that seemed most threatening.

Evangelical feminists came into contact with the secular feminist movement fairly late in the day—typically in the early 1970s or very late 1960s.[102] Their awareness came in a variety of ways. An evangelical feminist named Sharon Gallagher recalled that her first brush with the movement came when the editor of the Christian paper for which she worked asked her to do a piece on "women's lib," hoping, Gallagher surmised, that such a piece might convert some women in the movement to the evangelical faith.[103] Other evangelicals came in contact with the movement through talks with friends[104] and neighbors,[105] the popular press, or feminist classics such as Betty Friedan's *Feminine Mystique*.[106]

Many evangelicals were profoundly affected by their contact with secular feminism. Some found it presented an uncannily accurate analysis of the way that they and their mothers and grandmothers lived their lives.[107] Others reported that secular feminists helped them organize and make sense of their experiences: one evangelical spoke movingly of the way in which the ideas of the secular feminists had enabled her to give a name to her anger.[108]

Caught up in the excitement of the 1970s, a few evangelical feminists seemed to put their allegiance to the goals of feminism before their commitment to the evangelical tradition. Virginia Ramey Mollenkott admitted that she might well have been forced to abandon her faith if she had been convinced that the Bible called for the subjugation of women.[109]

Most evangelical feminists insisted, however, that their identity as Christians was more important to them than their identity as feminists.[110] And though evangelical feminists spoke warmly of the work of the secular feminists and reported that secular feminists in return applauded their efforts,[111] relations between evangelical and secular feminists were often strained, and there was in fact only a limited amount of cooperation—or even communication—between the leaders of the two groups. Some evangelicals were not even quite willing to think of the secularists as allies. They were, rather, "co-belligerents."[112]

Evangelical feminists knew that many secular feminists believed that Christianity and feminism were incompatible.[113] They noted with a twinge that feminists such as Naomi Goldberg had forcefully argued that the work of Christian feminists, no matter how well-intentioned, was contradictory and self-deceptive. They knew too that some feminists were engaged in a direct frontal attack on orthodox Christianity; evangelicals noted, for example, that militant feminists in places like Berkeley were burning copies of the Bible to protest its patriarchialism.[114] And there were hints in their writings that evangelicals felt that even those secular feminists who did not openly object to Christian feminism sometimes seemed to view the occasional evangelical feminist who crossed their path with some condescension, thinking of her as the "house Christian."[115]

Most evangelical feminists were, in turn, deeply distressed by the secular feminists' agitation for less restrictive abortion laws and by their willingness to cooperate with lesbian activists.[116] Evangelicals who had been deeply involved in organizations dominated by secular feminists were repulsed by the "tawdry occultism" in which some members dabbled.[117]

Many evangelicals were confused or offended by the rhetoric of secular feminism. Evangelicals could not muster much enthusiasm for secular feminists' calls for an end to women's submission, for they believed that the failure of human beings to submit their wills to God was "the biggest problem in society."[118] Secular feminists' demand that women "must have the chance to develop their fullest human potential"[119] was also incongruent with elements of the evangelical tradition. Many evangelical feminists had been reared upon a steady diet of self-abnegation: they had been taught that a real Christian should expect to be "somewhat martyred,"[120] and Sunday after Sunday they had heard sermons advising them that they must "die to self." Occasionally they had even been advised to think of themselves as "meek, insignificant worms."[121]

The evangelical feminists' explorations of the evangelical past helped them to resolve some of the apparent contradictions between their faith and feminism. At their first major gathering they heard an enthusiastic explication of the links between evangelicalism and feminism; in subsequent years article after article and book after book energetically celebrated those strands of the evangelical tradition that were most compatible with women's liberation. According to these writings, the movement for women's rights was not merely the result of secular agitation, but rather— as the nineteenth-century women's movement demonstrated—a natural outgrowth of the evangelical genius.[122] According to evangelical feminists, the history of the church was full of women saints whose memory needed to be revived. We have all heard of Jerome, feminists noted, but Christians have failed to cherish properly the memory of Jerome's patron, Paula.[123]

As that comment suggests, evangelical feminists' search for a usable past sometimes had a somewhat strained quality, and they certainly did have to comb the historical record with some selectivity: in the nineteenth century evangelicals had been virulent foes as well as friends of the struggle for women's rights. Furthermore, some of the most influential evangelical women of the nineteenth century had stridently denounced the women's movement. Phoebe Palmer, the author of several devotional classics and a leading figure in nineteenth-century evangelicalism, stressed that women's proper place was not in the world of work and politics but rather in the domestic sphere. By speaking of the joys of complete surrender to Christ and writing hymns exalting the joys of putting one's all on the altar for Christ, she had also encouraged women to think of their relation to Christ in terms of absolute surrender. She thereby contributed directly to the tradition of self-abnegation that inhibited the development of an assertive feminism among evangelicals.

But evangelical feminists' basic point nevertheless held: the evangelical tradition, examined with care, undeniably did provide fertile soil for some varieties of feminism. There were links between the nineteenth-century women's rights movement and evangelical Christianity.[124] Indeed, not even Palmer's example was unambiguously antithetical to the feminists. She herself had not been content to labor only within the domestic sphere: she had pursued a life of public service to the faith. She said that her duties in the home were terrible obstacles to her own spiritual maturation. Most importantly, she had taught evangelical women to value personal growth and inner autonomy, developing what one scholar has called "a theology of self-actualization."[125] Evangelical feminists picked up these themes with great alacrity; for them, self-acceptance and a determination to cease thinking of themselves as the wormlike creatures that pastors had told them they were actually were rooted in doctrines like those Palmer taught. Her doctrine of the in-dwelling Christ—

with a few relatively minor modifications—made it possible to accept the secular feminists' emphasis on self-worth without rejecting the evangelical tradition. Armed with such doctrines, the evangelical feminists discovered, or at least thought they discovered, that Christianity taught them the importance of loving one's self.[126] The appeal to the evangelical tradition was helpful in establishing the legitimacy of evangelical feminism, but not decisive. Ultimately its legitimacy would have to be settled by appeals to the Scriptures. Evangelical feminists drew inspiration from the Bible. *All We're Meant To Be* was subtitled *A Biblical Approach to Women's Liberation*; the Evangelical Women's Caucus referred to its constituency as "biblical feminists" and periodically reasserted its conviction that the Bible was free from all error, while Virginia Ramey Mollenkott, one of the most widely respected evangelical feminists, insisted that it was precisely her study of the Scriptures that had "radicalized" her.[127] Appealing to the Scriptures was, however, a risky tactic. Evangelical feminists noted that for centuries the Bible had been uniformly quoted to support "tyranny and oppression," that nineteenth-century feminists had identified the "Bible problem" as one of the chief impediments to the advancement of women, and that most twentieth-century evangelicals believed that the Bible demanded inequality between the sexes.[128] In the jargon of popular evangelicalism a "very biblical husband" had become, evangelical feminists noted, a euphemism for a man who kept his wife in place by ruling the house with a heavy hand.[129]

The difficulties created by what evangelical feminists called the "Bible problem" were personal and practical rather than simply abstract and theological. One woman's thorough reading of St. Paul left her with the "distinct impression" that Paul thought women were "second-class citizens." Another reported that she could no longer find satisfaction in reading the Pauline letters because she sensed that Paul had a terrible "bias against women."[130] Participants at the first conference sponsored by evangelical feminists dramatized the problem: some of them had been on the verge of giving up on the Bible before attending the conference; others were on the verge of giving up on feminism.[131] Women discovered that their attempts to justify their commitment to feminism were nearly always met with scriptural quotes that spoke of wives' duty to submit to their husbands' authority. One evangelical feminist confessed that for a time she was reduced to answering such quotations by asserting that she knew she was right, that it must be that the Scriptures were wrong. It was, as she ruefully noted, an untenable position for any evangelical.

Evangelical feminists soon discovered, however, that the Bible was not as unambiguously chauvinist as traditionalists had made it out to be. Some of the most reactionary interpretations of the proper role of women in society clearly showed "the effect of secular culture on biblical interpretations."[132] Evangelical feminists insisted that it was not they but the traditionalists who had let the gospel be contaminated by secular influence. The translation of the Bible into English had, for example, been affected by the cultural conditioning of those who did the translating. For example, the men who had produced the King James Version of the Bible had translated a word which Romans 16:1 applied to a woman as "servant." Yet in each of the nearly two dozen other places where Paul employed the word, they had translated it as "deacon" or "minister." They had thus obscured an important precedent which could be used to show the propriety of ordaining women as officers in the church.[133]

Evangelical feminists also argued that previous generations of evangelicals had not grasped the revolutionary implications of Jesus' treatment of women. Born into a society where nearly all men treated women with great contempt, he had instead treated women with conspicuous respect and had gone out of his way to include them in his ministry.[134] In a culture in which the testimony of a woman was not admissible in a court of law, he had purposely made a woman the first witness to his resurrection.[135] All in all, the way that Jesus "related to women" made him a "revolutionary." His "lifestyle was so remarkable that one can only call it astonishing. He treated women as fully human, equal to men in every respect; no word of deprecation about women, as such, is ever found on his lips."[136] Then, too, evangelicals traditionally had been selective in their use of the Scriptures. They put a great deal more emphasis on some scriptural injunctions—"wives, submit yourselves unto your own husbands"—than on others—submit "yourselves one to another in the fear of God."[137] The Bible did not teach that submission per se was wrong; it did, however, teach that Christian marriage was characterized not by male domination and female submission but by "mutual submission" between husbands and wives.[138]

Again, evangelicals had failed to note the possibility that the Apostles were themselves aware that a thoroughgoing application of the gospel of Christ would demand a radical reordering of the relations between men and women, and shrank from proclaiming that truth only because they feared that "too radical" a departure from "Jewish customs" would distract their potential converts from the central core of their message: the power of the gospel.[139] Perhaps those passages of the New Testament which seemed most restrictive were, the feminists argued, the result of apostolic sail-trimming.

In the evangelical feminists' opinion, the traditionalists had also failed to note the tremendous importance of a passage in the third chapter of Galatians:

For ye are all the children of God by faith in Christ Jesus. For as many of you as have been baptized into Christ have put on Christ. There is neither Jew nor Greek, there is neither bond nor free, there is neither male nor female: for ye are all one in Christ Jesus.

That passage was in fact the key to understanding the New Testament message concerning women. It was a "revolutionary . . . new covenant of equality,"[140] "the magna charta of humanity," and a stunning theological "breakthrough."[141]

Such arguments took the feminist a long way, such a long way, in fact, that some feminists were convinced that all scriptural passages could be "explained in a completely harmonious egalitarian fashion."[142] So a thoroughgoing commitment to feminism did not, in their opinion, require that one reject—or even modify—the doctrine of biblical inerrancy: the Scriptures had been

full of feminist sentiment all along; only the prejudices produced by a male-dominated society had kept them hidden. But
the most reflective evangelical feminists knew better. Jewett refused to blink at the embarrassingly plain fact that "Paul, who
was an inspired apostle, appears to teach female subordination
in certain passages in the epistles";[143] Mollenkott refused to gloss
over those passages of Scripture which seemed to assume that
women were inferior to men.[144]

At such points, as Mollenkott understated the case, evangelical feminists had to "begin to face a serious problem in our
interpretation of the Bible." The only way to resolve such fundamental difficulties, concluded many evangelical feminists, was
to admit that "although the Bible is a divine book, it has come to
us through human channels," and to "recognize the human as
well as the divine quality of Scripture." Although the light of
revelation shines through it, that light is filtered through the
"dark glass" of "earthen vessels." The weight of the biblical witness, taken as a whole and "correctly" interpreted, told us that
female subordination must be rejected. In the final analysis we
must conclude that Paul had asserted that Christians had
to accept it only because of "his rabbinical training and human
limitations."[145]

Evangelical feminism was, then, both a natural culmination of
the previous course of evangelical history and a sharp break with
the evangelical past. The increasing prestige and influence of
feminism in American culture at large, the widespread disenchantment among evangelical housewives, the large numbers of
evangelical women working outside the home, and the increasingly "progressive" advice presented by evangelical leaders in
the 1950s, 1960s, and early 1970s made the emergence of evangelical feminism nearly inevitable. The way evangelical feminists handled the doctrine of biblical inerrancy was a dramatic
break with the past. Though they often proclaimed their loyalty

to that doctrine, the most prominent and reflective evangelical feminists had in effect gutted it of meaning. As their critics noted, they had abandoned the "high view of scripture" that played such a crucial role in twentieth-century evangelical history.[146] In so doing they made their way into a territory less secure and more interesting than any the fundamentalists had ever explored.

6

COUNTERFEMINISM

IN SPITE OF THEIR TRIUMPHS, a note of failure and disillusionment pervaded the writings of evangelical feminists for, as the 1970s wore on, it became increasingly clear that large segments of the evangelical mainstream were still worried by the changing role of women in American society.[1] They found themselves stuck in congregations in which two-thirds of the members were women, but all but three members of the ruling council were men. In some of their churches, women ushers were still nearly as unthinkable as women preachers. They found that they still had to attend worship services in which they were told that the key to women's living successful lives was their avoidance of alcoholism and women's liberation.[2]

When they asked evangelical bookstores to stock books written by evangelical feminists, their requests were viewed with grave suspicion. Their attempts to organize committees in local churches to work for sexual equality met with meager success. Three women would show up for the first two meetings of such a committee, two for the next. Plans for subsequent meetings would simply be canceled.

One evangelical feminist wrote despairingly of the unbelievable "hatred and fear of the women's liberation movement" that she encountered in even the "most liberal" evangelical churches.[3]

Another, outraged by a poster advertising a counterfeminist seminar prominently displayed outside her pastor's office, determined to leave her church to find an evangelical community "reasonably in line with God's will for women." After nine months of looking she gave up her search and joined a non-evangelical congregation.

These thoroughgoing counterfeminists seem not to have captured the evangelical mainstream. By the middle 1970s Billy Graham, always a good barometer of middle-of-the-road evangelicalism, was carefully distancing himself from thoroughgoing opposition to the feminist movement.[4] Interviews with rank-and-file evangelicals suggested that even those women who gave careful attention to the thoroughgoing traditionalists in the end simply ignored their advice.[5] But the counterfeminist writings did vividly demonstrate the tremendous difficulties involved in being both a fully committed evangelical Christian and a fully committed feminist. They showed with great clarity why the gap between secular feminism and the traditions of evangelical Christianity could not be bridged as quickly or as straightforwardly as the evangelical feminists had hoped. Those writings help explain, therefore, why the evangelical feminists encountered such stiff resistance.

The opening paragraphs of an article in a newsweekly described the ideas of one evangelical counterfeminist as "hogwash and bullshit," "sick," and "a patchwork quilt of impressions, intuitions and out-of-style dogma."[6] Such statements are indicative of the scorn with which evangelical counterfeminists have often been treated. Counterfeminists provoked such strong reactions because their writings helped buttress social injustice. Their ideas are hard to appreciate for the same reason that it is hard to appreciate George Fitzhugh's defense of the institution of slavery.

Yet considered in the abstract, without reference to their social implications, the arguments of the evangelical counterfeminists have many merits. Not all the women and men who framed the evangelical critique of feminism were the provincial fundamentalists that polemicists have suggested; the evangelical counterfeminists included some of the keenest intellects and most original perspectives within the evangelical subculture. And even those who would take umbrage at the conclusions reached by the counterfeminists might find themselves in agreement with them on certain points. Many secular feminists, for instance, could admire the skill with which evangelical counterfeminists explored the difficulty of combining a thoroughgoing commitment to orthodox Protestantism with a commitment to feminism.

Elisabeth Elliot, one of the most prominent evangelical counterfeminists, came from a family as distinguished as any within evangelicalism. Her great uncle, Charles G. Trumbull, played a crucial role in popularizing Keswick teaching in the United States. Her grandfather owned the company that published the *Sunday School Times*; her father edited that important journal.[7] Her siblings went on to distinguished careers as missionaries, writers, and educators.

Shortly after she graduated from Wheaton College, she married Jim Elliot, an intense and athletic Westerner determined to dedicate his life to strenuous service in the kingdom of God. The two of them soon became missionaries to Ecuador, and eventually they, along with other missionaries in the area, began to focus their energies upon the Auca Indians, a tribe that had very little previous contact with the outside world and that had killed several outsiders who had made contact with them. At first their efforts to win the Aucas' confidence seemed to go well, but then, in January 1956, the Aucas killed Jim Elliot and four missionary companions.[8]

Remarkably, Elisabeth Elliot then chose to go and live with the tribe that had killed her husband. Although she spent years learning their language and attempting to convert them, Elliot achieved no dramatic successes among the Aucas. Their language proved particularly difficult for her to decipher; the Aucas exhibited little interest in the gospel she had come to share, and differences between her and another woman working among the tribe eventually led to Elliot's departure. But the courage and grace of her decision to work with the Aucas were, in the eyes of most evangelicals, undimmed by the experiment's meager results.

Elliot's experiences among the Aucas led her to reconsider the initial impulse that had led her husband to them. She eventually arrived at a mature and sophisticated understanding of mission activity that differed dramatically from the aggressive and rather cocksure attitude that had impelled the first attempts to convert the Aucas.[9] And, as if to give further evidence that her mind was not constrained by the traditional fundamentalist shibboleths, while she was living among the Aucas, Elliot wrote a tightly reasoned tract upon the foolishness of fundamentalists' insistence upon the evil of drinking.[10]

Elliot was a particularly prominent critic of feminism. She had, for instance, been at the first conference of the Evangelical Women's Caucus, "forcefully" (a reporter in sympathy with the feminists could think of no kinder word) outlining her views.[11] But she was by no means the only thoughtful, thoroughgoing evangelical counterfeminist. Her younger brother, Thomas Howard, did not devote as much attention to the question of women's proper roles as did she, and—perhaps because of the rhetorical difficulties inherent in any male critique of feminism—his views were advanced less forcibly than his sister's. Yet his concise evaluation of feminism ably presented some of the central themes of the traditionalists' position. John Gerstner, whose theological training included work at Harvard as well as at the seminary founded by J. Gresham Machen, and Larry Christenson, the pastor of a Lutheran church in southern California, likewise presented able expositions of counterfeminism.

Judith Miles, the wife of another Lutheran pastor and the author of *The Feminine Principle*, was in many respects a surprising source of the slashing and intellectually rigorous critique of feminism that she actually produced. She was, for one thing, a self-effacing person: she saw to it that her book contained an author's sketch which described her as a woman to whom God had shown mercy in spite of her "hardness of heart." Then, too, Miles was deeply suspicious of intellectual endeavors. All such endeavors were, strictly speaking, redundant searches after that "which is realized in Jesus." Nor did she much value the written word: reading newspapers she felt to be a waste of time; what one had learned from books was not worth passing along to others. The only trustworthy lessons were those gleaned from one's own dealings with God. Yet for all that, Miles's writings, like those of Elliot, Howard, Gerstner, and Christenson, skillfully disclosed the vulnerability of the accommodation between religious tradition and women's liberation that the evangelical feminists had attempted.[12]

Traditionalists found the claim that "women are the largest oppressed group in the world," which they took to be at the heart of the feminist movement, simply incredible. To them, feminism seemed not so much a rebellion against oppression as a response to the affluence promised by American society, which tempted its members to emulate the "style of life" associated with the station in life of those just above them. Women had been convinced that they had to select their recreations, style their hair, buy their clothes, and decorate their homes in the manner dictated by those women who possessed more status than they. They had thus allowed themselves to be enslaved by a "tenuous," "shifting," and "unholy" authority.[13]

According to the counterfeminists, the feminist movement, if successful, would wrap women even more tightly in the constraints of the American economic system; women would be called upon to prove their worth in the realm of production of wealth as well as in its consumption. That was no real liberation; rather, it was an example of an essentially "materialistic" society, one that was obsessed with competition and acquisition, reeling in women who had in the past been free of its more terrible constraints. Claiming to free women from oppression, women's liberation instead incorporated them more fully into an essentially tyrannous system.[14]

Some counterfeminists accompanied this interpretation of American society with a repudiation of some of its central values— the importance of education, for instance. While evangelical feminists sometimes buttressed their arguments with references to the superior education they had enjoyed,[15] counterfeminists took pride in the support they received from those who were not well educated. They freely admitted that university-trained women were more likely than their less well-educated sisters to be attracted to feminism and that the feminist movement had achieved remarkable success in winning the allegiance of America's "more articulate and energetic women." That was, they insisted, the natural result of a basic spiritual truth: the most talented persons are, tragically, "the most susceptible to the sins of pride and independence."[16]

Some counterfeminists rejected as well the therapeutic culture that had nourished evangelical feminism. Elliot, for instance, stressed the absurdity of attempting to solve a problem by asking, "Who am I?" or "How do I really feel?"[17] "Feelings," she wrote, "are the least dependable things in the world."[18] Miles similarly spoke of the foolishness of "seeking to know ourselves." Such a search simply got one stuck in "mental mud." There was a basic error at the heart of all psychotherapies: the assumption that we should learn to "accept" our carnal, sinful nature. To Miles the therapeutic stress on self-acceptance sounded like a modern restatement of the ancient suggestion of the serpent: "Surely God did not intend that you . . . stifle your own potential; surely you will not die if you seek self-actualization."[19] When Miles wished to say that a certain truth was so obvious that the most ignorant dullard could not miss it, she wrote that "even psychotherapists knew that."[20]

Traditionalists argued that there was a sense in which feminists implicitly exaggerated the differences between the two sexes: they assumed that women were less prone to sin than men and that male power was the root of the world's evil. Traditionalists readily admitted that men were responsible for much of the evil and injustice in the world, but they stressed that converted men were no more sinful than converted women and that unregenerate women were no more virtuous than unregenerate men. "Natural women on top of the power heap are just as cruel and repressive" as men, they asserted; "it is the nature of the human, unregenerated, to repress someone weaker."[21]

But there were other, more important ways in which feminists had underestimated the differences between men and women.

They had, first of all, disregarded the biological differences between the sexes. Traditionalists insisted that many fundamental distinctions between the roles society assigned to men and women were dictated by biology. Thus in all cultures in all ages women had the responsibility for taking care of the home. Men had been dominant in every society that had ever existed and would inevitably dominate all future societies. These transcultural patterns were, Elliot bluntly asserted, "a matter of hormones."[22]

Furthermore, the social subordination of women was in accord with God's will and the spiritual principles through which he governed the universe. Hierarchy and subordination were rooted in the nature of the spiritual universe as well as in biology: "As long as God has been," traditionalists said, "there has been a chain of command." Indeed a pattern of hierarchy and submission was embedded in the Trinity itself, with the second and third persons of the Trinity selflessly recognizing and rejoicing in their subordinate relation to God the Father.

Human beings by nature were far less willing to recognize their place in the scheme and they stubbornly rebelled against submitting their wills to the will of God. Yet in order for their souls to be saved their wills had to be broken.[23] The details of how God broke men's wills were beyond the ken of the counterfeminist argument, which was, after all, addressed primarily to women. Counterfeminists only hinted that to accomplish it God often had to resort to strenuous and dramatic tactics.[24] But such forcible methods were less often necessary with women. The structure of society taught them humility—the lesson that all humans have to learn in order to be saved. By learning to conform to the will of their husbands and to defer to them, women learned how to conform to the will of God and to submit their wills to his.

Counterfeminists conceded that throughout history some women had indeed been mistreated and some men had behaved outrageously. But the abuse of women could sometimes be a good thing in the way that Adam's fall was fortunate or in the way that Good Friday was good. Even those women who were abused often found that their mistreatment served to "turn their hearts in submission to God." And whether they were treated well or ill by men, women's submission to their husbands served as a crucial model for others to follow. It awakened in others "an ineffable longing" for "union with Christ."[25]

So some Christians wondered aloud if the "doctrinaire egalitarianism of our culture, which makes the concept of 'the place of women' seem either laughable or boorish" would not turn out, on closer inspection, "to be demonic, uncharitable, destructive of personality [and] disrespectful of creation."[26] Others asserted that the feminist movement was Satan's effort to destroy a divine economy that had saved countless human souls.[27] In any case, it was clear that feminism was a rebellion against "the central principle of Christianity: the laying down of one's own life for another,"[28] and that resisting subordination was in the final analysis simply a "part of being sinful."[29] The goals for which feminists struggled were a terrible departure from the "Divine Order."[30]

The argument that traditionalists advanced most frequently was that feminism and the Bible were incompatible. They claimed that evangelical feminists' unreflective adherence to the notion that "subordination per se is evil" forced them into "absolute virtuoso performances of exegetical fancy."[31]

Traditionalists announced that the feminists did not take the Scriptures as seriously as did they. They were not, of course, able to prove that assertion but—since traditionalists unquestionably did apply the words of the Scriptures to their own lives with a stunning, literalistic rigor—it did possess a certain plausibility. Miles's full embrace of the "feminine principle," for instance, resulted from a reexamination of her relations with her husband in light of Saint Paul's demand that wives be subject to their husbands "as unto the Lord."[32] She asked herself if she would ever nag the Lord to finish up a household chore or remind him that he was not driving with the proper care. Would she, she wondered, seek to modify his taste in clothes or sit in judgment—even in silent judgment—of any of his actions?[33]

A number of skillful and sometimes mildly taunting appeals to such proof texts were included in the traditionalist response. Elliot directed her readers' attention to Paul's assertion that "man was not made from woman, but woman from man" and more especially to the corollary he deduced from it: "Neither was man created for woman but woman for man." Although some verses in the Bible might be plausibly interpreted in several different ways, readers who approached this text without axes to grind could not possibly find any ambiguity in this passage.[34] The traditionalists also dealt with the feminists' emphasis on the cultural limitations of the human authors of the Bible. They claimed that feminists realized that a close reading of the Biblical text would demolish their position; the feminists' invocation of the cultural contamination argument and appeal to the spirit of the Bible were desperate attempts to shift the grounds of the debate. That tactic could not simply be dismissed out of hand, for it was quite true that the Scriptures were shaped by the culture in which they were produced. It was also quite true that the precise cultural patterns of the New Testament era could not be taken as infallible guides for our present situation; there was, obviously, no need for modern Christians to wear togas.[35] On the other hand, there was no reason to assume arrogantly that the culture of the modern West was in every single respect superior to that of ancient Palestine. Modern men and women knew more about the material realm than did the earliest Christians, but their preoccupation with material things had left them ignorant of spiritual matters.[36] There was therefore no reason to assume that modern notions of gender were superior to those that had prevailed when the Scriptures were written.

In any case, it was risky to attempt to separate the essential core of the Christian revelation from the external forms that supposedly obscured its pure essence. Whoever made such an attempt would unconsciously skew that meaning so that it accorded more closely to his or her own cultural preconceptions. "We have the divine content only in the cultural forms in which it was originally given to us," asserted one evangelical theologian. "For better or worse, we hear the witness to Jesus Christ only through the expression and imagery of patriarchy."[37]

If God had wanted to make himself known in a matriarchal culture or in an egalitarian one, he could have done so; he could have shaped history in such a way that Israel would not have been patriarchical. Feminists' suggestion that God's ability to reveal himself faithfully was inhibited by the cultural limitations of the human authors of the Bible was, when carefully considered, simply absurd. God had not been forced to take his cues from Israel; rather, Israel had taken its patriarchal values from him. "It was not," therefore, "a random happenstance that Yahweh picked a patriarchal society to exhibit His Name in":[38] a patriarchical culture revealed essential truths about his nature.

It was only natural that in such a culture the imagery used to describe God was overwhelmingly masculine. And that sort of imagery was crucial to the Christian understanding of the universe. Substituting a mother goddess for a heavenly father was not a matter of tinkering with an inessential bit of imagery. It in effect created a new religion, one that saw the universe as an emanation of God.[39]

The traditional critique of evangelical feminism was an impressive achievement. Responding to the sophisticated arguments of the evangelical feminists, the traditionalists went well beyond a mere regurgitation of the dyspeptic remarks of earlier conservatives such as Rice; theirs was a far more sophisticated position than was his. Nor was it a mere restatement in religious language of the cultural assumptions of white middle-class America; indeed, in several important respects it was a critique of those assumptions. Evangelicals, unlike nearly all other critics of feminism, could ground their opposition to the movement on a coherent and transcendent understanding of the nature of the universe. Many other critiques of feminism, which seemed to rest ultimately on simple self-interest or fear of change, appeared scattered and superficial—or merely cranky—by comparison.

The traditionalists' position was, however, an extremely difficult one to popularize. For one thing, it offered American women few concrete improvements in their lot. Traditionalists admitted that their position did imply that women were left with "the dishwater and diapers and scrub brushes" as well as with "suckling and singing lullabies."[40] Indeed, according to Miles, there was an iron law in the universe that unless the wife continually decreased her husband would be "thwarted and diminished."[41] Wives were advised to make all their decisions in light of that terrible danger.

The only solace traditionalists could, without inconsistency, offer to a single woman was that she could avoid having to subordinate herself to a husband by remaining single throughout her entire life; all they could tell those already married was that no biblical injunction prevented those husbands who wanted to do a little housework every now and again from doing so. Those were not, as the counterfeminists themselves admitted, messages that women who had been exposed to the feminist movement were likely to find appealing.[42]

The slogans with which the traditionalists' message was expressed were bound to strike many twentieth-century women as paradoxical at best. One of the "freedoms" Miles offered her readers was freedom from seeking success. She promised them that by following her guidelines they could free themselves from the "sin" of "independence." At times she seemed on the verge of proclaiming, "Women of the world, submit; you having nothing to lose but your pride."[43] Elliot spoke of gaining freedom through subjection to discipline and explained that women could obtain strength and power only through submission.[44] To many women, the traditionalists' careful distinctions between a woman's being submissive and her being a doormat and between men being naturally more suited to leadership and men being superior sounded suspiciously like doubletalk.[45]

It was, furthermore, difficult to establish one of the main points upon which the traditionalists' argument rested: the correctness of a hierarchical view of the universe. They quite correctly noted that most of their opponents simply assumed the superiority of egalitarianism, and by showing that a hypothetical alternative existed, they did call that assumption into question. But their writings did not present a compelling rationale for the superiority of hierarchicalism to egalitarianism.

And hierarchicalism was not congruent with the religious experiences and traditions of most evangelicals. The traditionalists generally belonged to denominations that had never cut themselves off from the heritage of medieval Christianity: Miles and Christenson were Lutherans; Elliot and Howard were Episcopalians. A hierarchical view of the universe was not out of place in either of those traditions. Respect for hierarchy is, for instance, embedded in the minutest details of the liturgy of the Episcopal church: its Book of Common Prayer directs that priests should receive communion before the cup has touched lay lips. It was only natural, then, that Elliot could appeal to the words of the prayer book to buttress her position. But, as evangelical feminists noted with pleasure, such appeals had little resonance for most evangelicals: most of them belonged to denominations that viewed the medieval heritage with great suspicion and that took great pride in their democratic polity.[46]

Nor was a hierarchical view of the world congruent with the way evangelicals conducted their lives outside their homes. Even the most thoroughgoing of traditionalists admitted that the hierarchical scheme was inapplicable to every other aspect of life. Attempts to apply it, for example, to the governing of the nation or to the organization of the workplace were bound to end in disaster. The traditionalists argued that its unworkableness in all other spheres of life made it all the more important that hierarchicalism—with its witness to the basic spiritual laws of the universe—find expression in the one sphere in which it was workable: the Christian family.[47] But the general inapplicability of hierarchicalism also cut the other way: it required that evangelicals behave antihierarchically at school, at work, and in their relations with their neighbors and then somehow jettison all the habits and assumptions that grew out of that behavior as soon as they entered the home.

Such difficulties help explain why thoroughgoing traditionalism did not capture the evangelical mainstream. They also account for the remarkable concessions to the feminists that crept into the writings of even those authors with the keenest sense of the incompatibility between feminism and evangelicalism. Those concessions resulted, finally, in a position closer to feminism than to the earlier traditionalism of Rice. Howard, for instance, emphasized that there was no biblical warrant for "bossism" in the home.[48] The Bible did not command that husbands be domineering or that wives be servile; after all, Jesus had come not to lend his support to oppression but to loose the captive.[49] Traditionalists stressed, furthermore, that a husband's authority in the home was rooted in his willingness to put the interests of his wife and children above his own desires. The good husband had "died to self."[50] Nor could the traditionalists quite resist the use of the language of the therapeutic. Miles, for example, insisted that she too was a feminist, if being a feminist meant seeking "the highest potential of each individual woman."[51]

Some traditionalists professed complete sympathy with feminists' demands for an end to discrimination against women in the workplace. Christian women might well conclude that they would be violating the will of God if they put their own careers ahead of their families; indeed, they might decide that working wives were a terrible departure from the divine order of creation.[52] Nevertheless, there could no longer be any serious debate over whether or not women should be given equal pay for equal work. And all jobs had to be open to anyone, male or female, who was qualified to perform them.[53]

Underlying the traditionalists' apparent resistance to feminism were a number of significant concessions to that movement. That same pattern was also evident in the writings of Marabel Morgan. But her resistance to feminism was not nearly so firm nor her accommodations nearly so subtle as those of writers like Elliot and Miles.

Some controversies are the result of persons having so little in common that they cannot even begin to understand each other, but others result, in a sense, from how much the parties in the controversy have in common. Sharing many assumptions, speaking the same language, and having common experiences, the disputants cannot abide the differences that separate them. Most commentators have assumed that the controversy between counterfeminists and feminists was an instance of the first sort of controversy. Morgan's writings suggest it may, in fact, properly be seen as an example of the second.[54]

Morgan's early years were difficult. Her parents were poor and they were in the "throes of divorce" by the time she was in the third grade; her father died when she was fourteen.[55] She attended Ohio State University (working as a beautician to support herself) and while there was converted to Christianity—largely through the efforts of a friend who told her, as Morgan later recalled, "that God loved me and had a wonderful plan for my life."[56] At the time Morgan wrote *The Total Woman* and *Total Joy*—bestselling books that purported to tell women how they could improve their lives and their marriages—she was in her late thirties and married to an attorney.

Morgan's books were concerned largely with secular matters. They included, for instance, suggestions on how wives could better manage their time and how they could improve their sexual relations with their husbands. The books also discussed the way that following biblical principles could provide the solution to women's problems. Chief among these principles was that of adapting to one's husband's will.

The Total Woman sold over 3 million copies. It achieved such prominence in conservative Protestant circles that evangelical writers assumed that "everyone is familiar with the Total Woman phenomenon."[57] Evangelical celebrities such as Anita Bryant came to Morgan for help;[58] evangelical humorists parodied her ideas;[59] evangelical theologians sandwiched discussions of Karl Barth's view of the sexes between responses to her writings;[60] and Billy Graham alluded to them in his sermons.[61]

Morgan's ideas circulated well beyond the evangelical subculture. Secular women's magazines printed excerpts from her books. Network news organizations devoted segments of documentaries to the "total woman" phenomenon. The *National Review* and the *New York Times* commented on her writings, and newsweeklies placed her picture on their covers. Feminist activists subjected her books to skeptical scrutiny,[62] and a group at Princeton University tried to sponsor a debate between her and Betty Friedan.[63]

Scholars came to see Morgan as a central figure in the backlash against feminism. Articles in *Feminist Studies* saw Morgan's seminars as representative of a broader pattern of resistance to the feminist movement.[64] Social scientists noted the apparent link between Morgan's writings and the anti-ERA movement.[65] Textbooks in American history, adjusting their accounts of the history of women in America in light of the growing opposition to the feminist movement, began to single out the "total woman" as one of the "slogans" around which opponents of the women's liberation movement and the Equal Rights Amendment rallied.[66]

Yet in spite of all the attention they have received, the precise significance of Morgan's writings has not been widely recognized. They have, for instance, sometimes been interpreted as promising a panacea for domestic difficulties. Her books were indeed filled with testimonials from women who had found happiness by following her suggestions, and in interviews Morgan insisted that her principles worked "99 times out of 100."[67] But elsewhere Morgan explicitly warned that "the Total Woman principles" would not "solve every woman's problems."[68] Indeed the principles she enumerated were no panacea even in her own life: her husband and children sometimes responded poorly to her best efforts to apply those principles; good friends who tried to live up to them found their marriages ending in divorce, and Morgan admitted that it was quite possible that those principles might not prevent even her own marriage from falling apart. She admitted also that her dreams of transforming herself into the "total woman," of changing her husband into the "total man," and of making their daily life together "super great" had all gone unfulfilled.[69]

Morgan has usually been cast as a reactionary, firmly rejecting all attempts to modify traditional notions concerning the proper relations between men and women. She has been seen as the opposite pole of the feminist movement and as more reactionary than writers such as Elliot. Morgan did indeed believe that women needed to choose between a career and being a wife or mother.[70] She did argue that women who had been convinced that fulfillment was to be found in careers rather than in the home had "been sold a bill of goods."[71] And she did indeed tell her readers that a good wife "reveres and worships" her husband.[72]

But there are several difficulties connected with interpreting Morgan as a thoroughgoing traditionalist. She insisted on describing herself as "liberated,"[73] and she claimed that feminists familiar with her program said that it was "exactly what we're promoting—getting organized, expressing yourself, and being your own person."[74] Then too there is the somewhat grudging, but entirely sincere, praise that Morgan won from some evangelical feminists familiar with her works.[75] And conservative evangelicals saw her books as dangerous departures from tradition: *Moody Monthly* refused to carry advertisements for *The Total Woman;*[76] fundamentalists called Morgan heretical and "satanic."[77]

There were in fact several striking similarities between Morgan and the mainstream feminist movement. Far from offering a sanguine view of the wisdom of men, her writings presented such an unflattering portrait of her husband that Morgan had to explicitly confute the notion that he was feeble-minded.[78] Nor were her books based on an idyllic assessment of the lot of most wives and mothers, for she saw their lives as being comparable to that of a prisoner of war shackled, gagged, and locked in a six-foot by six-foot room surrounded by stone.[79]

Morgan's reaction to that confinement was not unlike that of many feminists. She took courses in self-improvement, read books on the proper relations between men and women, and she began to study psychology.[80] The result was an agenda comparable to some of the aims of feminists. Morgan called for human autonomy and for control of one's own life. She wanted women to escape from their old and rutted mental habits and learn that they were not enslaved by their past. She worked to eradicate the drabness that marred most women's lives and to foster human fulfillment. She hoped to produce resilient, "adventuresome" women who could announce, after months of struggle to create a better life for themselves, "it's been awfully hard going, but we're going to make it."[81]

Morgan's position, like that of some feminists, was open to the charge of materialism: her program promised greater access to the material benefits of a prosperous society. But on closer inspection her position, like that of the feminists, was more complex. Possessions were valued less for themselves than as tangible recognition of one's worth, and were seen as far less important than other, less tangible, signs of recognition.[82]

Her stress on the principle of adaptation was not in fact the sweeping repudiation of feminism that at first glance it appeared to be. She was, for instance, quick to point out that it had little to do with a woman's career. The Scriptures commanded that a wife adapt to her husband, not "to all men in general." Outside the home a woman might properly "compete with anybody in any realm." She could in fact become the president of the company for which she worked without in any way violating Morgan's principles.[83]

Nor were the principle's implications in the home what one might at first expect. They did not preclude women telling their husbands with great emphasis precisely what course of action they thought their families should take. Indeed, in practice the concept led Morgan herself to do more shouting at her husband than she had before she had begun to adapt to his will.[84] Nor did the principle mean that Morgan simply did whatever her husband told her to do.

Thus when Morgan's husband requested that she skip a tennis tournament in which she had planned to play so the family could go on a fishing trip, a two-hour argument ensued. Morgan's husband eventually gave in and withdrew his request, so in that particular case the discussion never moved beyond what Morgan somewhat euphemistically called the "compromise level": "the principle of adapting," she explained, "never came into play, mainly because I wouldn't let it."[85]

In practice, then, the principle seemed to mean simply that if a husband and wife were in total disagreement and no suitable compromise was possible, then the husband should make the final decision—not merely on the basis of his own wishes but rather in accord with what he honestly thought to be the best interests of the family.

Yet even after narrowly circumscribing its applicability and carefully qualifying its meaning, Morgan still displayed considerable ambiguity toward the principle of adapting. She confessed that adhering to the principle was for her "the most difficult part" of her life. She said she was certain that "no matter how [much] I dislike the principle of adapting," it was God's will. "As much as lies within me," she said, "I try to do it." Sometimes, however, Morgan herself simply could not or would not force herself to adhere to the principle she had introduced into so many other women's lives.[86]

Morgan thus managed to cling to the biblical injunction that wives must submit themselves to their husbands, but she did so only by gutting the notion of most of its meaning. Her clinging to that injunction therefore carried almost exactly the same significance as did the evangelical feminists' allegiance to the doctrine of biblical inerrancy. Thus her "resistance" to the feminist movement was, in a way, a testimony to its influence.

7

MODERN PSYCHOLOGY

The unceasing battle between faith and unbelief keeps shifting ground from time to time. In one era Christianity is attacked vehemently and particularly from the standpoint of history. In another era it is attacked vehemently and particularly from the standpoint of geology. In a third era it is attacked vehemently and particularly from the standpoint of biology. Today, however, it is being attacked vehemently and particularly from the standpoint of psychology.

—Vernon Grounds,
Dean of the Conservative
Baptist Theological
Seminary in Denver, 1955.[1]

TWENTIETH-CENTURY AMERICAN EVANGELICALS often commented upon the rise of "modern psychology." The term was an elastic one. They used it to describe the ideas and practices associated with psychoanalysis, with other forms of psychiatry, and with "clinical psychology"—the form of psychology directly concerned with relieving mental illness or emotional distress. They also applied the term to popular writers whose works reflected the influence of psychiatrists and psychologists. Thus in evangelicals' minds, Norman Vincent Peale and Dale Carnegie as well as Freud and Jung were linked to "modern psychology."

Evangelicals believed that modern psychology had profoundly influenced the American people. They believed that they were living in a "psychological" age, an age in which a "therapeutic emphasis" suffused books, magazines, and daily conversation.[2] Troubled persons who in previous eras would have turned to pastors for help now turned to psychiatrists. Evangelicals discerned, in fact, a general tendency for psychology to take over roles traditionally performed by religion.[3]

Evangelicals' descriptions of twentieth-century American society parallel the observations of those scholars—Philip Rieff, T. J. Jackson Lears, and Christopher Lasch, for example—who argue that a pervasive "therapeutic culture," associated with the rise of psychiatry and clinical psychology, has profoundly shaped the modern world. Modern Americans were, according to evangelical observers, obsessed with finding happiness in this world and uninterested in the fate of their souls in the next. The American people tended to see disease where a previous generation would have seen sin. They seemed to doubt that self-denial was a good thing. Instead, Americans prized self-improvement, self-actualization, and self-realization. They seemed more interested in developing a pleasing personality than in building a virtuous character.[4]

Between 1925 and 1950 fundamentalism was a bulwark against the onslaughts of the therapeutic culture: fundamentalists did not allow therapeutic ideas to shape their view of the world, but mounted numerous direct attacks upon modern psychology. It seemed clear in those years that if the therapeutic culture were going to triumph in America, it was going to do so in spite of significant fundamentalist opposition.

Evangelical hostility to psychology has not yet completely disappeared. But in the 1950s a number of influential evangelicals adopted a new, less belligerent stance toward psychology. They muzzled their criticisms of modern psychology and began presenting Christian versions of it. In the 1960s and 1970s most evangelical spokespersons embraced modern psychology with great enthusiasm and only minor reservations. By then, the evangelical subculture was less a bulwark against than a variant of the therapeutic culture.

In 1929, A. Z. Conrad, pastor of the prestigious Park Street Congregational Church in Boston, pronounced his verdict on modern psychology. It came in the course of a "great address" (so contemporaries described it) delivered at a conference sponsored by the Moody Bible Institute and held at Clarence Macartney's huge First Presbyterian Church in Pittsburgh.

Conrad briefly discussed the distinctive emphases of Freud, Jung, William McDougall, J. B. Watson, and Wolfgang Köhler,[5] indicating as he went that some of these men were more impressive than others. He stressed, however, what they had in common: an essentially "materialistic" outlook. Conrad made it clear that fundamentalists would find little common ground with such men. His address was reprinted under the title "Modern Psychology the Foe of Truth." The article began by declaring that "of all the modern confederacy of foes which Christianity has to face there is none more subtle, more dangerous than materialistic psychology."[6]

Conrad's salvo was one of the earliest systematic fundamentalist attacks upon modern psychology. It was by no means the last: in the next twenty years fundamentalists resisted modern psychology with tenacity and a good deal of success.

One of the most effective methods of resistance they employed was a stubborn refusal to let the ideas associated with the rise of modern psychology affect their own view of the world. They continued to judge human behavior in terms of virtue or vice and good or evil rather than in terms of health or illness. Fundamentalists downplayed the importance of developing a pleasing personality.[7] Developing one's personality was no great accomplishment if the personality that was being developed was sinful.[8] Instead they stressed the importance of "building character through self-denial."[9] They spoke frequently of the need for "self-crucifixion."

Fundamentalist writers and preachers naturally discussed how one should live one's life in this world, but they insisted that the fate of one's eternal soul was more important than obtaining this worldly happiness and that life in this world should be lived with that in mind. A true Christian viewed life in this world not as an end in itself but as a preparation for the next.[10] Accordingly, a Christian would not be overly concerned with obtaining earthly happiness: a godly life was not marked by complete happiness or satisfaction, but rather by a sort of "contented discontent."[11]

Fundamentalists combined this consistent eschewal of therapeutic themes with direct attacks upon the various manifestations of modern psychology. Pamphlets published by Moody dismissed popular psychology as "nonsense" and "flapdoodle"; they implied that many, even most, of its proponents were either charlatans or cranks.[12] Popular psychologists viewed the world, the *Sunday School Times* told its readers, in a manner that would most likely doom those psychologists and their followers to eternal perdition.[13]

Fundamentalists' attacks upon Freud's ideas were particularly vehement and sometimes verged on hysteria;[14] Walter A. Maier called Freudianism "pornographic";[15] other fundamentalist spokespersons called attempts to use concepts drawn from Freud's work to elucidate Christian dogma blasphemous. They were only slightly less hostile toward psychiatry in general. For instance, the editors of *Revelation* linked psychiatry with Christian Science and with medical quackery. They interpreted the widespread interest in psychiatric ideas as a sign of the sinful stubbornness of unregenerate human nature.[16]

Fundamentalists attacked the most prominent academic approaches to psychology. They alleged that McDougall's theories concerning human instincts were, in effect, a virtual declaration that there was no difference between human beings and animals.[17] They called gestalt a "monkey psychology."[18] They found behaviorism—which in its more moderate forms had become by

1919 the "normal science" of American university psychology departments—even more blameworthy.[19] They called Watson "a freak."[20]

Some of its proponents insisted that modern psychology was entirely compatible with Christianity, and most fundamentalists conceded that there were many similarities between the gospel and modern psychology. They nevertheless viewed all attempts to unite modern psychology with Christianity with great suspicion.

If modern psychology was as crucial an "adjunct" to the Christian faith as its proponents claimed, then it was "strange indeed" that God had refused to reveal it to his people for 1,900 years and had thus left them "in ignorance" and bereft of its benefits.[21] Modern psychology was in fact inferior at all points to the gospel. It was related to the true gospel in the same way that tinsel was related to gold.[22] It offered medicines for which Bible-believing Christians had no use. A person who really knew Christ had no need for self-improvement courses.[23] True Christians could not possibly suffer from an inferiority complex[24] nor could they possibly gain anything from taking up the "day by day, in every way . . ." chant that Emile Coué suggested.[25]

Psychology, therefore, was not simply a paler version of Christianity. When carefully scrutinized it turned out to be a satanic view of the world that was radically at odds with the gospel.[26] Fundamentalists charged that modern psychology's leading proponents did not believe that one's impulses needed to be checked. They viewed sin as nothing more serious than the transgression of ancient and entirely arbitrary standards.[27] They generally did not believe that humans were powerless to do good. Instead, they emphasized human potential.[28] Rather than teaching humans to rely on God, proponents of modern psychology advocated putting one's trust in oneself.[29]

In the 1920s, 1930s, and 1940s, fundamentalists repeatedly warned that attempts to appropriate the insights of modern psychology were likely to weaken rather than strengthen traditional religion. True believers, lulled by smooth assurances that they did not have to reject Christianity in order to accept modern psychology, would find that their thoughts and actions were increasingly governed by modern psychology. Gradually, very likely without the victims ever realizing what was happening, they would have their faith painlessly extracted.[30]

In the summer of 1946, *Moody Monthly* published an article by Virginia Whitman, a youth counselor associated with a Bible institute in Missouri, called "God's Psychiatry." The article emphasized the remarkable parallels between the Bible and the insights of psychiatry. It explained in some detail the difference between repression and suppression, emphasizing that psychoanalysts, like Christians, were convinced of the necessity of the latter. It outlined contemporary psychological views of man's basic needs and argued that Christianity fulfilled those needs. Departing sharply from the party line on the evils of modern psychology, Whitman argued that evangelicals were wrong to suppose that modern psychology was "humbug" and called for evangelicals to appropriate its insights.[31]

Whitman's stance was a courageous one, for at that time evangelicals who spoke kindly of modern psychology were still viewed with considerable suspicion. But the future belonged to Whitman, not her critics. Within a decade of the publication of "God's Psychiatry," a host of prominent evangelicals had expressed similar views. Several developments seemed to have worked together to produce the change.

It was in the 1940s and 1950s that evangelicals settled on their policy of constructive engagement with the rest of American society.[32] That policy naturally led them toward a less belligerent position concerning modern psychology. Determined to show that they were not obscurantists and that their gospel was not irrelevant to the needs of modern America, evangelicals now thought twice before attacking any respected and influential set of ideas.

In the postwar years, it was apparent to the evangelicals that modern psychology was not, as they sometimes had suspected earlier, a mere fad:[33] modern psychology's prestige and power were now beyond doubt.[34] It seemed clear that Americans' voracious interest in psychology was not going to disappear. It seemed clear, too, that it would be better if their appetite for psychology were satisfied by sound Christians rather than by secularists.

The changing nature of the psychological ideas they encountered lessened evangelicals' resistance to modern psychology. Popular psychology seemed less dangerous than it had in the 1930s. To be sure, it was still not fully Christian in its outlook.[35] Sometimes it was remarkably banal. But the most prominent popular psychologists of the day often couched their message in religious language, and evangelicals had to admit that their books contained a good deal of common sense.[36] Evangelicals also believed that practicing psychiatrists were becoming less hostile to Christianity: articles in evangelical magazines noted that psychiatrists now sometimes told potential patients to seek counseling from a minister before undergoing psychiatric treatment. Evangelicals noted too—with great relief—that the sinister influence of Freud seemed to be waning.[37] They took comfort in the growing prominence of ideas drawn from psychologists and psychiatrists—Adler, Fromm, Horney, Erikson, Jung, Rogers—who seemed to possess a solicitous attitude toward religion, or who at least did not wear their lack of piety on their sleeves.[38]

Evangelicals' new, less hostile, attitude toward modern psychology infused the first annual Calvinistic Conference on Psychology and Psychiatry, convened in 1954. Participants called for an appropriation of modern psychology's insights and for encouraging more young Christians to pursue careers in psychotherapy. They also tried to use concepts drawn from psychology to illuminate the nature of Christ: he had, one participant argued, a human psyche and a "Divine Ego."[39]

Hildreth Cross's *An Introduction to Psychology* (1952)—purportedly the first "textbook in general psychology screened

through the Word of God"[40]—chided evangelicals for their prejudices against psychology[41] and decried popular resistance to
modern methods of curing mental illness.[42] Cross, chairman of
the department of psychology at Taylor University, left his
readers with the comforting impression that Christians had no
quarrel with the data that psychological research unearthed;
Christians and secular psychologists simply disagreed on how
that data should be interpreted.[43] Psychology was no less a legitimate field of study than biology. Evangelicals had not let Darwin's errors frighten them into rejecting all forms of biological
inquiry. Neither should they let the errors of Watson and Freud
keep them from the study of psychology.

In the 1950s, evangelicals also began to present the gospel in a
new way, as a solution to the maladies that psychologists described. Typically, they accepted psychologists' diagnosis of the
human condition, argued that secular psychology could not fully
cure the problems it uncovered, and then showed that the prescriptions offered by Christianity were more effective than those
offered by secular psychologists. Their basic message was, as one
evangelical put it, "faith can cure our emotional sickness."[44]

To be sure, some of the works published in this decade made
only superficial accommodations to modern psychology. They
presented the traditional faith to their readers with only the thin-
nest of therapeutic veneers. "The Art of Living"—an eleven-part
series written by Godfrey C. Robinson and Stephen F. Winward
and published by *Eternity* in 1951–52—was closer in spirit to
nineteenth-century advice manuals than to contemporary popular psychology. It was in fact conceived as a distinctively Christian response to best sellers such as *How to Win Friends and
Influence People* and *Peace of Mind*. "The Art of Living" did,
however, present Christianity in a new way: the answer to problems like "anxiety" and an "inferiority complex"[45] and the path
to "a full and happy life."[46]

Many prominent evangelical writers, among them Charles L.
Allen and Clyde M. Narramore, embraced modern psychology
with greater gusto. Allen, the pastor of a large Methodist church
in Atlanta and the author of *In Quest of God's Power* (1952) and
God's Psychiatry (1953), preached a message of positive think-

ing. He cited Dale Carnegie[47] and Rabbi Joshua Liebman[48] with warm approval and some reverence. The human predicament, as he diagnosed it, was that people have a tendency to become "negative" in their "thinking."[49] He ebulliently passed on ten-word cures to those suffering from psychological complexes[50] and told his readers how they could make good things come about by visualizing them in advance.

Narramore, who had been reared on a Western ranch and educated at Columbia University, eventually became the most prominent of all evangelical psychologists. Like Allen, he was a self-conscious popularizer, and his works did not always demonstrate a familiarity with recent psychological literature or a grasp of the complexity of the topics he discussed.[51]

Narramore was, however, considerably more sophisticated than Allen, and he drew his ideas from more respectable sources. Carl Rogers shaped his thinking about counseling. Narramore recommended that counselors use open-ended questions and repeat the statements made by their counselees. He emphasized the importance of communicating unconditional acceptance and of helping counselees claim their feelings.[52] Narramore never tired of repeating a lesson that he learned from Adler: the importance of self-esteem.

McDougall's ideas provided the framework of an influential series of articles Narramore published in 1954 and 1955 called "Your Psychological Needs." Each article in the series focused on a particular human need; each presented advice drawn from contemporary psychologists and from the Scriptures on how to deal with that need. Narramore discussed a wide range of psychological needs—freedom from guilt, belonging, freedom from fear, learning and gaining knowledge, and love and affection, among others. Each article pointed, however, toward the same conclusions: Christians, like everyone else, had needs which had to be met; Christians should consult the insights of secular psychology as well as those of the Christian tradition.[53]

The new approach to modern psychology formulated by evangelicals such as Narramore was a prudent response to the circumstances in which evangelicals found themselves in the 1950s. Disengaging themselves from a few-holds-barred fight with an increasingly powerful foe, evangelicals made the survival of the faith more likely. Aligning themselves with an increasingly powerful impulse in American culture, evangelical writers and pastors bolstered their own authority and prestige.

The new strategy involved no wholesale acceptance of secular psychology. Evangelical writers all drew on modern psychology with great selectivity. They spoke of "fixations"[54] and of "a sense of inferiority"[55] but not of the collective unconscious. Some concepts—ambivalence and the Oedipus complex, for instance—they rejected outright.[56] The psychological terms they incorporated into their works were usually fenced in by inverted commas and by scriptural language.

Evangelicals often emphasized secular psychology's limitations. They never supposed that modern psychology was a substitute for the gospel. It was, they carefully specified, merely an "adjunct."[57] They consistently emphasized that modern psychology could not by itself solve the problems it described. Psychologists were correct, Vernon Grounds noted, to say that all humans had a need for "unconditional love," but they were wrong to suppose that such a love was a human possibility.[58] Narramore said that psychological needs met at "a merely human level" had not really been met at all.[59]

The new response seemed, furthermore, to require no repudiation of the evangelical faith. Certainly, the books and articles that exemplified the new approach to modern psychology were filled with signs of the piety and thoroughgoing orthodoxy of their authors. Cross's preface disclosed that he had prayed for divine guidance as he struggled to get the wording of his textbook right.[60] Narramore's books showed that he had no doubts concerning the reality of demonic possession or the efficacy of petitionary prayer. His works showed too that the ultimate objective of all his counseling was to deepen the spiritual lives of those who came to him for help.

However, the worldview associated with the evangelical proponents of modern psychology differed in several significant respects from the evangelical tradition. Sometimes those proponents seemed to deemphasize the importance of purely spiritual matters. Narramore, for instance, pictured human nature as three intersecting circles arranged in a manner that suggested that the spiritual aspect of man was no more important than the physical or emotional.[61]

These evangelicals began to see the Bible in a new light. Its power seemed to rest as much on the fact that it presented a positive, hopeful approach to life as upon the fact that it was the Word of God.[62] Its power was interpreted in explicitly therapeutic terms: a man who came to Allen nervous and tense was "prescribed" 245 doses of the Twenty-Third Psalm.[63]

Evangelical writers came to think of ministers as, in effect, a special variety of psychiatrists.[64] Increasingly, they assumed that all ministers would want to be of help in the "here and now," and that in order to do so they would have to be acquainted with the insights of modern psychology.[65] While ministers were seldom particularly competent psychologists, often they would encounter parishioners who needed professional help. Ministers thus became little more than the first line of defense in the campaign against mental illness: they spotted the more seriously troubled individuals and sent them to their superior officers. Ministers could only be trusted to handle the little problems.

Then, too, there were surprisingly few direct references to God in the works produced by the evangelical proponents of modern psychology. God had left us with a set of biblical principles which, if followed faithfully, would make our lives more rewarding. He comforted us when we were in trouble. He approached us too by offering us a "vision of our better selves."[66] God did not, however, burst upon one's life "unbidden." He was, according to Allen, "unobtrusive." His presence in the world was so faint that if one did not make a point of setting aside an hour or two a week to look for him, God would simply fade from view.[67]

Billy Graham's *Peace with God* (1953) used a revealing metaphor to explain God's presence in our life. A Christian was like a little boy flying a kite. God was the kite. The kite had soared so high that it had become invisible. The boy knew it existed only because "every little while" he felt a tug on the kite string.[68]

Modern psychology did not win complete acceptance in the evangelical subculture. Scattered echoes of an older, non-therapeutic form of evangelicalism reverberated through the literature of evangelicalism throughout the 1960s and 1970s. An article in *Moody Monthly* advised, for instance, that Christians view loneliness as a stage on their journey to God rather than as a problem to be overcome.[69] An article in *Eternity* resisted the temptation to classify all human problems as a form of illness: alcoholism was first and foremost, it insisted, a sin.[70] A writer in another magazine argued that most pastoral counseling was a waste of time.[71]

Even in the 1970s, decades after evangelicals had begun to make their peace with modern psychology, some evangelicals continued to attack psychology head-on. Oliver W. Price suggested that the therapeutic themes embedded in a particular bestseller were ultimately demonic in origin.[72] Paul T. Brownback produced a careful and telling comparison of "biblical concepts" and the ideas espoused by Narramore.[73] John Piper, writing in *Christianity Today*, argued that the concept of self-esteem that writers such as Narramore insisted was embedded in the Bible was in fact a modern idea, and one deeply at odds with the biblical view of man.[74] In *Psychology as Religion*, Paul Vitz presented an extended discussion of the works of Fromm, Rogers, Maslow, and May that was intended to show that those works were essentially anti-Christian.[75]

Jay E. Adams, a professor at Westminster Seminary, was a particularly thoroughgoing and fearless opponent of modern psychology. His first manifesto, *Competent to Counsel*, appeared in 1970; his ideas were elaborated in a collection of essays, *The Big Umbrella*, published in 1972, and in numerous subsequent works. He questioned whether there was "any legitimate place" for the psychiatrist in "the economy of God." The territory psychiatrists had won for themselves had largely been taken over from pastors. It was, Adams averred, "stolen property."[76]

Adams rejected the notion that there was such a thing as mental illness.[77] The problems that psychiatrists grouped under that category were in reality simply manifestations of a sinful failure to follow God's dictates.

Adams denounced the Rogerian techniques of counseling advocated by Narramore as unscriptural.[78] Problems could not legitimately be solved by any sort of client-centered therapy, for any counseling that moved Christ from the center was non-Christian.[79] Men and women who came to a counselor should be told that their problems were rooted in their own sins. The counselor's job was simply to help identify precisely what those sins were and then to suggest techniques to help avoid further sins. A wise counselor would not try to empathize with a teen-age boy who transgressed biblical standards of sexual conduct. The counselor would, rather, tell the adolescent that he was sinning, impress upon him the enormity of his sins, and warn him to stop his evildoing.[80]

The significance of the continuing evangelical resistance to modern psychology and of the "cure of souls" tradition that lingered in the evangelical subculture may be easily exaggerated. A willingness to criticize some forms of psychology is not a sign that one has rejected modern psychology per se. Psychologists, after all, are famous for their zestful dissections of other schools of thought. Many evangelicals criticized certain forms of psychology while embracing others: Mark Cosgrove wrote both *Psychology Gone Awry*[81] and *Mental Health: A Christian Approach*.[82]

Even Adams was touched by modern psychology. He adopted some of its argot, speaking, for instance, of "intrapersonal relations." He adopted some of its practices as well: he used behavior modification to eradicate the sinful practices of those he counseled. Interestingly enough, writers within the evangelical camp described his work as a form of popular psychology.[83]

In any case, the influence of men like Adams was circumscribed. Their fellow evangelicals sometimes gave them a hearing, but the hearing they received was not the sort one accords an orthodoxy. The general trend in the 1960s and 1970s was in the other direction: far from retreating from the accommodations worked out in the 1950s, evangelicals actually went well beyond them.

In the 1960s and 1970s evangelical magazines often seemed to be little more than self-help compendiums. Evangelical bookstores were full of books that treated subjects such as family relations, alcoholism, old age, and death in a way that did not "bore" the reader "with clarifications and lengthy explanations."[84] Evangelical readers were told "How to Fight Depression and Win"[85] and offered "God's Rx for Depression."[86] They were told how to be calm[87] and content[88] and how to avoid fatigue.[89] They were advised to "Help Yourself to Happiness";[90] they were told "How to Live in Heaven on Earth."[91]

Guidance in how to live life in this world was drawn largely, if indirectly, from the work of secular psychologists. *Christianity Today* published a review of a book called *Improving Your Self Image* that communicated the nature of much of the evangelical literature in this era. The book read in places, said the reviewer, exactly like "fourteen other" books of "popular-psychology-with-a-little-religion-added-for-flavor." He recommended it highly.[92]

Evangelical books explained how to maintain a "balanced and integrated personality."[93] They stressed the importance of living in "the now,"[94] taking risks, and allowing oneself to be vulnerable.[95] Readers were assured that feelings, even negative feelings, "can work toward our wholeness as persons."[96] Evangelical books promised to divulge "the path that leads through complete forgiveness to self-acceptance, spontaneous freedom, and exhilarating growth."[97]

Evangelicals used the terms and concepts they borrowed from secular psychologists in ways that indicated that they had forgotten some basic distinctions about which their predecessors had been quite clear. In this era, evangelicals used "heart" and "personality" as though they were synonymous. The "deeper life" became something that one arrived at by reading books that disclosed "psychological insights."[98] The "abundant life" Christ promised became associated in evangelicals' minds with ensuring mental health and avoiding nervous breakdowns.[99] A positive self-image was synonymous with a biblical self-image.[100]

M. N. Beck, writing in *Christianity Today*, marveled at the similarities between Jesus' injunction to go "and teach all nations, baptizing them in the name of the Father, and of the Son and of the Holy Ghost" and the views of a contemporary psychiatrist:

> our greeds, our lusts, our aggressions, present major difficulties for preventative and therapeutic medicine, and for society. These are the very problems that psychiatry has struggled with for over the past forty years. We need to increase our effectiveness in dealing with human personality. In the meanwhile we can do better than we are now doing by psychological support, by counseling and truly accepting the model that we care for people irrespective of their disease.

"What is this," marveled Beck, "but a modern expression of the Great [Commission]."[101]

Evangelicals displayed in these decades a remarkable tolerance for psychological ideas which their predecessors would have attacked. Sometimes they doubted the orthodoxy of Robert Schuller, a protégé of Peale and an advocate of "self-love." But his books were published by evangelical houses and sold in evangelical bookstores. He was warmly praised by Graham and by *Christianity Today*.[102] Evangelicals noted that Paul Tournier, a Swiss psychiatrist whose books blended psychiatric and theological concepts, had an extraordinarily vague theological position.[103] But in spite of his inability to spell out an orthodox position, Tournier gained almost universal approbation among evangelicals: criticizing Tournier was as unthinkable as criticizing "Grandma Moses" or "apple pie."[104] Magazines such as *Eternity* praised books which in their judgment gave the impression that the truths discovered by psychology were more exciting and interesting than those taught by Jesus.[105] Fuller Seminary, eager to win a scholarly reputation for its fledgling school of psychology, required only that its professors not be notoriously hostile to religion. Fuller considered—apparently quite seriously—trying to lure Rollo May onto its faculty.[106]

As they became more tolerant of modern psychology, evangelicals became more sensitive to the dangers of an excessive attachment to traditional religious ideas and practices. *Christianity Today* disparaged the notion that troubled Christians should simply be content to "turn their problems over to Jesus" and "trust the Lord." Basil Jackson warned in his *Moody Monthly* column, "Clinically Speaking," that it was dangerous to pray over one's emotional problems.[107] Gene A. Getz, writing in the same magazine, argued that wise counselors would hesitate to either pray or quote Scripture during counseling sessions. They would also generally avoid concluding that a person was encountering troubles because of a "lack of faith."[108] *Christianity Today* warned pastors that they might give their listeners a negative self-image if they spent too much time preaching about sin.[109]

One final sign of evangelicals' acceptance of modern psychology should be noted. In the 1970s, prominent conservative evangelicals such as Marabel Morgan, Tim LaHaye, Bill Gothard, and James Dobson did not resist modern psychology's penetration of the evangelical subculture. They in fact promoted it. Like those evangelicals to their theological, social, and political left, they stressed the here and now rather than the hereafter. They, like other evangelicals, drew heavily on concepts and terms whose origins were in secular psychology.

Morgan, the most prominent of all the evangelical counterfeminists, affirmed that Christians' "future destination is truly out of this world." But she did not see life in this world simply as a preparation for life in the next. Instead, she emphasized the importance of Christians living up to their human potential and learning to express their real selves here on earth.[110] She admired the work of men such as Dale Carnegie[111] and Viktor Frankl.[112] She credited Clyde Narramore's ideas with having changed her life.[113]

Tim LaHaye, co-founder of the Moral Majority, wrote scores of popular books which presented a consistently conservative—even reactionary—interpretation of Christianity and of current events. But many of his books were devoted to telling Christians how to find contentment in this world. He told his readers how to improve sex lives,[114] how to "win over depression,"[115] how to cope with guilt feelings, and how to overcome anxiety.[116] He told "self-rejecting" Christians that they were rebelling against God.[117]

Bill Gothard was an implacable foe of modernism, socialism, and secular humanism. His remarkably popular seminars in "Basic Youth Conflicts" presented an extraordinarily authoritarian vision of how a Christian family should be run.[118] Yet his seminars repeatedly stressed the importance of learning to accept one's self;[119] they were regarded within the evangelical subculture as a form of popular psychology, comparable in some respects to Transactional Analysis.[120]

James Dobson, author of *Dare to Discipline* (1970), a conservative guide to child rearing viewed as nearly canonical in most evangelical circles, presented his advice as an antidote to the excessive permissiveness of American society. But it would be hard to argue that his thinking was distinctively Christian rather than distinctively psychological. His *Hide and Seek* (1974) gave about the same sort of advice that secular psychologists such as William Glasser dispensed. The book was devoted primarily to showing how parents could give their children a sense of self-esteem.[121] *Dare to Discipline* relied heavily upon the techniques of behavior modification.[122] There were in fact no fundamental differences between its outlook and the worldview that had informed John Watson's *Psychological Care of the Infant and Child* (1928). Pejorative language aside, Jay Adams's analysis of *Dare* was essentially accurate: it was indeed "basically a godless humanistic book."[123]

By the 1960s, popular evangelicalism had been profoundly influenced by its encounter with modern psychology. A stress on the here and now, a lack of concern for the afterlife, and a constant emphasis on the importance of self-esteem—these were some of the hallmarks of popular evangelicalism in the 1960s and 1970s.

The significance of the vitality of contemporary evangelicalism therefore needs to be reassessed. The common assumption that evangelical vitality is a sign that the "old-time" religion is alive and doing well in America is simply incorrect.

There is good reason to believe that a culture—or a subculture—that is shot through with therapeutic ideas and practices is one in which traditional religion is declining. Most scholars who have explored the development of America's therapeutic culture see its hypertrophy as a sign of the decline of traditional religion. The leading evangelicals of the 1920s and 1930s would have worded this point differently: modern psychology is at war with the gospel; whatever victories psychology wins are, in a sense, defeats for Christianity.

If therapeutic world views are symptomatic of the declining power of traditional religion and if evangelicalism is at base a therapeutic subculture, then the vitality of evangelicalism is not a sign that traditional religion is flourishing in America. It is rather a sign that a new sort of faith, one that owes at least as much to modern psychology as to Paul, is being born.

APPENDIX:
WHAT IS EVANGELICALISM?

MANY DIFFERENT ATTEMPTS have been made in recent years to define evangelicalism. As one reads over them it becomes clear that it is impossible to produce a perfect, once-and-for-all definition of the word. The word has and still does have many different meanings. It follows then that definitions of the word that pretend to be universal are less helpful than those that are contextual.[1]

In the present context, two of evangelicalism's many meanings are particularly relevant. Evangelicalism is, first off, often used in a way that I seldom use it in the main body of this book: as a synonym for conservative Protestantism. In this sense of the word evangelicalism refers to an aggregate of people who would give certain answers to certain questions. It could, for instance, be defined as that group of people who would, when asked the five questions listed in Table A, answer no to questions one and two and yes to all the others.[2]

Evangelicalism, thus construed, seems to be predominantly— but not overwhelmingly—white and disproportionately female. Its adherents are somewhat older than are the adherents of other religious communities in the United States. Most of them are married. Although evangelicals can be found in every region of the nation, they are dramatically underrepresented in New

APPENDIX

TABLE A.
EVANGELICAL BELIEFS

---

1. Do you believe that the Bible is a book of fables, legends, history, and moral precepts recorded by men?
2. Do you believe that Jesus was simply a great moral teacher?
3. Do you believe that the contents of the Bible are true and trustworthy?
4. Do you believe that Jesus was the Messiah and the Son of God?
5. Was there a definite time in your life when you accepted Christ as your personal Savior?

England and dramatically overrepresented in the South. They are also overrepresented in rural areas, small towns, and (in the South and the Midwest) in medium-sized cities. Relatively few of them live in large cities. They are, as a very general rule, not as well educated or as prosperous as the average American. They tend to belong, again as a very general rule, to either the working class or to the lower middle class.[3]

Recent scholarship emphasizes that evangelicalism is not a monolithic whole. It refers rather to what may be thought of as a mosaic made up of a number of discrete and heterogenous tiles. An essay published in 1984 nicely illustrates the point.

So on one side of evangelicalism are black Pentecostals and on another are strict separatist fundamentalists, such as at Bob Jones University, who condemn Pentecostals and shun blacks. Peace churches, especially those in the Anabaptist-Mennonite tradition, make up another discrete group of evangelicals. And their ethos differs sharply from that of the Southern Baptist Convention, some fourteen million strong and America's largest Protestant body. Southern Baptists in turn, have had experiences quite different from those of the evangelicals who have kept the traditional faith within the more liberal "mainline" northern churches. Each of these predominately Anglo groups is, again, very different from basically immigrant church bodies like the Missouri Synod Lutheran or the Christian Reformed, who have carefully preserved Reformation confessional heritages. Other groups have held on to heritages less old but just as distinctive: German Pietists and several evangelical varieties among Methodists preserve traditions of eighteenth-century Pietism. The spiritual descendants of Alexander Campbell, especially in the Churches of Christ, continue to proclaim the nineteenth-century American ideal of restoring the practices of the New Testament church. Holiness and Pentecostal groups of many varieties stress similar emphases that developed slightly later and in somewhat differing contexts. Black Christians, responding to a cultural experience dominated by oppression, have developed their own varieties of most of the major American traditions especially the Baptist, Methodist, and Pentecostal.[4]

The evangelical aggregate is not the sort of thing about which historians like to write monographs. Such books, we tend to assume, are best devoted to movements or impulses rather than aggregates. In the present case, at least, that convention makes a good deal of sense. I do not think that a monograph can really do justice to the experience of Bob Jones's followers and those of the black Evangelicals they scorn. Writing a history of the evangelical aggregate seems to be a little like—though not exactly like, of course—writing a history of the people who are on L. L. Bean's mailing list.

The word evangelical can also refer, as George Marsden has helpfully argued, to something like a denomination. As I said at the beginning of this book, I think of this denomination (which, following convention, I refer to as the evangelical mainstream) as a network of born-again Protestants associated with organizations such as the National Association of Evangelicals, the Billy Graham Evangelistic Association, and Campus Crusade; magazines such as *Christianity Today*, *Eternity*, and *Moody Monthly*; schools such as Wheaton College and the Moody Bible Institute; and publishing firms like Eerdmans and Zondervan. The roster of the landmarks of the evangelical mainstream I have provided

APPENDIX

TABLE B.
EVANGELICAL LANDMARKS

Baker Book House. Publisher. Grand Rapids, Michigan. 1939–.

Biola University. Educational Institution. La Mirada, California. 1908–.

Billy Graham Evangelistic Association. Evangelistic Organization. Minneapolis, Minnesota. 1950–.

Campus Crusade for Christ. Evangelistic Organization which works primarily with college students. Arrowhead Springs, California. 1951–.

Campus Life. Periodical. Carol Stream, Illinois. 1965–.

Christianity Today. Periodical. Carol Stream, Illinois. 1956–.

Dallas Theological Seminary. Educational Institution. Dallas, Texas. 1924–.

Decision. Periodical. Minneapolis, Minnesota. 1960–.

Eternity. Periodical. Philadelphia, Pennsylvania. 1950–1989.

Fleming H. Revell Company. Publisher. Old Tappan, New Jersey. 1870–.

Fuller Theological Seminary. Education Institution. Pasadena, California. 1947–.

Gordon College. Educational Institution. Wenham, Massachusetts. 1889–.

Gordon-Conwell Theological Seminary. Educational Institution. South Hamilton, Massachusetts. 1889–.

HIS. Periodical. Downer's Grove, Illinois. 1941–1986.

Inter-Varsity Christian Fellowship. Evangelistic association which works primarily with college students. Madison, Wisconsin. 1938–.

Inter-Varsity Press. Publisher. Downer's Grove, Illinois. 1947–.

Moody Bible Institute. Educational Institution. Chicago, Illinois. 1886–.

Moody Monthly. Periodical. Chicago, Illinois. 1900–.

Moody Press. Publisher. Chicago, Illinois. 1894–.

APPENDIX

National Association of Evangelicals. Organization which promotes cooperation between conservative Protestants. Wheaton, Illinois. 1942–.
Navigators. Evangelistic Organization. Colorado Springs, Colorado. 1933–.
Nyack College. Educational Institution. Nyack, New Jersey. 1882–.
Our Hope. Periodical. Waretown, New Jersey. 1894–1957.
Revelation. Periodical. Philadelphia, Pennsylvania. 1931–1950.
Sunday School Times. Periodical. Philadelphia, Pennsylvania. 1859–1966.
Tyndale House. Publisher. Wheaton, Illinois. 1962–.
Westmont College. Educational Institution. Santa Barbara, California. 1940–.
Wheaton College. Wheaton, Illinois. 1852–.
Wm. B. Eerdman's Publishing Company. Publisher. Grand Rapids, Michigan. 1911–.
World Vision. Relief Organization. Monrovia, California. 1950–.
Wycliffe Bible Translators. Missionary Organization. Huntington Beach, California. 1934–.
Young Life. Evangelistic Organization which works primarily with high school students. Colorado Springs, Colorado. 1941–.
Youth for Christ. Evangelistic Organization which works primarily with high school students. Carol Stream, Illinois. 1944–.
Youth for Christ. Periodical. Wheaton, Illinois. 1943–1965.
Zondervan Publishing House. Publisher. Grand Rapids, Michigan, 1931–.

in Table B is reasonably comprehensive, but hardly exhaustive. Neither is it "definitive": another researcher would probably produce a slightly different list, for such a compilation has less in common with a table of the chemical elements than it does with a list of the most prestigious preparatory schools in contemporary America. There is, however, a surprising amount of agreement upon what the landmarks of the evangelical denomination are: there is a sense, then, in which my roster simply systematizes an informal but widely-shared set of assumptions.

Although there is very little hard statistical data on the women and men that are a part of this network, most scholars who have worked in the primary sources that it produced would agree with the following generalizations. The members of the evangelical mainstream are mostly women. They are overwhelmingly white. As Table B suggests, few of the mainstream's bastions are located in the South. Some of them are located in the Northeast and some in the Far West. A great number of them are in the Midwest. The evangelical mainstream is less rural, less poorly educated and more prosperous than is conservative Protestantism as a whole. It draws fewer of its adherents from the working class and more from the middle class than does the evangelical aggregate.

In light of these demographic differences it is not surprising that the evangelical "denomination's" view of its relationship to other forms of conservative Protestantism was, on occasion, somewhat presumptuous. It did sometimes seem to assume that it was the most important tile in the evangelical mosaic and that it was the tile with the greatest claim to evangelical legitimacy. Thus one essayist, who was reared at the heart of the evangelical denomination, recently wrote: "The evangelicalism of which I speak differs from what one finds in Southern Baptist, Wesleyan, Pentecostal, or Missouri Synod Lutheran circles, even though all of these may lay claim to being evangelical in some sense."[5]

The evangelical mainstream is important. No account of conservative Protestantism in the middle decades of the twentieth century could claim to be comprehensive if it ignored all the landmarks listed in Table B. But of course the evangelical mainstream's view of its relationship to conservative Protestantism as a whole simply cannot be taken at face value. As scholars such as Timothy Smith and Donald Dayton have argued, the idea that the other tiles in the evangelical mosaic are less important and less legitimate versions of the real thing is itself a cultural artifact to be analyzed (analyzed for instance to see what it tells us about the power struggles within conservative Protestantism)—not an opinion which any self-respecting scholar can uncritically incorporate into her own work.[6] I want, accordingly, to repeat a point I made in the introduction. The evangelical denomination is related to conservative Protestantism as a whole in roughly the same way that New England is related to the entire United States. Anyone who read a history of New England and thought that she knew the history of the United States would be making a serious mistake. I hope that as you read this book you will continually remind yourself that it is, so to speak, about New England rather than about America.

One other point needs to be made here. The evangelical mainstream is, as the second chapter of this book relates and as Joel Carpenter's essays demonstrate, a group with deep roots in the fundamentalist movement. In the 1940s and 1950s the evangelical mainstream was made up in very large measure of the spiritual heirs of the fundamentalist movement. And yet those heirs were determined to reach out to a broader constituency of conservative Protestants and that determination met with considerable success. The evangelical mainstream therefore became increasingly broad as time went on. Thus the evangelical mainstream as it presently exists is still in a real sense the successor to the fundamentalist movement: indeed nearly all of the landmarks listed in Table B were linked to the fundamentalist movement. But it is also drawing increasingly on other varieties of conservative Protestantism that were never a part of the fundamentalist movement. This broadening constituency is one of the factors that produced changes described in the main text of this book.[7]

NOTES

INTRODUCTION

1. "The Year of the Evangelicals," *Newsweek*, 25 October 1976, 68–78. Cf. "The Evangelicals—New Empire of Faith," *Time*, 26 December 1977, 52–58.

2. Richard Quebedeaux, *The Young Evangelicals: Revolution in Orthodoxy* (New York, 1974), Carol Flake, *Redemptorama: Culture, Politics, and the New Evangelicalism* (New York, 1984), and Randall Balmer, *Mine Eyes Have Seen the Glory: A Journey into the Evangelical Subculture* (New York, 1989) are all useful popular accounts of the contemporary state of conservative Protestantism. More scholarly works on the same topic include: Nancy Tatom Ammerman, *Bible Believers: Fundamentalists in the Modern World* (New Brunswick, N.J., 1987); Steve Bruce, *The Rise and the Fall of the New Christian Right: Conservative Protestant Politics in America, 1978–1988* (Oxford, 1988); Susan Harding, "Convicted by the Holy Spirit: The Rhetoric of Fundamental Baptist Conversion," *American Ethnologist* 14 (1987): 167–181; James Davison Hunter, *American Evangelicalism: Conservative Religion and the Quandary of Modernity* (New Brunswick, N.J., 1983); James Davison Hunter, *Evangelicalism: The Coming Generation* (Chicago, 1987); Erling Jorstad, *The New Christian Right 1981–1988: Prospects for the Post-Reagan Decade* (New York, 1987); Alan Peshkin, *God's Choice* (Chicago, 1986); Susan D. Rose, *Keeping Them Out of the Hands of Satan: Evangelical Schooling in America* (New York, 1988); Ellen M.

Rosenberg, *The Southern Baptists: A Subculture in Transition* (Knoxville, Tenn., 1989); Corwin Smidt, ed., *Contemporary Evangelical Political Involvement* (Lanham, Md., 1989); and R. Stephen Warner, *New Wine in Old Wineskins: Evangelicals and Liberals in a Small-Town Church* (Berkeley, 1988). The two classic studies of conservative Protestantism in the years between 1875 and 1925 are George M. Marsden, *Fundamentalism and American Culture: The Shaping of Twentieth-Century Evangelicalism, 1870–1925* (New York, 1980) and Ernest R. Sandeen, *The Roots of Fundamentalism: British and American Millenarianism, 1800–1930* (Chicago, 1970). For the years between 1925 and 1975 see Joel A. Carpenter, *Revive Us Again: The Recovery of American Fundamentalism, 1930–1950* (New York, 1991); George M. Marsden, *Reforming Fundamentalism: Fuller Seminary and the New Evangelicalism* (Grand Rapids, Mich., 1987); Leo P. Ribuffo, *The Old Christian Right: The Protestant Far Right from the Great Depression to the Cold War* (Philadelphia, 1983); and Robert Wuthnow, *The Restructuring of American Religion: Society and Faith Since World War II* (Princeton, N.J., 1988). See, too, a series of important articles written by Carpenter that appeared throughout the 1980s: "From Fundamentalism to the New Evangelical Coalition," in *Evangelicalism and Modern America*, ed. George M. Marsden (Grand Rapids, Mich., 1984), 3–16; "Fundamentalist Institutions and the Rise of Evangelical Protestantism, 1929–1942," *Church History* 49 (1980): 62–75; "The Fundamentalist Leaven and the Rise of an Evangelical United Front," in *The Evangelical Tradition in America*, ed. Leonard I. Sweet (Macon, Ga., 1984), 257–288; and "Revive Us Again: Alienation, Hope, and the Resurgence of Fundamentalism, 1930–1950," in *Transforming Faith: The Sacred and the Secular in Modern American History*, ed. M. L. Bradbury and James B. Gilbert (New York, 1989), 105–125. For more bibliographic information on these topics see Edith L. Blumhofer and Joel A. Carpenter, eds., *Twentieth-Century Evangelicalism: A Guide to the Sources* (New York, 1990)—it is a splendid guide to the secondary literature as well as to the primary sources.

    3. Cf. Bernard Bailyn, "The Challenge of Modern Historiography," *American Historical Review* 87 (1982): 24. "In the end . . . historians must be . . . narrators of worlds in motion. . . . The historian must re-tell . . . the story of what some one of the worlds of the past was, how it ceased to be what it was, how it faded and blended into new configurations, how at every stage what was, was the product of what had been, and developed into what no one could have anticipated. . . ."

4. Raymond Williams, "Base and Superstructure in Marxist Cultural Theory," in *Problems in Materialism and Culture* (London, 1980), 31–50 is a classic explication of the concept of hegemony. See, too, Cornell West, "Marxist Theory and the Specificity of Afro-American Oppression," in *Marxism and the Interpretation of Culture*, ed. Cary Nelson and Lawrence Grossberg (Urbana, Ill., 1988), 17–29.

5. Even works as fine as William J. Bouwsma, "Intellectual History in the 1980s," *Journal of Interdisciplinary History* 12 (1981): 279–291, Robert Darnton, "Intellectual and Cultural History," in *The Past Before Us*, ed. Michael Kammen (Ithaca, N.Y., 1980), 327–354, and Lynn Hunt, ed., *The New Cultural History* (Berkeley, 1989) are not entirely free from this tendency.

6. Phillip E. Hammond, "In Search of a Protestant Twentieth Century: American Religion and Power Since 1900," *Review of Religious Research* 24 (March 1983): 281–294; James A. Beckford, "The Restoration of 'Power' to the Sociology of Religion," *Sociological Analysis* 44 (1983): 11–31; George M. Marsden, "Preachers of Paradox: The Religious New Right in Historical Perspective," in *Religion and America: Spirituality in a Secular Age*, ed. Mary Douglas and Steve M. Tipton (Boston, 1983), 150–168; and R. Laurence Moore, *Religious Outsiders and the Making of Americans* (New York, 1986), 150–172.

7. Carpenter, "Revive Us Again," 109–110.

8. Lears, "Hegemony," 572.

9. For a much more thorough exploration of that topic, see Balmer, *Mine Eyes*.

10. See especially the articles by Joel Carpenter cited in note 2.

1 THE FOUR SPIRITUAL LAWS

1. My account of Miller's conversion comes from his first book, *The Taste of New Wine* (Waco, Tex., 1965), 31–39.

2. Miller, *Wine*, 39. The "extraordinary lives" phrase comes from Sam Shoemaker, *Extraordinary Living for Ordinary Men* (Grand Rapids, Mich., 1965).

3. Jackson W. Carroll, Douglas W. Johnson and Martin E. Marty, *Religion in America, 1950 to the Present* (San Francisco, 1979), 117.

4. Hugh T. Kerr and John M. Mulder, eds., *Conversions: The Christian Experience* (Grand Rapids, Mich., 1983) is a good anthology of conversion stories drawn from the whole sweep of church history.

5. Pat Robertson and Jamie Buckingham, *Shout It from the Rooftops* (South Plainfield, N.J., 1972); Elisabeth Elliot, *Through Gates of Splendor* (New York, 1957); Will D. Campbell, *Brother to a Dragonfly* (New York, 1977).

6. Bill Bright, *Have You Heard of the Four Spiritual Laws?* (San Bernardino, Calif., 1965.)

7. Richard Quebedeaux, *I Found It!: The Story of Bill Bright and Campus Crusade* (San Francisco, 1979), 93–97. Except where noted, the following account of Bright's career is based on this book.

8. Quebedeaux, *I Found It!*, xi–xii.

9. Readers interested in the details of Bright's ministry should consult the periodical *Worldwide Challenge* (formerly *Worldwide Impact* and *Collegiate Challenge*).

10. "Big Bucks for Evangelism," *Christian Century*, 3–10 June 1981, 632–633.

11. Bill Bright, *Come Help Change the World* (Old Tappan, N.J., 1970), 27.

12. Quebedeaux, *I Found It!*, 24–25, 118.

13. Connie Paige, *The Right to Lifers: Who They Are, How They Operate, Where They Get Their Money* (New York, 1983), 251–253.

14. For a blistering, but poorly documented, critique of Bright's politics, see Jim Wallis and Wes Michaelson, "The Plan to Save America," *Sojourners*, April 1976, 3–12.

15. Bright, *Come Help*, 42–46.

16. Bright, *Come Help*, 42–46.

17. G. Christian Weiss, *On Being a Real Christian* (Chicago, 1951), 9.

18. Bright, *Laws*, 2.

19. Quebedeaux, *I Found It!*, 97.

20. Bright, *Laws*, 4.

21. Bright, *Laws*, 6.

22. The sign, closely associated with the "Jesus People" movement of the late 1960s, is made by pointing the index finger skyward.

23. Mike Yaconelli, "Spiritual Smugness," *Wittenberg Door*, February-March 1977, 21.

24. Bright, *Laws*, 8.

25. See, for example, the following works: *Have You Made the Wonderful Discovery of the Spirit-Filled Life?* (San Bernardino, Calif., 1966);

Ten Basic Steps to Christian Maturity, 10 vols. (San Bernardino, Calif., 1968); *Transferable Concepts Series*, 9 vols. (San Bernardino, Calif., 1971–72).

26. Quebedeaux, *I Found It!*, 87.
27. C. S. Lewis, *The Abolition of Man* (New York, 1947), 11.
28. Carl F. H. Henry, "Dare We Renew the Controversy? The Evangelical Responsibility," *Christianity Today*, 22 July 1957, 23.
29. Francis A. Schaeffer, *The Complete Works of Francis A. Schaeffer*, 5 vols. (Westchester, Ill., 1982).
30. Paul K. Jewett, *Man as Male and Female: A Study in Sexual Relations from a Theological Point of View* (Grand Rapids, Mich., 1975). See, too, Harold Lindsell, *The Battle for the Bible* (Grand Rapids, Mich., 1976).
31. "Door Interview: Eddie Dobson," *Wittenberg Door*, December 1982-January 1983, 12–16.
32. James Davison Hunter, *American Evangelicalism: Conservative Religion and the Quandary of Modernity* (New Brunswick, N.J., 1983), 142–143.
33. Quebedeaux, *I Found It!*, 179 summarizes this critique.
34. Dave Sheffel, "Fishers of Men," *Wittenberg Door*, February-March 1977, 25.
35. Wayne Rice, "You Can't Take it With You," ibid., pp. 16–17.
36. Billy Graham, *Peace with God* (Garden City, N.Y., 1953), 156.
37. David F. Wells, "Reservations about Catholic Renewal in Evangelicalism," in *The Orthodox Evangelicals: Who They Are and What They Are Saying*, ed. Robert E. Webber and Donald Bloesch (Nashville, Tenn., 1978), 213–214. See, too, Peter Clecak, *America's Quest for the Ideal Self* (New York, 1983), 115–156.
38. Ronald J. Sider, ed., *The Chicago Declaration* (Carol Stream, Ill., 1974), 1–2; J. Lawrence Burkholder, "Popular Evangelicalism: An Appraisal," in *Evangelicalism and Anabaptism*, ed. C. Norman Kraus (Scottsdale, Pa., 1979), 31–32. But note that Burkholder rather surprisingly concludes with a positive assessment of popular evangelicalism.
39. Bright, *Laws*, 10.
40. Bright, *Laws*, 14–15. See also Graham, *Peace with God*, 163, 178.
41. Hunter, *American Evangelicalism*, 65–67.
42. Bright, *Laws*, 9.
43. Bright, "Door Interview," *Wittenberg Door*, February-March 1977, 8–12. Scholars have not tested Bright's assertion that the pamphlet

succeeded on that score. Quantitative analysis does suggest, however, that in the postwar era evangelical churches have done a better job of deepening the religious commitment of the sort of persons to whom the pamphlet was addressed than have mainline churches. Their success in that endeavor accounts in large part for their ability to maintain and increase their membership roles. See Reginald Bibby, "Why Conservative Churches Really Are Growing: Kelley Revisited," *Journal for the Scientific Study of Religion* 17 (1978): 129–137.

44. Bright, *Spirit-Filled Life*, 6–7. Graham's position on these matters is similar to Bright's. See Billy Graham, *The Holy Spirit* (Waco, Tex., 1978).

45. Phillip Greven, *The Protestant Temperament* (New York, 1977), 12–13.

46. Richard Foster, *Celebration of Discipline* (San Francisco, 1978); Bill Gothard, *Research in Principles of Life* (Oak Park, Ill., 1968), 1–8.

47. Bright, *Spirit-Filled Life*, 5.

2 THE FUNDAMENTALIST CONTROVERSIES

1. "More Trouble for Jonah," *Literary Digest*, 4 January 1930, 22.

2. Margaret Sherwood, "Intellectual Death and Spiritual Life," *Atlantic*, December 1926, 794.

3. Henshaw Ward, "Uncle Jasper and Mr. Bryan: Fundamentalism and Absurdity," *Independent*, 2 May 1925, 494.

4. Miriam Allen De Ford, "After Dayton: A Fundamentalist Survey," *Nation*, 2 June 1926, 604. De Ford's article attempted to refute that view.

5. "Vanishing Fundamentalism," *Christian Century*, 24 June 1926, 799.

6. Richard Hofstadter, *Anti-intellectualism in American Life* (New York, 1963), 131; George M. Marsden, *Fundamentalism and American Culture* (New York, 1980), 204–205.

7. John D. Hicks, *Republican Ascendancy* (New York, 1960), 182.

8. John M. Blum et al., *The National Experience*, 4th ed. (New York, 1977), 599.

9. George M. Marsden, "From Fundamentalism to Evangelicalism: A Historical Analysis," in *The Evangelicals: What They Believe, Who*

They Are, Where They Are Changing, ed. by David F. Wells and John D. Woodbridge (Nashville, Tenn., 1975), 127.

10. Stewart G. Cole, *The History of Fundamentalism* (New York, 1931), 95. Cole was referring specifically to the controversy among the Northern Baptists, but the remark is representative of the tenor of the entire book.

11. James Davison Hunter, *American Evangelicalism: Conservative Religion and the Quandary of Modernity* (New Brunswick, N.J., 1983), 37.

12. Sydney E. Ahlstrom, *A Religious History of the American People* (1972; reprint, Garden City, N.Y., 1975), 2:403.

13. A convenient summary of the signs of current evangelical vitality, an intelligent discussion of works which assume evangelical vitality is a recent phenomenon, and a telling critique of that assumption may be found in Grant Wacker, "Searching for Norman Rockwell: Popular Evangelicalism in Contemporary America," in *The Evangelical Tradition in America*, ed. Leonard I. Sweet (Macon, Ga., 1984), 289–315.

14. Joel A. Carpenter, "Fundamentalist Institutions and the Rise of Evangelical Protestantism," *Church History* 49 (1980):62–75.

15. Harold E. Fey, "What About 'Youth for Christ'?" *Christian Century*, 20 June 1945, 729–731.

16. "Fundamentalist Revival," *Christian Century*, 19 June 1957, 749–751.

17. See "The Basis of the Evangelical Alliance," in *History, Essays, Orations, and Other Documents of the Sixth General Conference of the Evangelical Alliance*, ed. Philip Schaff and S. Iranaeus Prime (New York, 1874), 760.

18. Robert Baird, *Religion in America* (New York, 1844), 292.

19. John Hughes, *Complete Works*, ed. Lawrence Kehoe (New York, 1866), 1:57.

20. William G. McLoughlin, ed., *The American Evangelicals: An Anthology* (1968; reprint, Gloucester, Mass., 1976), 1. Important recent studies include Mary P. Ryan, *Cradle of the Middle Class: The Family in Oneida County, New York, 1790–1865* (Cambridge, Mass., 1981); Paul E. Johnson, *A Shopkeeper's Millennium: Society and Revivals in Rochester, New York, 1815–1837* (New York, 1978); Ronald P. Formisano, *The Birth of Mass Political Parties: Michigan 1827–1861* (Princeton, N.J., 1971); and Bruce Kuklick, *Churchmen and Philosophers: From Jonathan Edwards to John Dewey* (New Haven, Conn., 1985). These studies only begin, however, to suggest the vast literature that details evangelicalism's influence on nineteenth-century America.

Leonard I. Sweet, "The Evangelical Tradition in America," in *Evangelical Tradition*, ed. Sweet, 1–86, provides a useful guide to that literature.

21. James J. Thompson, Jr., *Tried As by Fire: Southern Baptists and the Religious Controversies of the 1920s* (Macon, Ga., 1982), 76.

22. Ernest R. Sandeen, *The Roots of Fundamentalism: British and American Millenarianism 1800–1930* (Chicago, 1970); Marsden, *Fundamentalism and American Culture*. Defining evangelicalism and fundamentalism presents many difficulties. Indeed some liberal Protestants—persons that the fundamentalists would regard as heterodox—thought of themselves as evangelicals, a confusing situation indeed. In hopes of avoiding as much confusion as possible, I use the phrase "conservative Protestants" to describe all those evangelical Christians who had not actively embraced liberal theology. Thus all fundamentalists are conservative Protestants, but not all conservative Protestants are fundamentalists.

23. J. Gresham Machen, "Christianity in Conflict," in *Contemporary American Theology: Theological Autobiographies*, ed. Vergilius Ferm (New York, 1932), 1:263.

24. Machen, "Christianity in Conflict," 272.

25. Harry Emerson Fosdick, *The Living of These Days* (New York, 1956), 145.

26. Bob Jones, Sr., quoted in Louis Gaspar, *The Fundamentalist Movement* (The Hague, 1963), 13.

27. Thomas Howard, *Christ the Tiger: A Postscript to Dogma* (Philadelphia, 1967), 22.

28. Cole, *Fundamentalism*, 95–97, 129–130.

29. "Vanishing Fundamentalism," 798. The observation applied specifically to the controversy in the Northern Baptist Convention.

30. Not all were clearly evangelical, or even in existence, in 1942: Fuller opened its doors in 1947; *Eternity* and *Christianity Today* commenced publication in the 1950s. Standard accounts of the emergence of what became the evangelical mainstream include: Joel A. Carpenter, "From Fundamentalism to the New Evangelical Coalition," in *Evangelicalism and Modern America*, ed. George M. Marsden (Grand Rapids, Mich., 1984), 3–16; Joel A. Carpenter, "The Fundamentalist Leaven and the Rise of an Evangelical United Front" in *The Evangelical Tradition in America*, ed. Leonard I. Sweet (Macon, Ga., 1984), 257–288; Joel A. Carpenter, "Revive Us Again: Alienation, Hope, and the Resurgence of Fundamentalism, 1930–1950," in *Transforming Faith: The Sacred and the Secular in Modern American History*, ed. M. L. Bradbury and James

B. Gilbert (New York, 1989), 105–125; Joel A. Carpenter, *Revive Us Again: The Recovery of American Fundamentalism, 1930–1950* (New York, 1991); and George M. Marsden, *Reforming Fundamentalism: Fuller Seminary and the New Evangelicalism* (Grand Rapids, Mich., 1987).

31. *Evangelical Action! A Report of the Organization of the National Association of Evangelicals for United Action* (Boston, 1942), 28, 31.

32. Joel Carpenter, "The Fundamentalist Leaven and the Rise of an Evangelical United Front," in *Evangelical Tradition*, ed. Sweet, 257–288.

33. *Evangelical Action*, 149.

34. *Evangelical Action*, 27, 158, vi.

35. *Evangelical Action*, 33.

36. "Evangelicals Discuss Stand on Councils," *St. Louis Post Dispatch*, 8 April 1942.

37. "St. Louis Meeting Sets up Tentative Association," *Christian Beacon*, 7 May 1942, 1.

38. See, for example, "Which Council?" a pamphlet prepared and released by the American Council of Christian Churches, probably in 1945, Iowa Right Wing Collection.

39. "Theology, Evangelism, Ecumenism," *Christianity Today*, 20 January 1958, 23.

40. Erling Jorstad, *The Politics of Doomsday: Fundamentalists of the Far Right* (Nashville, Tenn., 1970), 67.

41. Ed Reese, *The Life and Ministry of Carl McIntire* (Glenwood, Ill., 1975) presents a concise summary of McIntire's career.

42. T. T. Shields, "The Necessity of Making War on Modernism," *Christian Beacon*, 4 June 1942, 5.

43. See "Which Council?," cited in note 39 above.

44. Carl McIntire, *Twentieth Century Reformation*, 2d ed. (Collingswood, N.J., 1945), 204–205.

45. Hunter, *American Evangelicalism*, 39.

46. For criticism of fundamentalism on these grounds, see John W. Sanderson, "Fundamentalism and Its Critics," *Sunday School Times*, 21 January 1961, 58–59, 66.

47. George W. Dollar, *A History of Fundamentalism in America* (Greenville, S.C., 1973), 248. See also Ralph Lord Roy, *A Study of Organized Bigotry and Disruption on the Fringes of Protestantism* (Boston, 1953), 196–198, 393–398.

48. *Evangelical Action*, 53–54, 59.

49. Robert O. Ferm, *Cooperative Evangelism* (Grand Rapids, Mich., 1950).
50. Ronald H. Nash, *The New Evangelicalism* (Grand Rapids, Mich., 1963), 93.
51. *Evangelical Action*, 19.
52. James DeForest Murch, *Cooperation Without Compromise* (Grand Rapids, Mich., 1956), 62.
53. Nash, *New Evangelicalism*, 91.

3 POLITICS

1. Except where otherwise indicated, the material in the first four paragraphs of this chapter is drawn from Robert Booth Fowler, *A New Engagement* (Grand Rapids, Mich., 1982).
2. James Davison Hunter, "Religion and Political Civility: The Coming Generation of American Evangelicals," *Journal for the Scientific Study of Religion* 23 (December 1984): 364–380.
3. Fowler, *New Engagement*; Timothy L. Smith, "Protestants Falwell Does Not Represent," *New York Times*, 22 October 1980, A31; and Richard Quebedeaux, *The Young Evangelicals* (New York, 1974), 99–135. All stress the importance of the emergence of the evangelical left.
4. See, for instance, Ronald J. Sider, ed., *The Chicago Declaration* (Carol Stream, Ill., 1974), and Richard V. Pierard, *The Unequal Yoke* (Philadelphia, 1970).
5. William C. Ringenberg, "Must a Christian's Politics Be Conservative?" *Eternity*, July 1970, 13.
6. "Stacking Sandbags Against a Conservative Flood," *Christianity Today*, 2 November 1979, 77. Steven Bruce, *The Rise and the Fall of the New Christian Right: Conservative Protestant Politics in America, 1978–1988* (Oxford, 1988) is, I think, the best single account of this conservative flood.
7. Donald Grey Barnhouse, "Tomorrow: The Decline of Civil Liberties," *Revelation*, September 1938, 398.
8. "The Radical Change in a Radical's Heart," *Sunday School Times*, 24 May 1930, 319–320.
9. Barnhouse, "Decline," 398.
10. Donald Grey Barnhouse, "President Roosevelt's Error," *Revelation*, April 1938, 146.

11. "Calvin Coolidge on Easter Sunday," *Moody Bible Institute Monthly*, March 1934, 301.

12. "Coolidge on Present Tendencies," *Moody Bible Institute Monthly*, July 1934, 512.

13. See, for example, "Lexington Protests Loss of Liberty," *Moody Bible Institute Monthly*, July 1934, 507. See, too, Robert E. Wenger, "Social Thought in American Fundamentalism, 1918–1933" (Ph.D. diss., University of Nebraska, 1973); George M. Marsden, *Fundamentalism and American Culture* (New York, 1980), 207, 287.

14. Arno C. Gaebelein, *World Prospects* (New York, 1934), 128.

15. "Notes on Open Letters: Should Christians Try to Reform the World?" *Sunday School Times*, 29 June 1935, 430.

16. E. B. Dwyer, "The Parable of the Favored Land," *Moody Bible Institute Monthly*, July 1931, 545.

17. "'Labor's Fight for Power,'" *Moody Bible Institute Monthly*, November 1934, 100.

18. "Notes on Open Letters: Is Interest on Money Wrong?" *Sunday School Times*, 13 September 1930, 522.

19. "Seven Work Days," *Moody Bible Institute Monthly*, April 1930, 398.

20. "Stock Gambling and Legitimate Investment," *Moody Bible Institute Monthly*, February 1930, 290.

21. See, for instance, Donald Grey Barnhouse, "Social Gospel," *Revelation*, May 1938, 194.

22. I. M. Haldeman, *Socialism* (New York, 1933), 3–5.

23. William F. E. Hitt, "Why the Hard Times?" *Moody Bible Institute Monthly*, November 1932, 105–106.

24. F. W. Haberer, "Socialism and First Century Christianity," *Moody Bible Institute Monthly*, July 1933, 482.

25. C. H. Heaton, "Pink Communism in the Churches," *Moody Bible Institute Monthly*, May 1935, 415.

26. I. V. Neprash, "When a Communist Leader Was Brought to Christ," *Sunday School Times*, 12 January 1935, 23.

27. Haldeman, *Socialism*, 25–26. See, too, "Should Christians," 430.

28. Wenger, "Social Thought"; Timothy P. Weber, *Living in the Shadow of the Second Coming*, enl. ed. (Grand Rapids, Mich., 1983).

29. [Filler at the bottom of a column], *Moody Bible Institute Monthly*, July 1931, 544.

30. E. J. Pace, "The Way Out," *Sunday School Times*, 9 November 1935, 774. See, too, E. J. Pace, "Where He Belongs," *Sunday School Times*, 19 January 1935, 37.

31. A. J. Nesbit, "How to Bring Back Prosperity," *Moody Bible Institute Monthly*, October 1931, 64–65.

32. "Why Business Depression?" *Sunday School Times*, 27 September 1930, 549.

33. Walter A. Maier, *Christ for Every Crisis* (St. Louis, 1935), 52–53.

34. William Dean Allen, "Young People's Topics: The Sacredness of Marriage and the Home," *Revelation*, July 1934, 266.

35. H. Ellis Lininger, "Religion in the Home," *Revelation*, October 1936, 428.

36. Arno C. Gaebelein, *Hopeless—Yet There Is Hope* (New York, 1935), 79.

37. "Bureaucratic Dictatorship," *Moody Bible Institute Monthly*, August 1932, 576.

38. Maud Howe, "Atheism's Attack on Home and Marriage," *Sunday School Times*, 5 July 1930. Howe was quoting Senator Thomas F. Bayard.

39. James D. Gilbert, "Reading the Bible in High School," *Sunday School Times*, 1 February 1930, 62; William H. Richie, "The Bible in Southern Night Schools," *Sunday School Times*, 13 December 1930, 741.

40. Raymond M. Hudson, "Bible Instruction Alone Will Save Our Public Schools," *Moody Bible Institute Monthly*, December 1934, 166–167.

41. "The Pope's Encyclical on Marriage, Divorce and Birth Control," *Revelation*, February 1931, 74.

42. "Why Missions to Catholics?" *Sunday School Times*, 1 June 1935, 369.

43. Review of *Will America Become Roman Catholic?* by John F. Moore, *Revelation*, December 1931, 444.

44. "Atheists Petition the President," *Sunday School Times*, 6 December 1930, 717.

45. Weber, *Living in the Shadow*, 188.

46. "An Inflammable World," *Moody Bible Institute Monthly*, May 1935, 410.

47. William B. Riley, "Why We Believe the Lord's Return Is Near," *Sunday School Times*, 6 April 1935, 237.

48. Weber, *Living in the Shadows*, 189–201, *passim*.

49. Joseph Taylor Britan, "An Appeal for Persecuted Israel," *Moody Monthly*, February 1939, 316, 345.

50. "The Nazi and the Jew," *Moody Bible Institute Monthly*, January 1934, 208.

51. See Arno C. Gaebelein, *The Conflict of the Ages* (New York, 1933).

52. "An Open Letter from Patriots to Christians," *Moody Bible Institute Monthly*, July 1931, 545.

53. William McLoughlin, *Billy Graham: Revivalist in a Secular Age* (New York, 1960).

54. George Marsden, "From Fundamentalism to Evangelicalism: A Historical Analysis, in *The Evangelicals: What They Believe, Who They Are, Where They Are Changing*, ed. David F. Wells and John D. Woodbridge (Nashville, Tenn., 1975).

55. Louis Gaspar, *The Fundamentalist Movement* (The Hague, 1963), 121–124.

56. Robert D. Linder, "The Resurgence of Evangelical Social Concern," in *Evangelicals*, ed. Wells and Woodbridge, 201–202.

57. Thomas A. Askew, "Foundations of the Evangelical Resurgence," in *Eerdman's Handbook to Christianity in America*, ed. Mark A. Noll et al. (Grand Rapids, Mich., 1983), 465.

58. Robert Booth Fowler, *New Engagement*, 77–93.

59. Askew, "Foundations," 466.

60. James DeForest Murch, *Cooperation without Compromise* (Grand Rapids, Mich., 1956), 166.

61. Dennis P. Hollinger, *Individualism and Social Ethics* (Lanham, Md., 1983), 187.

62. George H. Williams and Rodney L. Petersen, "Evangelicals: Society, the State, the Nation (1925–1975)," in *The Evangelicals*, ed. Wells and Woodbridge, 226–227.

63. Williams and Petersen, "Evangelicals," 225–226.

64. See, for instance, Carl F. H. Henry, "Perspective for Social Action," *Christianity Today*, 19 January 1959, 11.

65. "Report of the Editor to the June 18, 1959, Meeting of the Board of Directors of *Christianity Today*," The Archives of the Billy Graham Center, Wheaton, Ill., 8:1:10.

66. William Ward Ayer, "Shall the Church Concern Itself with Society's Problems?" *Moody Monthly*, January 1948, 342.

67. "Social Problems," *Eternity*, January 1955, 9.

68. Carl F. H. Henry, *The Uneasy Conscience of Modern Fundamentalism* (Grand Rapids, Mich., 1947), 36–45.

69. Ayer, "Shall the Church," 342.

70. Ayer, "Shall the Church," 343.

71. Billy Graham, "The Answer to Broken Homes" (Minneapolis, 1955).

72. Henry, *Uneasy Conscience*, 88.

73. Billy Graham, "The Mystery of Conversion," The Archives of the Billy Graham Center, Wheaton, Ill., 221:P4. For a fascinating, extreme manifestation of this habit of mind, see Billy Graham, "Highway Safety . . . A Spiritual Problem" (Minneapolis, 1955).

74. Wilbur M. Smith, *The Increasing Peril of Permitting the Dissemination of Atheistic Doctrines on the Part of Some Agencies of the United States Government* (Chicago, 1947), 27, 28. But for a contrasting view, see Frank E. Gaebelein, *Christian Education in a Democracy* (New York, 1951), 91.

75. "Resolutions Adopted by the Eighth Annual Convention of the National Association of Evangelicals" (1950). The Archives of the Billy Graham Center, Wheaton, Ill. 20:67:9.

76. "The State in Welfare Work," *Christianity Today*, 18 January 1960, 23.

77. Donald W. Dayton, "The Social and Political Conservatism of Modern American Evangelicalism: A Preliminary Search for the Reasons," *Union Seminary Quarterly Review* 32 (1977):71.

78. Bell to Pew, 4 September 1956, The Archives of the Billy Graham Center, Wheaton, Ill., 8:1:57. (It was Pew, not Bell, who suspected Henry of such tendencies.)

79. Carl F. H. Henry to Frank W. Price, 3 November 1958, The Archives of the Billy Graham Center, Wheaton, Illinois, 8:15:9.

80. Billy Graham, "Organized Labor and the Church" (Minneapolis, 1952).

81. William G. McLoughlin, *Modern Revivalism* (New York, 1959), 509.

82. A. Herman Armerding, "Industrial Evangelism," *Moody Monthly*, March 1946, 417–418.

83. Billy Graham to J. Howard Pew, 15 July 1960, The Archives of the Billy Graham Center, Wheaton, Ill., 8:1:58.

84. Smith, *Increasing Peril*, 5–6.

85. Youth for Christ, "Here We Stand," (n.p., n.d.), The Archives of the Billy Graham Center, Wheaton, Ill., 70:72:24. See, too, Billy Graham, "Americanism" (Minneapolis, 1956).

86. "End or Beginning" (n.p., 1959), The Archives of the Billy Graham Center, Wheaton, Ill., 20:72:4.

87. "Resolutions of the National Association of Evangelicals [1950]," The Archives of the Billy Graham Center, Wheaton, Ill., 20:67:9.

88. "Resolutions of the National Association of Evangelicals [1950]," The Archives of the Billy Graham Center, Wheaton, Ill., 20: 67:9. For a fuller discussion of the issue, see Murch, Cooperation, 137–152.

89. Clyde W. Taylor, "The Slaughter of Protestants in South America" (August 1951), The Archives of the Billy Graham Center, Wheaton, Ill., 20:67:17.

90. Herbert Henry Ehrenstein, review of The Other Side of Rome by John B. Wilder, Eternity, February 1960, 40–41.

91. Richard V. Pierard, "Billy Graham and the U.S. Presidency," Journal of Church and State 22 (Winter 1980):121.

92. Smith, Increasing Peril, 40. On the growing influence of the anti-religionists, see also Murch, Cooperation, 137.

93. See, for instance, Bruce W. Dunn, "Why the U.S. Is in Trouble," Moody Monthly, February 1968, 20–22; "Radicals on a Rampage," Christianity Today, 6 November 1970, 33–34; Francis A. Schaeffer, How Should We Then Live? (Old Tappan, N.J., 1976), 205–227.

94. Harold B. Kuhn, "The Nuclear Family," Christianity Today, 23 May 1975, 62–64; Tim F. LaHaye and Beverly LaHaye, Spirit-Controlled Family Living (Old Tappan, N.J., 1978), 15–36; James Dobson, Dare to Discipline (Wheaton, Ill., 1970), 2–5; Grant Wacker, "Searching for Norman Rockwell: Popular Evangelicalism in Contemporary America," in The Evangelical Tradition in America, ed. Leonard I. Sweet (Macon, Ga., 1984), 307–309.

95. Evangelicals' response to the perceived crisis of the 1960s and 1970s was more complex and less narrowly political than most outsiders realize. It included new efforts to develop Christian alternatives to the nation's secular public schools and to its godless and immoral—so evangelicals perceived them—national media. Evangelicals responded to the 1960s and 1970s, too, with a new focus on the possibilities for finding private hopes in the midst of public despair. As Chapter 5 argues, in these years a great many evangelicals became increasingly fascinated with the possibility that Christ would soon return to take his people out of a world drifting toward disaster; even more devoted much of their energy to creating strong families.

96. "Assignment for Christian Citizens," Christianity Today, 15 September 1972, 34.

97. For a discussion of the sources of the concept of secular humanism, see George Marsden, "Preachers of Paradox," in Religion and America, ed. by Mary Douglas and Steven Tipton (Boston, 1983), 157–158.

Robert E. Webber, *Secular Humanism* (Grand Rapids, Mich., 1982), is a book-length explication of that topic written by a respected evangelical theologian.

98. Harold O. J. Brown, "The Passivity of American Christians," *Christianity Today*, 16 January 1976, 10.

99. Brown, "Passivity," 10; Larry Christenson, *Social Action: Jesus Style* (Minneapolis, 1974), 20–21.

100. Donald Tomaskovic-Devey, "The Protestant Ethic, the Christian Right, and the Spirit of Recapitalization," in *The Political Role of Religion in the United States*, ed. Stephen D. Johnson and Joseph B. Tamney (Boulder, Colo., 1986), 150, points out that evangelicals were opposed to governmental legitimation of cultural innovation as well as to the government's actually fostering departures from tradition.

101. Pierard, "Graham and the U.S. Presidency," 111. On the topic of other evangelicals' views of the decision, see James Davison Hunter, *American Evangelicalism: Conservative Religion and the Quandary of Modernity* (New Brunswick, N.J., 1983), 105; Hollinger, *Individualism*, 201; and Williams and Petersen, "Evangelicals," 230–231.

102. "Revolt at the Grassroots," *Moody Monthly*, May 1974, 21.

103. "Abortion and the Court," *Christianity Today*, 16 February 1973, 32–33.

104. Paul Vitz, *Psychology As Religion* (Grand Rapids, Mich., 1977), 114.

4 THE PRIVATE AND PUBLIC SPHERES

1. Timothy P. Weber, *Living in the Shadow of the Second Coming*, 2d ed. (Grand Rapids, Mich., 1983), and George M. Marsden, *Fundamentalism and American Culture* (New York, 1980), 43–71 are two recent, extremely helpful, discussions of fundamentalists' views concerning the End Times. Both books focus particular attention on dispensationalism.

2. Curriculum materials, file 4, The Archives of the Moody Bible Institute, Chicago, Ill.

3. Weber, *Living*, 178–181.

4. "The Blue Eagle," *Revelation*, August 1933, 329.

5. Ernest Sandeen, *The Roots of Fundamentalism* (Chicago, 1970) exaggerates but also effectively documents dispensationalism's role in shaping the fundamentalist movement.

6. Marsden, *Fundamentalism*, 64.

7. Arno C. Gaebelein, *Hopeless—Yet There Is Hope* (New York, 1935), 10; William Wonderly, "Hope Amid Anxiety," *Moody Bible Institute Monthly*, November 1933, 103; "Why We Believe the Lord's Return Is Near," *Sunday School Times*, 6 April 1935, 237–238; 20 April 1935, 277; and 27 April 1935, 293.

8. Donald Grey Barnhouse, "Tomorrow: Summer Is Nigh," *Revelation*, September 1934, 342.

9. Marsden, *Fundamentalism*, 63.

10. Gaebelein, *Hopeless*, 10; Wonderly, "Hope Amid Anxiety," 103; and Barnhouse, "Tomorrow: Summer Is Nigh," 342.

11. Barnhouse, "Tomorrow: Summer Is Nigh," 352.

12. Cecil V. Phillips, "Why Preach the Second Coming?" *Moody Bible Institute Monthly*, February 1935, 298, asserted that preaching on the Second Advent could excite sinners to turn from their sins, accept Christ, and thus place themselves in a position where they could look to the Second Coming with hope rather than dread.

13. Ruth Paxson, *Life on the Highest Plane* (Chicago, 1928) is one standard discussion of the victorious life. For Paxson's assessment of general world conditions, see pages 40, 50, 85, and 142–143 of that book.

14. See, for example, Helen Miller Lehman, "The Church and World Peace," *Moody Bible Institute Monthly*, November 1934, 102–103, and George W. Toms, "How Shall We Meet the Current Need of the World?" *Moody Bible Institute Monthly*, February 1933, 263.

15. Kirk Jeffrey, "The Family as Utopian Retreat From the City: The Nineteenth-Century Contribution," *Soundings* 55 (1972): 21–40, and Christopher Lasch, *Haven in a Heartless World* (New York, 1977).

16. Seven E. Ozment, *When Fathers Ruled* (Cambridge, Mass., 1983) and Colleen McDannell, *The Christian Home in Victorian America, 1840–1900* (Bloomington, Ind., 1986).

17. R. A. Torrey, Jr., "Dr. R. A. Torrey in His Home," *Moody Bible Institute Monthly*, October 1929, 68–70; J. Henry Allen, "The Home, A Divine Institution," *Moody Bible Institute Monthly*, July 1930, 531–532; and Peter Stam, "The Influence of a Christian Home," *Moody Bible Institute Monthly*, May 1937, 466, 478 illustrate the way that fundamentalists thought about the family.

18. Weber, *Living*, 204, 274.

19. "Foretaste," *Eternity*, May 1974, 2. See, too, William S. Sailer, "A Second Look at the Second Coming," *Eternity*, May 1974, 36–37, 62.
20. Wilbur M. Smith, "Wilbur M. Smith Comments on Mid-East Crisis," *Moody Monthly*, July-August 1967, 58.
21. John F. Walvoord, "Is the Lord's Coming Imminent?" *Eternity*, January 1954, 48. William Petersen and Stephen Board, "The Kingdom and the Power: Main Street in Evangelicalville," *Eternity*, November 1981, 20–21 discusses dispensationalism's continuing importance at the Moody Bible Institute and at Dallas Theological Seminary. Weber, *Living*, 204–226, and Albert F. Schenkel, "The Second Coming and Cultural Engagement: Varieties of Premillennialism in Twentieth-Century America" (Seminar paper, Harvard Divinity School, Cambridge, Mass., 1984) demonstrates dispensationalism's vitality in postwar America.
22. James Davison Hunter, *American Evangelicalism: Conservative Religion and the Quandary of Modernity* (New Brunswick, N.J., 1983).
23. See, for example, B. A. Gerrish, *Tradition and the Modern World* (Chicago, 1978), and Grant Wacker, *Augustus H. Strong and the Dilemma of Historical Consciousness* (Macon, Ga., 1985).
24. Alan Brinkley, "Writing the History of Contemporary America: Dilemmas and Challenges," *Daedalus* 119 (1984):121–141, Louis Galambos, "The Emerging Organizational Synthesis of Modern American History," *Business History Review* 44 (1970):279–290, and Louis Galambos, "Technology, Political Economy, and Professionalization: Central Themes of the Organizational Synthesis," *Business History Review* 57 (1983):471–493 seem to me to suggest such an understanding of modernity.
25. Richard Wightman Fox and T. J. Jackson Lears, eds., *The Culture of Consumption* (New York, 1983) and Christopher Lasch, *The Culture of Narcissism* (New York, 1978).
26. Wilbur M. Smith, "The Testimony of Bible Prophecy," *Moody Bible Institute Monthly*, September 1949, 14 and [Billy Graham?], "Signs of the Times," an undated sermon manuscript, The Archives of the Billy Graham Center, Wheaton, Ill., 15:1:11.
27. Herbert Henry Ehrenstein, review of *The Basis of the Premillennial Faith* by Charles C. Ryrie, *Eternity*, March 1954, 40.
28. Carl F. H. Henry, *The Uneasy Conscience of Modern Fundamentalism* (Grand Rapids, Mich., 1947), 48–57.
29. George E. Ladd, *Crucial Questions About the Kingdom of God* (Grand Rapids, Mich., 1952), and George E. Ladd, "Historic Premillennialism," in *The Meaning of the Millennium*, ed. Robert G. Clouse

(Downers Grove, Ill., 1977), 17–40. Schenkel, "The Second Coming," provides a helpful analysis of Ladd's work. For other indications of evangelicals' wavering commitment to dispensationalism, see Richard Quebedeaux, *The Young Evangelicals* (New York, 1974), 38; Richard D. Reiter, "A History of the Development of Rapture Positions," in *The Rapture* by Richard R. Reiter et al. (Grand Rapids, Mich., 1984), 34–44; Weber, *Living*, 241–242; and Petersen and Board, "The Kingdom," 22.

30. See, for example, Billy Graham, *World Aflame* (Garden City, N.Y., 1965), 189–263, and Billy Graham, "The Second Coming of Christ," *Eternity*, December 1970, 14.

31. Wilbur M. Smith, *The Atomic Bomb and the Word of God* (Chicago, Ill., 1945), 9–10, and Raymond L. Cox, "Will the Real Antichrist Please Stand Up!" *Eternity*, May 1974, 15–17, 60.

32. William Culbertson, "Perspective in Prophecy," *Moody Monthly*, July-August 1964, 50, reports that the staff of the *Moody Monthly* was puzzled by the emphasis earlier generations had placed on prophecy.

33. Wilbur M. Smith, "World Crisis and the Prophetic Scriptures," *Moody Monthly*, June 1950, 679, lamented "how little is prophecy discussed in our religious journals; how few the ministers who speak of the return of the king!"

34. *Revelation*, January-December 1935, and *Eternity*, January-December, 1975.

35. Frank E. Gaebelein, "Christian Education and the Home: Part II," *Moody Monthly*, December 1950, 254.

36. John R. Rice, *The Home, Courtship, Marriage, and Children* (Wheaton, Ill., 1945), 7–8.

37. Lars I. Granberg, review of *Design for Christian Marriage* by Dwight Hervey Small, *Eternity*, June 1959, 38.

38. Granberg, review of *Design*, 38.

39. *Moody Monthly*, January-December, 1975.

40. Billy Graham, "10 Commandments for the Home," *Decision*, June 1974, 1.

41. Hunt, *Focus on Family Life* (Grand Rapids, Mich., 1970), 12.

42. Roy B. Zuck, "Churches Focus on the Family," *Moody Monthly*, July-August 1967, 32 and Herbert Henry Ehrenstein, "Your Questions Answered," *Eternity*, May 1964, 39.

43. Seminars on the family are discussed in Wilfred Bockelman, *Gothard: The Man and His Ministry* (Santa Barbara, Calif., 1976) and Denny Rydberg, "Getting a Loose Leaf on Life," *Wittenberg Door*,

April-May 1973, 6–18. On national conferences on the family, see "We Are Planning to Affect Your Family!" [an advertisement], *Eternity*, August 1975, 3.

44. Robert Booth Fowler, *A New Engagement* (Grand Rapids, Mich., 1982), 191–212 and Grant Wacker, "Searching for Norman Rockwell," in *The Evangelical Tradition in America*, ed. Leonard I. Sweet (Macon, Ga., 1984), 289–315.

45. See for instance the September-October 1976 issue of *The Other Side*, one of the most prominent publications associated with the evangelical left: that issue was devoted entirely to the family. See, too, the roster of conference participants listed in "We Are Planning to Affect Your Family!" 3: it included "progressive" evangelicals such Letha Scanzoni, Nancy Hardesty, and David Moberg.

46. For expressions of such sentiments, see Dwight Hervey Small, *Design for Christian Marriage* (Old Tappan, N.J., 1959), 41–42, and Hunt, *Family Life*, 9, 55.

47. Merla Jean Sparks, *The Creative Christian Home* (1974; reprint, Grand Rapids, Mich., 1975), 87, asserts that it is proper for Christians who wish to improve their family life to see non-Christian psychologists; "Books to Strengthen Your Marriage," *Eternity*, May 1965, 21 recommends Christians read books by non-evangelicals. My conclusion that evangelicals' fundamental assumptions on the family were similar to those of their non-evangelical neighbors is based on a comparison between the views analyzed in David M. Schneider and Raymond T. Smith, *Class Differences and Sex Roles in American Kinship and Family Structure* (Englewood Cliffs, N.J., 1973) and the views expressed in evangelical works such as Norman V. Williams, *The Christian Home* (Chicago, 1952); Small, *Design*; Henry R. Brandt and Homer E. Dowdy, *Building a Christian Home* (Wheaton, Ill., 1960); David Allan Hubbard, *Is the Family Here to Stay?* (Waco, Tex., 1971); Gene A. Getz, *The Christian Home in a Changing World* (Chicago, 1972); Graham, "10 Commandments," 1–2; and Lois Bock and Miji Working, *Happiness Is a Family Time Together* (Old Tappan, N.J., 1975).

48. Frank E. Gaebelein, "Christian Education and the Home: Part II," *Moody Monthly*, November 1950, 149; Lacey Hall as told to Robert Flood, "What's Happening to the American Family?" *Moody Monthly*, July-August 1967, 26–28, 42; and Gary Collins, "What Threatens the Family?" *Eternity*, August 1975, 14–15.

49. S. Maxwell Coder, "The Christian Family and the Word of God," *Moody Monthly*, August 1971, 15.

50. Larry Christenson, *The Christian Family* (Minneapolis, 1970).

51. For Graham's use of statistics, see Graham, "10 Command-ments," 2. For his thoughts on how conversion would affect one's fam-ily, see Billy Graham, "The Answer to Broken Homes" (Minneapolis, 1955), and Billy Graham, *The Christ-Centered Home* (Minneapolis, 1961), 32.

52. The fragility of Christian families is discussed in Horace A. Larsen, "How To Be Happy Though Married," *Moody Monthly*, April 1949, 564; Lars I. Gransberg, "Why Christian Homes So Often Fail," *Eternity*, May 1965, 20–21; and "Foretaste," *Eternity*, March 1981, 2. See, too, "The Christian Worker's Forgotten Family," *Moody Monthly*, January 1962, 34–35; "I Prayed for the Other Woman," *Christian Life*, October 1971, 35, 44, 46, and 62; "What I Learned When My Daughter Ran Away," *Eternity*, January 1972, 23–24; and Marilee P. Dunker, *Days of Glory, Seasons of Night* (Grand Rapids, Mich., 1984).

53. Tim LaHaye and Beverly LaHaye, *Spirit-Controlled Family Liv-ing* (Old Tappan, N.J., 1978), 16.

54. Granberg, "Christian Homes," 20, and "Foretaste," *Eternity*, Au-gust 1975, 2.

5 FEMINISM

1. Susan Harding, "Family Reform Movements: Recent Feminism and Its Opposition," *Feminist Studies* 7 (1981): 57.

2. Elaine Tyler May, "Expanding the Past: Recent Scholarship on Women in Politics and Work," *Reviews in American History* 10 (1982): 222.

3. Kent L. Tedin et al., "Social Background and Political Dif-ferences Between Pro- and Anti-ERA Activists," *American Politics Quarterly* 5 (1977): 398–405. Other useful accounts of conservative Protestants' reactions to the changing role of women include: Margaret L. Bendroth, "The Search for 'Women's Role' in American Evangelical-ism, 1930–1980" in *Evangelicalism and Modern America*, ed. George Marsden (Grand Rapids, Mich., 1984), 122–134; Carol Flake, *Re-demptorama: Culture, Politics, and the New Evangelicalism* (New York, 1984), 63–88; and Susan D. Rose, *Keeping Them Out of the Hands of Satan: Evangelical Schooling in America* (New York, 1988), 60–68.

4. David W. Brady and Kent L. Tedin, "Ladies in Pink: Religion and Political Ideology in the Anti-ERA Movement," *Social Science Quarterly* 56 (1976): 574.

5. Brady and Tedin, "Ladies," 573–575.

6. *The Baltimore Sun*, 8 July 1924, 10 and 7 July 1924, 18. See also Wilbur M. Smith, *Before I Forget* (Chicago, 1971), 61.

7. George W. Dollar, *A History of Fundamentalism in America* (Greenville, S.C., 1973), 355, 253.

8. *National Cyclopedia of American Biography* (New York, 1891—), 42: 197–198.

9. Dollar, *Fundamentalism*, 207.

10. John Pollock, *Billy Graham* (New York, 1966), 92, 173.

11. "Dull Sword," *Christianity Today*, 26 February 1971, 39.

12. See photograph and caption in Charles J. Woodbridge, "The Streams of Protestantism," *Moody Monthly*, May 1948, 636.

13. For warm praise of Maier's *For Better Not For Worse: A Manual for Christian Matrimony*, see the book notices column in *Moody Monthly*, June 1947, 725.

14. See photograph and caption in Ruth Lindal, "Making Family Worship Work," *Moody Monthly*, April 1948, 561.

15. Louis Gaspar, *The Fundamentalist Movement* (The Hague, 1963), 143.

16. Pollock, *Graham*, 92.

17. John R. Rice, *Bobbed Hair, Bossy Wives and Women Preachers: Significant Questions for Honest Christian Women Settled by the Word of God* (Wheaton, Ill., 1941), 13, 84.

18. John R. Rice, *The Home—Courtship, Marriage and Children: A Bible Manual of Twenty-Two Chapters on the Christian Home* (Wheaton, Ill., 1945), 8.

19. Rice, *The Home*, 101.

20. Rice, *The Home*, 129, 109, 105–107. But compare Walter A. Maier, *For Better Not For Worse: A Manual of Christian Matrimony*, 3d. ed. (St. Louis, 1939), 462.

21. Rice, *Bobbed Hair*, 38–65.

22. Maier, *For Better*, 480.

23. Maier, *For Better*, 4, 166.

24. Maier, *For Better*, 399.

25. Rice, *The Home*, 154.

26. Rice, *The Home*, 174–175.

27. Rice, *The Home*, 156. See also Maier, *For Better*, 346.

28. Rice, *The Home*, 136.

29. Rice, *The Home*, 112.
30. Maier, *For Better*, 455.
31. Maier, *For Better*, 460.
32. [Billy Graham?] "Signs of the Times," an undated sermon manuscript, The Archives of the Billy Graham Center, Wheaton, Ill., 15:1:11. Internal evidence suggests that this sermon was composed shortly before America's entrance into the Second World War.
33. Billy Graham, "Problems of the American Home," 9 May 1964, The Archives of the Billy Graham Center, Wheaton, Ill., 113:F27.
34. Billy Graham, "How to Save Your Marriage," 15 June 1968, The Archives of the Billy Graham Center, Wheaton, Ill., 113:F182.
35. Alfred C. Murray, *Youth's Marriage Problems* (Grand Rapids, Mich., 1947), 141–143.
36. Norman V. Williams, *The Christian Home* (Chicago, 1952), 31–37.
37. C. C. Ryrie, *The Place of Women in the Church* (New York, 1958), 139, 146. Ryrie was a professor at Dallas Theological Seminary.
38. Rice, *The Home*, 101.
39. Rice, *Bobbed Hair*, 22–24.
40. Graham, "Problems," 113:F27.
41. *The Baltimore Sun*, 7 July 1924, 18.
42. Maier, *For Better*, 453.
43. Theodore Caplow et al., *Middletown Families: Fifty Years of Change and Continuity* (Minneapolis, 1983), 112–113. The degree to which the religious life of this community is dominated by conservative Protestantism is discussed in Theodore Caplow et al., *All Faithful People: Fifty Years of Change and Continuity* (Minneapolis, 1983), 269.
44. Rice, *The Home*, 102.
45. Maier, *For Better*, 460.
46. *The Baltimore Sun*, 8 July 1924, 10.
47. Mildred Cooper and Martha Fanning, *What Every Woman Still Knows: A Celebration of the Christian Liberated Woman* (New York, 1978), 48.
48. Sharon Gallagher, "When You Are . . . ," in *Our Struggle to Serve: The Stories of 15 Evangelical Women*, ed. Virginia Hearn (Waco, Tex., 1979), 93.
49. Virginia Hearn, "Woman's Place in the Evangelical Milieu . . . ," in *Struggle*, ed. Hearn, 14.
50. Patti Roberts with Sherry Andrews, *Ashes to Gold* (Waco, Tex., 1983), 88.

51. Clyde Narramore, *A Woman's World: A Christian Psychologist Discusses Twelve Common Problem Areas* (Grand Rapids, Mich., 1963), 206.
52. Cooper and Fanning, *What Every*, 145.
53. Cooper and Fanning, *What Every*, 82.
54. Lois C. Anderson, "It Was Sometimes Amusing . . . ," in *Struggle*, ed. Hearn, 168.
55. Narramore, *Woman's World*, 12–14. There are few reliable statistics concerning the proportion of evangelical women who continued their schooling past high school, but clearly a good number of them did so. As early as 1930, half of the students in the graduating class at Moody Bible Institute were women. The class presidency at that school seems to have traditionally been reserved for men, but, interestingly, in many years over half the class offices were held by women.
56. Narramore, *Woman's World*, 15.
57. Narramore, *Woman's World*, 15–17.
58. Gladys Hunt, *Ms. Means Myself* (Grand Rapids, Mich., 1972), 15.
59. Marabel Morgan, *Total Joy* (Old Tappan, N.J., 1976), 62.
60. Virginia Ramey Mollenkott, "Evangelical Feminism . . . ," in *Struggle*, ed. Hearn, 156–157.
61. Morgan, *Joy*, 18.
62. Louis H. Evans, *Your Marriage: Duel or Duet?* (Westwood, N.J., 1967), 11–12.
63. Eugenia Price, *The Unique World of Women: In Bible Times and Now* (Grand Rapids, Mich., 1969), 84.
64. Morgan, *Joy*, 149–150, 60–61. See also Dwight Hervey Small, *After You've Said I Do: New Ways to Communicate in Marriage* (Old Tappan, N.J., 1968), 128–131.
65. Morgan, *Joy*, 111.
66. Caplow et al., *Middletown Families*, 358.
67. Hearn, "Woman's Place," 13.
68. Narramore, *Woman's World*, 56–58.
69. Virginia Ramey Mollenkott, *Speech, Silence, Action!: The Cycle of Faith* (Nashville, 1980), 18. Mollenkott was describing the situation in which she found herself in 1965.
70. Lareta Halteman Finger, "I Would Read . . . ," in *Struggle*, ed. Hearn, 29.
71. See, for example, Francis Adney, "Traditionally, the Husband Has Been Given Freedom . . . ," in *Struggle*, ed. Hearn, 86–87.

72. G[ertrude] D. Clark to Herbert J. Taylor, 25 September 1944, The Archives of the Billy Graham Center, Wheaton, Ill., 20:66:10.
73. Adney, "Husband," 85.
74. Winnie Christenson, "What Is a Woman's Role?," *Moody Monthly*, June 1971, 82.
75. Ethel May Baldwin and David V. Benson, *Henrietta Mears: And How She Did It!* (Glendale, Calif., 1966), 121.
76. Baldwin and Benson, *Mears*, 3, 231–232.
77. In the late 1950s and early 1960s, the editor of *Christianity Today* was, in the opinion of one of that magazine's directors, "utterly dependent" upon the aid of his wife, Helga Henry, in editing that journal (L. Nelson Bell to Harold Ockenga, 15 April 1961, The Archives of the Billy Graham Center, Wheaton, Ill., 8:1:56; Bell to Carl Henry, 3 December 1959, The Archives of the Billy Graham Center, Wheaton, Ill., 8:1:13). Helga Henry was eventually awarded a salary for her efforts, but her contributions to the magazine were not reflected in its masthead. The contributions of other women to evangelical publishing were more openly acknowledged: in 1971 30 percent of the bylines in magazines such as *Eternity* went to women ("Foretaste," *Eternity*, January 1971, 2). Even at that late date a man's name had to be at the top of the masthead, but by then few evangelicals objected to women serving as assistant editors.
78. Mary Stewart, "The Movement of the Spirit Challenges a Feminist," *Vanguard*, March-April 1975, 11.
79. Narramore, *Woman's World*, 53–60.
80. Dorothy Canfield Fisher, "Danger for American Women," *The Christian Herald*, March 1941, 32.
81. Dwight Hervey Small, "Christian Married Love," *Eternity*, August 1955, 19.
82. Dwight Hervey Small, "Whom God Hath Joined," *Eternity*, June 1955, 41. Small, educated at Wheaton and at Dallas Theological Seminary, was a prominent evangelical writer and educator. He eventually became a professor of marriage and family studies at Westmont College.
83. Joe Burton, *Tomorrow You Marry* (1950; reprint, Nashville, Tenn., 1957), 3, 113–115.
84. For a discussion of Narramore's career and his role in the development of therapeutic evangelicalism, see Chapter 7.
85. Narramore, *Woman's World*, 103, 88–89, 53–55, 60, 65–66. Narramore also discussed the liabilities of women working outside the home.

86. "The Feminine Bid for the Pulpit," *Christianity Today*, 30 August 1963, 38–39.

87. "Sunday School Materials Stereotype Women," *Christianity Today*, 31 March 1972, 64.

88. "That Women's Rights Amendment," *Christianity Today*, 6 November 1970, 34.

89. "First at the Cradle, Last at the Cross," *Christianity Today*, 16 March 1973, 26–27.

90. Billy Graham, "The Revolution in the Family Home," 12 May 1976, The Archives of the Billy Graham Center, Wheaton, Ill., 13:V14–15.

91. Ruth Schmidt, "Second-Class Citizenship in the Kingdom of God," *Christianity Today*, 1 January 1971, 13–14.

92. Nancy Hardesty, "Women: Second-Class Citizens?" *Eternity*, January 1971, 14–16, 24–29.

93. Letha Scanzoni and Nancy Hardesty, *All We're Meant To Be: A Biblical Approach to Women's Liberation* (Waco, Tex., 1974).

94. Paul K. Jewett, *Man as Male and Female: A Study in Sexual Relationships from a Theological Point of View* (Grand Rapids, Mich., 1975).

95. Anderson, "Sometimes Amusing," 171.

96. Anne Eggebroten, "I Was Convinced . . . ," in *Struggle*, ed. Hearn, 117–118.

97. Virginia Ramey Mollenkott, foreword to Jewett, *Man as Male and Female*, 7.

98. Wes Michaelson, "Neither Male Nor Female: The Thanksgiving Conference on Biblical Feminism," *Sojourners*, January 1976, 11.

99. David Scholer, in John Gerstner and David Scholer, "Is Women's Ordination Unbiblical? An Areopagus Discussion Forum with John Gerstner and David Scholer," sponsored by the Current Affairs Committee, Student Government Association, Gordon-Conwell Theological Seminary, South Hamilton, Mass., 1980, 34.

100. Princeton Religion Research Center, *Religion in America, 1982* (Princeton, 1982), 162.

101. Mollenkott, *Speech*, 26.

102. Finger, "I Would Read," 33; Lorraine Peters, "Finally I Had the Courage . . . ," in *Struggle*, ed. Hearn, 78.

103. Gallagher, "When You Are," 95.

104. Peters, "Courage," 79.

105. Richard Quebedeaux, *I Found It!: The Story of Bill Bright and Campus Crusade* (San Francisco, 1979), 115–116.

106. Finger, "I Would Read," 30.
107. Mildred Meythaler, "I Was Freed to Face the Differences . . . ," in *Struggle*, ed. Hearn, 50.
108. Gallagher, "When You Are," 95.
109. Mollenkott, "Evangelical Feminism," 158.
110. See, for example, Ruth A. Schmidt, "I Did Not Need to Conform to the Stereotypes," in *Struggle*, ed. Hearn, 101.
111. Letha Scanzoni and Nancy Hardesty, "Beyond the Barriers and the Stereotypes: All We're Meant To Be," *Vanguard*, March-April 1975, 14.
112. Gallagher, "When You Are," 98.
113. Mollenkott, *Speech*, 76.
114. Anderson, "Sometimes Amusing," 170.
115. Schmidt, "Conform," 106.
116. Gallagher, "When You Are," 99.
117. Stewart, "Movement," 11.
118. Stewart, "Movement," 11.
119. The National Organization for Women's statement of purpose, quoted in Gayle Graham Yates, *What Women Want: The Ideas of the Movement* (Cambridge, Mass., 1975), 6.
120. Linda Coleman, "Forging Chains of Command," *Daughters of Sarah*, May–June 1980, 7.
121. Katie Funk Wiebe, "What Would Happen If My Husband Died?" in *Struggle*, ed. Hearn, 137–138.
122. For sophisticated versions of this argument see Lucille Sider Dayton and Donald W. Dayton, "'Your Daughters Shall Prophesy': Feminism in the Holiness Movement," *Methodist History* 14 (1976): 67–92 and Donald W. Dayton, *Discovering an Evangelical Heritage* (New York, 1976), 85–98.
123. Scanzoni and Hardesty, "Beyond the Barriers," 15.
124. Scanzoni, "Feminists," 10.
125. Theodore Hovet, "Phoebe Palmer's 'Altar Phraseology' and the Spiritual Dimension of Women's Sphere," *Journal of Religion* 63 (1983): 264–280.
126. Wiebe, "Husband," 137.
127. Mollenkott, *Speech*, 26.
128. Scanzoni, "Feminists," 11.
129. Anderson, "Sometimes Amusing," 165–166.
130. Christenson, "Woman's Role," 22.
131. Michaelson, "Neither Male," 10.
132. Coleman, "Forging," 4.

133. Scanzoni, "Feminists," 12.
134. Gerstner and Scholer, "Women's Ordination," 16–17.
135. Mollenkott, *Women, Men, and the Bible* (Nashville, Tenn., 1977), 19.
136. Jewett, *Man as Male and Female*, 94. In the original all of the material I have quoted was printed in italics.
137. Gallagher, "When You Are," 95–96. The injunctions come from Eph. 5: 21–22.
138. Mollenkott, *Women*, 25.
139. Mollenkott, *Women*, 30.
140. Ruth Schmidt, "What Did Saint Paul Want?" *His*, May 1973, 13.
141. Jewett, *Man as Male and Female*, 142, 144.
142. Mollenkott, *Women*, 95. Mollenkott was summarizing a view that she disagreed with.
143. Jewett, *Man as Male and Female*, 134.
144. Mollenkott, *Women*, 90–106.
145. Mollenkott, *Women*, 95; Jewett, *Man as Male and Female*, 134–135.
146. Judith Ann Craig Piper, "I Probably Don't Fit . . . ," in *Struggle*, ed. Hearn, 71–72. The most famous elaboration of the point is Harold Lindsell's pugnacious *The Battle for the Bible* (Grand Rapids, Mich., 1976), 117–121.

6   COUNTERFEMINISM

1. Except where noted otherwise, this paragraph and the two that follow are based on "Consciousness Raising in the Church," in *Our Struggle to Serve: The Stories of 15 Evangelical Women*, ed. Virginia Hearn (Waco, Tex., 1979), 184–188.
2. Mildred Meythaler, "I Was Freed to Face the Differences . . . ," in *Struggle*, ed. Hearn, 53.
3. Virginia Hearn, "Woman's Place in the Evangelical Milieu . . . ," in *Struggle*, ed. Hearn, 23.
4. Billy Graham, "The Revolution in the Family Home," 12 May 1976, The Archives of the Billy Graham Center, Wheaton, Ill., 13: V14–15.
5. Wilfred Bockelman, *Gothard: The Man and His Ministry* (Santa Barbara, Calif., 1976).

6. "The New Housewife Blues," *Time*, 14 March 1977, 62.

7. Thomas Howard, *Christ the Tiger: A Postscript to Dogma* (Philadelphia, 1967), 20–22, 31; George Marsden, *Fundamentalism and American Culture* (New York, 1980), 96. Keswick teachings explained how a Christian could live a "victorious life" on earth. See J. C. Pollock, *The Keswick Story* (London, 1964).

8. Elisabeth Elliot, *Through Gates of Splendor* (New York, 1957).

9. Elisabeth Elliot, *The Savage My Kinsman* (Ann Arbor, Mich., 1981), 147–148.

10. Elisabeth Elliot, *The Liberty of Obedience* (1968; reprint, Nashville, 1981), 41–53.

11. Wes Michaelson, "Neither Male Nor Female: The Thanksgiving Conference on Biblical Feminism," *Sojourners*, January 1976, 12.

12. Judith M. Miles, *The Feminine Principle* (Minneapolis, 1975), 7, 96, 66.

13. Miles, *Principle*, 79–80.

14. Miles, *Principle*, 24–26.

15. Linda Coleman, "Forging Chains of Command," *Daughters of Sarah*, May-June 1980, 7.

16. Miles, *Principle*, 96.

17. Elisabeth Elliot, *Let Me Be a Woman: Notes on Womanhood for Valerie* (Wheaton, Ill., 1976), 13.

18. Elliot, *Let Me*, 176.

19. Miles, *Principle*, 125–126.

20. Miles, *Principle*, 47.

21. Miles, *Principle*, 17.

22. Elliot, *Let Me*, 58, 143.

23. John Gerstner, in John Gerstner and David Scholer, "Is Women's Ordination Unbiblical? An Areopagus Discussion Forum with John Gerstner and David Scholer," sponsored by the Current Affairs Committee, Student Government Association, Gordon-Conwell Theological Seminary, South Hamilton, Mass., 1980, 2–3.

24. Miles, *Principle*, 45.

25. Miles, *Principle*, 152–153.

26. John Howard Yoder, quoted in Donald G. Bloesch, *Is the Bible Sexist?* (Westchester, Ill.,1982), 15.

27. Miles, *Principle*, 152.

28. Elliot, *Let Me*, 115.

29. Gerster, in Gerstner and Scholer, "Women's Ordination," 3.

30. Larry Christenson, *The Christian Family* (Minneapolis, Minn., 1970), 127.

31. Gerstner, in Gerstner and Scholer, "Women's Ordination," 22.
32. Eph. 5:22.
33. Miles, Principle, 44.
34. Elliot, Let Me, 22.
35. Thomas Howard, in Thomas Howard and Donald W. Dayton, "A Dialogue on Women, Hierarchy and Equality," Post-American, May 1975, 12.
36. Christenson, Christian Family, 213.
37. Bloesch, Is the Bible Sexist?, 34.
38. Howard, in Howard and Dayton, "Dialogue," 9.
39. Bloesch, Is the Bible Sexist?, 80.
40. Howard, in Howard and Dayton, "Dialogue," 14.
41. Miles, Principle, 99.
42. Howard, in Howard and Dayton, "Dialogue," 14.
43. Miles, Principle, 63, 96, 40.
44. Elliot, Let Me, 50, 103.
45. Coleman, "Forging," 6.
46. Donald W. Dayton, in Howard and Dayton, "Dialogue," 9–11.
47. Howard, in Howard and Dayton, "Dialogue," 13.
48. Howard, in Howard and Dayton, "Dialogue," 11.
49. Elliot, Let Me, 142.
50. Christenson, Christian Family, 127–138.
51. Miles, Principle, 16.
52. Christenson, Christian Family, 127.
53. Howard, in Howard and Dayton, "Dialogue," 11.
54. Here I have in mind the sort of feminism associated with Betty Friedan and not that associated with more thoroughgoing feminists.
55. Marabel Morgan, Total Joy (Old Tappan, N.J., 1976), 25–26.
56. Marabel Morgan, The Total Woman (1973; reprint, Old Tappan, N.J., 1975), 232.
57. Coleman, "Forging," 3.
58. Morgan, Woman, 120.
59. "What If . . . ," Christianity Today, 18 July 1975, 17.
60. Bloesch, Is the Bible Sexist?, 12, 14, 127–128.
61. Billy Graham, "What It Costs You Not to Follow Christ," 19 August 1976. The Archives of the Billy Graham Center, Wheaton, Ill., 113:V33.
62. Andrea Dworkin, Right Wing Women (New York, 1978), 25–26.
63. Telephone interview with Marabel Morgan's husband, Charles, 19 May 1984.

64. Susan Harding, "Family Reform Movements: Recent Feminism and Its Opposition," *Feminist Studies* 7 (1981): 57.

65. David W. Brady and Kent L.Tedin, "Ladies in Pink: Religion and Political Ideology in the Anti-ERA Movement," *Social Science Quarterly* 56 (1976): 564.

66. John M. Blum et al., *The National Experience*, 4th ed. (New York, 1977), 835.

67. Marabel Morgan, "Door Interview," *Wittenberg Door*, August–September 1975, 9.

68. Morgan, *Joy*, 19. See also Morgan, *Woman*, 20.

69. Morgan, *Joy*, 31, 16; Morgan, *Woman*, 120; Morgan, "Door Interview," 9.

70. Morgan, "Door Interview," 12.

71. Morgan, "Door Interview," 10.

72. Morgan, *Woman*, 96.

73. Morgan, *Joy*, 196.

74. Marabel Morgan, "Preferring One Another," *Christianity Today*, 10 September 1976, 12.

75. Kay Lindskoog, "Reactions from a Partial Woman," *Wittenberg Door*, August–September 1975, 16–17.

76. Telephone interview with Charles Morgan, 19 May 1984.

77. Morgan, "Door Interview," 14.

78. Morgan, "Door Interview," 13.

79. Morgan, *Joy*, 216.

80. Morgan, *Woman*, 14. While writing her first book she solicited the advice of Christian psychologists such as Clyde Narramore and Keith Miller (telephone interview with Charles Morgan, 19 May 1984).

81. Morgan, *Joy*, 31, 30, 22, 140, 205.

82. Morgan, *Woman*, 18–19, 88.

83. Morgan, *Joy*, 86.

84. Morgan, "Door Interview," 15.

85. Morgan, *Joy*, 86–89.

86. Morgan, *Joy*, 85, 92–93.

7 MODERN PSYCHOLOGY

1. Vernon Grounds, "Modern Psychology and the Gospel [Part One]," *Eternity*, April 1955, 12. Grounds was the dean of the Conservative Baptist Theological Seminary in Denver, Colorado.

2. Charles C. Cook, "Psychology the Latest Craze" (Chicago, n.d.), 3, copy in Press Booklets Collection, Archives of the Moody Bible Institute, Chicago, Ill.; L. Gilbert Little, *Nervous Christians* (Lincoln, Neb., 1956), 10, quoted in Donald Meyer, *The Positive Thinkers*, rev. ed. (New York, 1980), 291.

3. W. M. Frysinger, "Does Psychology Weaken or Strengthen the Inspired Records?" *Moody Bible Institute Monthly*, June 1925, 457; Cook, "Latest Craze," 3.

4. The term "therapeutic culture" is often used with some imprecision. (See Jack Jones, "Five Versions of Psychological Man," *Salmagundi* 20 [1972]: 106.) In this essay, it simply means a culture that displays the characteristics listed in the final five sentences of this paragraph.

For discussions of the attributes of a therapeutic culture see Philip Rieff, *Freud: The Mind of the Moralist*, 3d ed. (Chicago, 1979), 329–357; Philip Rieff, *The Triumph of the Therapeutic* (New York, 1966); Christopher Lasch, *Haven in a Heartless World* (New York, 1977); Christopher Lasch, *The Culture of Narcissism* (New York, 1978); T. J. Jackson Lears, *No Place of Grace* (New York, 1981); Robert Castel, Françoise Castel, and Anne Lovell, *The Psychiatric Society*, trans. Arthur Goldhammer (New York, 1982); Warren I. Susman, *Culture as History* (New York, 1984), 271–285; Michael Beldoch, "The Therapeutic as Narcissist," *Salmagundi* 20 (1972): 134–152; and Benjamin Nelson and Dennis Wrong, "Perspectives on the Therapeutic," *Salmagundi*, 20 (1972): 160–195.

This chapter discusses the relationship between evangelicalism and America's therapeutic culture, focusing specifically on evangelicals' reactions to (1) psychoanalysis, (2) psychiatry, (3) clinical psychology, and (4) popular writers whose works reflected the influence of 1, 2, or 3. Evangelical responses to academic and experimental psychology are considered only insofar as they illuminate 1, 2, 3, and 4.

E. Brooks Holifield, *A History of Pastoral Care in America* (Nashville, 1983), and Andrew Abbott, "Religion, Psychiatry, and Problems of Everyday Life," in *Religion and Religiosity in America*, ed. Jeffrey K. Hadden and Theodore E. Long (New York, 1983), 133–142, discuss the relationship between American Protestantism and therapeutic ideas and practices. Neither work focuses on evangelicalism.

5. Köhler was the author of *Gestalt Psychology* (New York, 1929).

6. A. Z. Conrad, "Modern Psychology the Foe of Truth," *Moody Bible Institute Monthly*, November 1929, 116.

7. "Self-Improvement," *Revelation*, December 1946, 535–536.

8. Godfrey C. Robinson and Stephen F. Winward, "The Art of Living," *Eternity*, October 1951, 6.

9. William Allan Dean, "Young People's Topics," *Revelation*, January 1937, 14, 28.

10. Godfrey C. Robinson and Stephen F. Winward, "Christ—The Beginning and the End," *Eternity*, September 1952, 32–33.

11. "Contended Discontent," *Revelation*, April 1939, 143.

12. Cook, "Latest Craze," 3.

13. H. V. Caneday, "Psychiana's Unholy Kin and False Promises," *Sunday School Times*, 25 September 1948, 5.

14. Ruby Y. Burgess, "What Behaviorism and Freud Psychology Have Done," *Moody Monthly*, March 1928, 316–317. See, too, Frances Arick Kolb, "The Reaction of American Protestants to Psychoanalysis, 1900–1950" (Ph.D. diss., Washington University, 1972), 196.

15. Walter A. Maier, *For Better Not For Worse: A Manual of Christian Matrimony*, 3d ed. (St. Louis, 1939), 132.

16. "Psychiatry," *Revelation*, August 1934, 298.

17. Conrad, "Foe of Truth," 116.

18. Conrad, "Foe of Truth," 116.

19. Michael M. Sokal, "The Gestalt Psychologists in Behaviorist America," *American Historical Review* 89 (1984): 1242.

20. Conrad, "Foe of Truth," 116.

21. Cook, "Latest Craze," 6.

22. Cook, "Latest Craze," 5.

23. "Self-Improvement," 535–536.

24. "Inferiority Complex," *Revelation*, May 1934, 174.

25. Lillian C. Galloway, "Reject Coueism If You Are a Christian!" *Moody Bible Institute Monthly*, March 1923, 292.

26. Donald Grey Barnhouse, "Emotions, Nerves, and Christianity," *Revelation*, June 1948, 249; "Psychology," *Revelation*, June 1937, 235.

27. "Inferiority Complex," 174.

28. Galloway, "Reject," 292.

29. Galloway, "Reject," 292.

30. E. E. P. [sic], "Words of Weight and Wisdom," appendix to Charles C. Cook, "The Savior and Psychology" (Chicago, n.d.), 28, copy in Press Booklets Collection, Archives of the Moody Bible Institute, Chicago.

31. Virginia Whitman, "God's Psychiatry," *Moody Monthly*, August 1946, 737–739.

32. See Chapter 2.

33. "Psychiatry," 298.

34. Maurice Green and R. W. Rieber, "The Assimilation of Psychoanalysis in America," in *Psychology: Theoretical-Historical Perspectives*, ed. R. W. Rieber and Kurt Salzinger (New York, 1980), 295, notes the "spectacular growth of psychoanalysis" in the 1950s and early 1960s. See, too, Albert R. Gilgen, *American Psychology since World War II* (Westport, Conn., 1982), 20–21, 25; and Paul Starr, *The Social Transformation of American Medicine* (New York, 1982), 344–346.

35. Godfrey C. Robinson and Stephen F. Winward, "The Art of Living," *Eternity*, September 1951, 13.

36. For evangelical attitudes on popular psychology see Herbert Henry Ehrenstein, review of *Life Is Worth Living* by Fulton J. Sheen, *Eternity*, February 1954, 34; Hildreth Cross, *An Introduction to Psychology* (Grand Rapids, Mich., 1952), 405 (on Dale Carnegie), and 424–425 (on Norman Vincent Peale); and Charles L. Allen, *In Quest of God's Power* (Westwood, N.J., 1952), 94 (on Joshua Liebman), and 85 (on Dale Carnegie).

37. "Freud Without Freud," *Eternity*, September 1953, 15. See, too, Robert S. Woodworth, *Contemporary Schools of Psychology*, rev. ed. (New York, 1948), 193–212.

38. *Proceedings of the First Calvinistic Conference on Psychology and Psychiatry* (April 7–8, 1954), 11, 20.

39. *Proceedings*, 5–6.

40. Cross, *Introduction*, 11.

41. Cross, *Introduction*, 12.

42. Cross, *Introduction*, 290–291.

43. R.L.K. [sic], review of *An Introduction to Psychology* by Hildreth Cross, *Eternity*, February 1953, 31.

44. Allen, *Quest*, 83.

45. Godfrey C. Robinson and Stephen F. Winward, "The Conquest of Temperament," *Eternity*, August 1952, 23, 34.

46. Robinson and Winward, "The Art of Living," *Eternity*, October 1951, 5.

47. Allen, *Quest*, 85.

48. Allen, *Quest*, 94.

49. Allen, *Quest*, 33.

50. Allen, *Quest*, 37.

51. Richard H. Cox, "Exploring Mental Health Problems," review of *Encyclopedia of Mental Health Problems* by Clyde M. Narramore, *Eternity*, February 1967, 62–63.

52. Clyde M. Narramore, *Counseling with Youth* (Grand Rapids, Mich., 1966), 47–51.

53. Clyde M. Narramore, "Your Psychological Needs: Freedom from Fear," *Moody Monthly*, February 1955, 16, 59, is typical of the entire series.

54. "Tension," *Eternity*, July 1954, 15.

55. Allen, *Quest*, 17; Cross, *Introduction*, 410.

56. Cross, *Introduction*, 409.

57. Vernon Grounds, "Has Freud Anything for Christians?" a review of *Christian Life and the Unconscious* by Ernest White, *Eternity*, July 1956, 9.

58. Vernon Grounds, "Modern Psychology and the Gospel: [Part Two]," *Eternity*, May 1955, 18.

59. Narramore, "Fear," 59.

60. Cross, *Introduction*, 12.

61. Narramore, *Youth*, 28.

62. Charles L. Allen, *God's Psychiatry* (Westwood, N.J., 1953), 14.

63. Allen, *Psychiatry*, 13.

64. Allen, *Psychiatry*, 7.

65. Norvel Peterson, review of *Understanding Grief* by Edgar N. Jackson, *Eternity*, December 1958, 42.

66. Allen, *Psychiatry*, 166.

67. Allen, *Psychiatry*, 59.

68. Billy Graham, *Peace with God* (Garden City, N.Y., 1953), 41–42.

69. Elisabeth Elliot, "When I'm Lonely," *Moody Monthly*, May 1977, 127.

70. Walter R. Martin, "What Can We Do about the Terrifying Trend of Alcoholism in America?" *Eternity*, August 1960, 19.

71. J. Grant Swank, Jr., "Counseling Is a Waste of Time," *Christianity Today*, 9 September 1977, 27.

72. Oliver W. Price, "Who's the Real Jonathan Livingston Seagull?" *Moody Monthly*, May 1973, 79.

73. Paul T. Brownback, "A Comparison of Narramore's Concept of Self-Love with Evangelical Theology" (Ph.D. diss., New York University, School of Education, 1980).

74. John Piper, "Is Self-Love Biblical?" *Christianity Today*, 12 August 1977, 6–9.

75. Paul Vitz, *Psychology as Religion* (Grand Rapids, Mich., 1977).

76. Jay E. Adams, *The Big Umbrella* (Grand Rapids, Mich., 1972), 5. For an analysis of Adams's work, see John D. Carter, "Adams' Theory of Nouthetic Counseling," *Journal of Psychology and Theology* 3 (1975): 143–155.

77. Adams, *Umbrella*, 4.
78. Jay E. Adams, *Competent to Counsel* (Nutley, N.J., 1970), 82–83.
79. Adams, *Competent*, 41.
80. Adams, *Umbrella*, 215–219.
81. Mark Cosgrove, *Psychology Gone Awry* (Grand Rapids, Mich., 1979).
82. Mark Cosgrove, *Mental Health: A Christian Approach* (Grand Rapids, Mich., 1977).
83. "New for Do-It-Yourselfers," *Christianity Today*, 31 January 1975, 14.
84. Cecil B. Murphey, "More Psychological Insights," *Christianity Today*, 9 September 1977, 23.
85. Carolyn Nystrom, "How to Fight Depression and Win," *Moody Monthly*, May 1978, 101–103.
86. James F. Conway, "God's Rx for Depression," *Moody Monthly*, January 1978, 86–89.
87. Robert Wise, "Anxiety: Mind Gnawing Devourer," *Moody Monthly*, September 1979, 47–48.
88. Bernard DeRemer, "How to Be Content," *Eternity*, July 1961, 30–31, 36.
89. Dwight L. Carlson, "Tired of Being Tired?" *Moody Monthly*, December 1974, 34–37.
90. Vernon C. Lyons, "Help Yourself to Happiness," *Moody Monthly*, January 1977, 29.
91. Oliver W. Price, "How to Live in Heaven on Earth," *Moody Monthly*, February 1975, 46.
92. Murphey, "Insights," 24.
93. Dickson, "Transactional Analysis," 34.
94. Craig Massey, "Forgive Yourself," *Moody Monthly*, January 1978, 83.
95. Murphey, "Insights," 20.
96. Murphey, "Insights," 23.
97. Advertisement for *There's Freedom in Christ* by Bruce Narramore and Bill Counts, *Moody Monthly*, June 1974, 7.
98. "Table of Contents," *Christianity Today*, 9 September 1977.
99. Stanley E. Lindquist, "How to Avoid Mental Breakdown," *Eternity*, November 1962, 23.
100. Anthony A. Hoekema, "Thinking Positively about Self," *Christianity Today*, 20 May 1977, 32.

101. M. N. Beck, "Christ and Psychiatry," *Christianity Today*, 25 October 1974, 10. Actually, Beck wrote "Commandment" rather than "Commission." Perhaps he had in mind Jesus' explication of the most important commandments of the Scriptures. More likely it was simply a slip of the pen.

102. Lawrence J. Crabb, Jr., "Counseling and Psychology," *Christianity Today*, 2 March 1973, 32.

103. Truman G. Esau, "The Problem of the Lonely Fellowship," review of *Escape from Loneliness* by Paul Tournier, *Eternity*, July 1962, 45.

104. Arthur W. Forrester, "Marriage As an Adventure," review of *To Understand Each Other* by Paul Tournier, *Eternity*, April 1970, 61.

105. Bert E. Van Soest, "Insights of a Psychologist," review of *The Psychology of Jesus and Mental Health* by Ramond L. Cramer, *Eternity*, May 1962, 46.

106. David A. Hubbard to Harold J. Ockenga, 27 March 1963, Charles E. Fuller Papers, Archives of Fuller Theological Seminary, Pasadena, Calif.

107. Basil Jackson, "The Psychology of Prayer," *Moody Monthly*, January 1971, 63.

108. Gene A. Getz, "So You'd Like to Learn to Counsel," *Moody Monthly*, July-August 1967, 39–40.

109. Hoekema, "Thinking Positively," 32.

110. Marabel Morgan, *Total Joy* (Old Tappan, N.J., 1976), 33.

111. Marabel Morgan, *The Total Woman* (1973; reprint, Old Tappan, N.J., 1975), 255.

112. Morgan, *Joy*, 32.

113. Morgan, *Woman*, v.

114. Tim F. LaHaye and Beverly LaHaye, *The Act of Marriage* (Grand Rapids, Mich., 1976).

115. Tim F. LaHaye, *How to Win over Depression* (Grand Rapids, Mich., 1974).

116. Tim F. LaHaye and Beverly LaHaye, *Spirit-Controlled Family Living* (Old Tappan, N.J., 1978), 61.

117. LaHaye and LaHaye, *Family Living*, 75.

118. Wilfred Bockelman, *Gothard: The Man and His Ministry* (Santa Barbara, Calif., 1976); Bill Gothard, *How to Understand the Purpose behind Humanism* (n.p., n.d.).

119. Bill Gothard, *Syllabus from Institute in Basic Youth Conflicts* (n.p., 1975).

120. "New for Do-It-Yourselfers," 14.
121. James Dobson, *Hide and Seek* (Old Tappan, N.J., 1974).
122. James Dobson, *Dare to Discipline* (Wheaton, Ill., 1970), 51–85.
123. Adams, *Big Umbrella*, 131.

APPENDIX

1. The discussion that follows is based on the following works: Nancy Tatom Ammerman, *Bible Believers: Fundamentalists in the Modern World* (New Brunswick, N.J., 1987), 3–6; Randall Balmer, *Mine Eyes Have Seen the Glory: A Journey into the Evangelical Subculture* (New York, 1989), ix–xii; Edith L. Blumhofer and Joel A. Carpenter, eds. *Twentieth-Century Evangelicalism: A Guide to the Sources* (New York, 1990), ix–xii; Joel A. Carpenter, "From Fundamentalism to the New Evangelical Coalition," in *Evangelicalism and Modern America* ed. George M. Marsden (Grand Rapids, Mich., 1984), 3–16; Joel A. Carpenter, "Fundamentalist Institutions and the Rise of Evangelical Protestantism, 1929–1942," *Church History* 49 (1980): 62–75; Joel A. Carpenter, "Revive Us Again: Alienation, Hope, and the Resurgence of Fundamentalism, 1930–1950," in *Transforming Faith: The Sacred and the Secular in Modern American History*, ed. M. L. Bradbury and James B. Gilbert (New York, 1989), 105–125; Donald W. Dayton, "Yet Another Layer of the Onion: Or Opening the Ecumenical Door to Let the Rifraff In," *Ecumenical Review* 40 (1988): 87–110; James Davison Hunter, *American Evangelicalism: Conservative Religion and the Quandary of Modernity* (New Brunswick, N.J., 1983), 139–141; George M. Marsden *Reforming Fundamentalism: Fuller Seminary and the New Evangelicalism* (Grand Rapids, Mich., 1987), 10–11, 165–171; George M. Marsden, "Introduction: the Evangelical Denomination," in *Evangelicalism and Modern America*, ed. George M. Marsden (Grand Rapids, Mich., 1984), vii–xix; George M. Marsden, "Defining Fundamentalism," *Christian Scholar's Review* 1 (1971): 141–151; Ernest R. Sandeen, "Defining Fundamentalism: A Reply to Professor Marsden," *Christian Scholar's Review* 1 (1971): 227–233; Timothy L. Smith, "The Evangelical Kaleidoscope and the Call to Christian Unity," *Christian Scholar's Review* 15 (1986): 125–140; Leonard I. Sweet, "Wise as Serpents, Innocent as Doves: The New

Evangelical Historiography," *Journal of the American Academy of Religion* 56 (1988): 397–416; R. Stephen Warner, *New Wine in Old Wineskins: Evangelicals and Liberals in a Small-Town Church* (Berkeley, 1988), 33–65.

2. For a different list of questions designed to separate evangelicals from non-evangelicals, see Hunter, *American Evangelicalism*, 139–141 and Blumhofer and Carpenter, *Twentieth-Century Evangelicalism*, x.

3. Hunter, *American Evangelicalism*, 49–69.

4. Marsden, "Introduction," viii–ix.

5. Thomas Howard, *Evangelical Is Not Enough: Worship of God in Liturgy and Sacrament* (San Francisco, 1984), 2.

6. Dayton, "Yet Another Layer" and Smith, "The Evangelical Kaleidoscope." See, too, Sweet, "Wise as Serpents" and James Leo Garrett, Jr., E. Glen Hinson, and James E. Tull, *Are Southern Baptists "Evangelicals?"* (Macon, Ga., 1983).

7. Carpenter, "From Fundamentalism" and George M. Marsden, *Fundamentalism and American Culture* (New York, 1980), 228.

INDEX

Adams, Jay E.: adoption of psychological principles by, 149–150; opposition of to modern psychology, 148–149
adaptation, principle of, 135–136
Agape, founding of, 19
Allen, Charles L.: acceptance of modern psychology by, 144–145; on unobtrusiveness of God, 147
All We're Meant to Be (Hardesty), 108; inspiration from, 113
American Council of Christian Churches: founding of, 42; vs. National Association of Evangelicals, 44
Ammerman, Nancy Tatom, 3
Anabaptist-Mennonite tradition, 156
Antichrist, 74, 83
anti-ERA coalitions, 94–95
anti-Semitism, 58
Armerding, A. Herman, on labor leaders, 64
"Art of Living, The," 144
atheism, influence of in American government, 57, 66–67
Athletes in Action, founding of, 18–19

Auca Indians, 121–122
Ayer, William Ward, social concern of, 61–62

Baird, Robert, on evangelicalism in pre–Civil War times, 36
Ballew, Dick, 20
Baptist Convention, liberals in, 42
Barnhouse, Donald Grey: on economic injustice, 53; growing audience of, 36; on sins of labor leaders, 51
beast, the, 74; mark of, 75
Beck, M. N., on Jesus' teaching and psychiatric concepts, 151–152
Beckford, James, 6
behaviorism, 140–141
believers, control over private fate of, 76–77
Bible: battle for the, 25; incompatibility of with feminism, 126–127; problem of, 113–114; therapeutic power of, 147; view of women in, 113–116
Bible-believing Christians, national association for, 43
biblical feminists, 113

INDEX

Big Umbrella, The (Adams), 148
Billy Graham Evangelistic Association: launching of, 10; publication of *Decision* by, 2
black Christians, 157
Bob Jones University, 156
Braun, Jon, 20
Bright, Bill: advice of to new converts, 29–30; campaigns of, 19; and Campus Crusade, 19–21; conversion of, 18; critics of, 26–27; founding of Athletes in Action by, 18–19; four spiritual laws of, 17–18; lack of dogmatism of, 24–25; ministry of, 19–21
Brownback, Paul T., on Narramore's ideas vs. biblical concepts, 148
Bruce, Steve, 3
Bryan, William Jennings, in Scopes trial, 34, 38–39
Burton, Joe, on women's place, 106–107
business leaders, denunciation of, 51

Calvinistic Conference on Psychology and Psychiatry, 143
Campbell, Alexander, spiritual descendants of, 157
Campus Crusade for Christ: Bill Bright and, 19–21; evangelicals involved in, 19–20; founding and growth of, 19
capitalism, fundamentalist view of, 53–54
Carnegie, Dale, 137, 145
Carpenter, Joel, on power, 6
Chafer, Lewis Sperry, dispensationalist position of, 80
change, 2–4
chiliasm: and familial hopes, 87–89; themes of, 74; uneasiness with, 83; vitality of, 78–80
Christ-directed life, 29–30
Christenson, Larry, on Christian family, 90

Christian Century: on strength of old-time religion, 36; on vanishing of fundamentalism, 34
Christian family: failure of, 90; health of, 90–91; resiliency of, 89–91. *See also* family
Christian Family, The (Christenson), 90
Christian Herald, The, on education for women, 106
Christian Home, The, 99
Christianity: America's drift away from, 67–69; emphasis on consolations of, 26–27
Christianity Today, 43; change in eschatology of, 84; on danger of rejection of psychology, 152; on ordaining women, 107
Christian life, fundamentalist view of, 25
Christians, spiritual vs. carnal, 30
Christian World Liberation Front, founding of, 19
civil governments, fundamentalist attitudes toward, 55–57. *See also* government
Civil Rights Act, 93
Civil War, evangelicalism during, 37
communism: conspiracy of, 57–58; fundamentalist view of, 54
Competent to Counsel (Adams), 148
Congress, Christian element in, 64–65
Conrad, A. Z., resistance of to psychology, 139–140
conservative Protestantism: change in, 2–4; and evangelical mainstream, 160–161; vs. evangelicalism, 155–156; membership in following 1920s controversies, 35; recent signs of vitality of, 34–35; scholarly studies of, 3
conservative Protestants: in counter-feminist movement, 94–95; in mainline denominations, 42; outside mainline denominations, 41–

204

archicalism in, 129–131; importance attached to, 55, 85–86; pressures on, 89; private hopes offered by, 77–78; resiliency of, 89–91; and Second Advent, 87. *See also* Christian family; marriage

family values, rejection of, 67–68

Federal Council of Churches: challenge to, 43–44; social creed of, 50

Feminine Mystique (Friedan), 110

Feminine Principle, The (Miles), 122

feminism, 93–117; and American economic system, 123; Bible problem in, 113–114; Billy Graham on, 98–99; and changing traditionalist evangelical views, 100–107; expression of in evangelical literature, 108–116; incompatibility of with Bible and Divine Order, 126–127; relationship between evangelical and secular, 109–116; rhetoric of secular, 111; Rice's view of, 97–98; search for usable past in Christianity, 112–114; traditionalists' resistance to, 128–131. *See also* counterfeminism

feminist movement, 86–87; backlash against, 93–94; in early 1970s, 93; women mobilized against, 94

feminists, evangelical, 100–101

Fitzhugh, George, defense of slavery by, 120

fixations, 146

foreign mission agencies, during 1930s, 35

Fosdick, Harry Emerson, "Shall the Fundamentalists Win?" sermon, 40

Four Spiritual Laws, The, 21; on conversion, 28; early draft of, 21–22; laws of, 22–25; message and challenge of, 25–31

free enterprise system, evangelical view of, 65

Freud, Sigmund, fundamentalist attack on, 140

Friedan, Betty, 110

Fuller, Charles, growing audience of, 36

Fuller, Dan, 19

Fuller Theological Seminary, 43; school of psychology faculty in, 152

fundamentalism: in 1920s, 10, 38–42; in 1930s, 41–42; against therapeutic culture, 138–139; Carl McIntire's influence on, 44–47; changes in eschatological tradition of in postwar years, 81–84; chiliastic hopes of, 78; conspiracy theories of, 57–59; dispensationalism in, 73–75; dogma of, 24; economic analysis of, 52–54; "errors" of, 47; evangelical roots in, 161; vs. evangelicalism, 43–44; on Freud, 140; interest of in eschatology, 78–80; as militantly antimodernist evangelicalism, 38; neglect of private hopes offered by family life, 77–78; patriotism of, 52; social and political views of, 50–51. *See also* evangelicalism; fundamentalist controversies

Fundamentalism and American Culture (Marsden), 3

fundamentalist controversies, 10, 33–48; aftermath of, 33–34, 41–42; response of fundamentalists to, 42–44

fundamentalist periodicals, increased circulation of in 1930s, 35

fundamentalist radio programs, growth of during 1930s, 35–36

Gaebelein, Arno C.: on conspiracy, 58; on need for strong homes, 55

Gallagher, Sharon: feminist views of, 101; first encounter of with secular feminists, 109–110

gender roles, changing evangelical views of, 105–107

INDEX

German Pietists, 157
Gerstner, John, counterfeminism of,
122
Gestalt psychology, 140
Getz, Gene A., on counseling, 152
Gillquist, Pete, 20
God: revelation of through patriarchical imagery, 127–128; unobtrusiveness of, 147
God's Psychiatry (Allen), 144–145
"God's Psychiatry" (Whitman), 142
Goldberg, Naomi, on Christian feminists, 110
gospel, without the cross, 27–28
Gothard, Bill, "Basic Youth Conflicts"
seminars of, 153
government: atheists' influence on,
57; evangelical attitudes toward,
62–63, 69; fundamentalist attitudes
toward, 55–57; influence of atheism in, 66–67; Roman Catholicism's influence on, 65–66
Graham, Billy, 19, 43; acceptance of
Kennedy's election, 66; on Christian family, 90; and counterfeminism, 120; emergence of, 36; focus
on family of, 85; on God's presence
in our life, 147–148; on husbands'
duty to wives, 107; on Kennedy's
campaign successes, 64; on labor
leaders, 63–64; link with Maier,
96–97; on modern women, 98–99;
premillennialism of, 83; on sex education, 70; social concern of, 61–
62; in White House, 60
Gramsci, Antonio, and hegemony, 5
Grounds, Vernon: on faith vs. unbelief, 137; on need for unconditional
love, 146

Haberer, F. W., on capitalism, 53
Hammond, Phillip, 6
Handelman, I. M., on economic con-
ditions, 53–54

Hardesty, Nancy, feminist view of,
108
Harding, Susan, 3; on feminism, 94
*Have You Heard of the Four Spiri-
tual Laws?* (Bright), 17–18. See
also *Four Spiritual Laws, The*
hegemony: and analysis of evangelicalism, 5; in evangelical history, 6–
7
Henry, Carl F. H., 43: on Christian
life, 25; and liberal evangelicalism,
59; premillennialism of, 82; on social issues, 61–63
"Here's Life, America" campaign, 19
"Here's Life, World" campaign, 19
Hide and Seek (Dobson), 153
hierarchicalism, vs. egalitarianism,
129–131
history, human inability to affect,
75–77
Hitt, William F. E., on America's
"ruling class," 53
Hofstadter, Richard, on fundamentalist controversies, 34
holiness groups, 157
home, importance of, 55. See also
family
Hoover, Herbert, Thanksgiving proclamation of, 57
Hopeless—Yet There Is Hope (Gaebelein), 55
Howard, Thomas: on "bossism" in
home, 130–131; counterfeminism
of, 122
Howe, Maud, on state in America, 56
Hughes, John, fight to circumscribe
evangelicalism, 36
human instincts, 140
human nature, psychological view of,
147
human progress, rejection of concept
of, 75–77
Hunt, Nelson Bunker, 19; and
Campus Crusade, 20

208

INDEX

Hunter, James Davison, 3; on evangelical world, 80

"I Found It" slogan, 19
Improving Your Self Image, 150
In Quest of God's Power (Allen), 144–145
Introduction to Psychology, An (Cross), 143–144
Israel, patriarchal values of, 127–128

Jackson, Basil, "Clinically Speaking" column of, 152
Jesus, relation of with women, 114–115
Jewett, Paul K., on women, 108, 116
Jewish conspiracy, 58
Jews, in new dispensation, 73–74
juvenile delinquency, answer to, 62

Kennedy, John F.: conspiratorial interpretation of success of, 64; evangelicals' acceptance of, 66

labor: antagonism toward leaders of, 51; evangelical attitudes toward, 63–64
Ladd, George E., premillennialism of, 82–83
LaHaye, Tim, on finding contentment in world, 153
Lasch, Christopher, 138
Late Great Planet Earth, The (Lindsey), 20, 79
Lears, T. J. Jackson, 138; on cultural authority and power, 7
Lewis, C. S.: view of Christianity of, 24–25
liberalism: evangelical attitudes toward, 63; relationship between political and religious, 52
Liebman, Rabbi Joshua, 145
Lindsey, Hal: in Bright's ministry,

19–20; royalties from sales of, 83–84; on Second Advent, 79
"Lutheran Hour, The," 96

Machen, J. Gresham: in fundamentalist controversy, 39–40; and McIntire, 45
Maier, Walter A.: ambivalence of toward feminism, 98, 100; on Freudianism, 140; links of with evangelical mainstream, 96–97; on need for strong homes, 55; theological and social views of, 96–97; on women, 96, 98
Man as Male and Female (Jewett), 108
marriage: biblical view of, 115; changing evangelical view of, 106–107; evangelical, 103–104; view of in evangelical literature, 103. *See also* family
Marsden, George, 3; on cultural authority, 6; on evangelicalism as denomination, 157; "From Fundamentalism to Evangelicalism," 59; on fundamentalist controversies, 34
McDougall, William, 140; influence of ideas of, 145–146
McDowell, Josh, 20
McIntire, Carl: and American Council of Christian Churches, 42; *Christian Beacon* paper of, 44; fundamentalist response of, 44–46
McLoughlin, William G., 59; on American evangelicalism, 37
Mears, Henrietta, influence of on Bright, 19
Mental Health: A Christian Approach (Cosgrove), 149
Middle East, interest in developments of, 79
Miles, Judith: counterfeminism of, 122–123; on feminine principle,